Meera Atkinson's creative non-fiction, poetry and short fiction have appeared in many publications, including *Best Australian Poems 2010*, *Best Australian Stories 2007*, *Salon.com*, *Meanjin* and *Griffith Review*. She was the recipient of the Varuna Dr Eric Dark Flagship Fellowship for 2017, awarded for a non-fiction application of outstanding quality in social, historical or political writing. She won the *Griffith Review* Contributors Circle competition in 2016 and the *Griffith Review* Emerging Writers' Prize in 2011, and she was shortlisted for the Alfred Deakin Prize for an Essay Advancing Public Debate in the Victorian Premier's Literary Awards 2007. Meera has a PhD from the Writing and Society Research Centre at Western Sydney University and also publishes academically. Her monograph, *The Poetics of Transgenerational Trauma*, was published by Bloomsbury in 2017, and she co-edited *Traumatic Affect*, an international volume of essays, published in 2013. Meera is half of the musical duo Theories of Everything, and she teaches writing, most recently at the University of Sydney.

TRAUMATA

MEERA ATKINSON

First published 2018 by University of Queensland Press
PO Box 6042, St Lucia, Queensland 4067 Australia

www.uqp.com.au
uqp@uqp.uq.edu.au

Cover design by Laura Thomas
Cover image by Christopher Wright
Author photo by Hugh Hamilton
Typeset in 11.5/15 pt Bembo Std by Post Pre-press Group, Brisbane
Printed in Australia by McPherson's Printing Group

Australian Government

Australia Council for the Arts

The University of Queensland Press is assisted by the Australian Government through the Australia Council, its arts funding and advisory body.

ISBN
978 0 7022 5989 0 (pbk)
978 0 7022 6085 8 (ePDF)
978 0 7022 6086 5 (ePub)
978 0 7022 6087 2 (Kindle)

NATIONAL LIBRARY OF AUSTRALIA
A catalogue record for this book is available from the National Library of Australia

University of Queensland Press uses papers that are natural, renewable and recyclable products made from wood grown in sustainable forests. The logging and manufacturing processes conform to the environmental regulations of the country of origin.

traumata (*plural of* **trauma**)
/trɔˈmətə/

1. *Pathology*
a. bodily injuries produced by violence, or any other extrinsic agent.
b. the conditions produced by this; traumatism.
c. the injurious agents or mechanisms themselves.

2. *Psychology* startling or distressing experiences which have a lasting effect on mental life; shocks.

[Greek: wound]

I wake up tense, nervous system switching onto the wild winds that have rattled the windows all night, making it hard to settle, trapping me in that thin top layer of sleep on which insistent thoughts intrude. I scan the room, tenderness at my temples, rise, and open the curtains. The branches of enormous eucalyptus trees dance out of time against the bruise-grey sky. The sun, breaking through, sparks off leaves. The power goes down.

Do I start with my mother's fear? My father's certainty? Or with the blackout rape I rarely think about that took place in a cheap Bondi hotel when I was a teenage alcoholic? I can still see the judgemental brow and hear the tone of the cop (you know the one: sneery, patronising, shaming) tasked with investigating after the police picked me up.

They're cruising down Campbell Parade in the early hours of a Sunday in 1981 and there on the side of the road stands a young woman holding the flattened side of a cardboard box against her naked body, having snatched it up while running through a fluoro-lit car park. Is it even necessary to tell that story? Haven't we heard enough? It occurs to me now I don't recall this rape ever coming up in therapy. It had some competition.

The poet Eileen Myles says that writers spend so much time 'processing, consuming [and] creating an alternative self that is entirely composed of language so that there are precise speeds or toxins or organs in it that work in concert with the state that you are in and can only neutralize your own pain by vanishing into a song composed of exactly that timbre'. I think she means there is a place we go for the magic of disappearing and arriving simultaneously – some kind of dissolving communion. I was lonely then. Or maybe I should say I was lonely then in a way I'm not lonely now. That's how I came to be at a bar, on my own, aged eighteen, letting some guy buy me drinks till I was drunk enough to go back to a hotel with him and his friends. This is not a confession or a hard-luck yarn, though there is some hard luck in it. This is not about me, or only me, my me-ness. There's a reason I'm telling you this.

I understand you want to know what kind of book this will be and whether you can count on me. I'm thinking about how to respond.

Einstein and the new generations of quantum physicists have been telling us for years that the past, present and future are illusions. Time is not what it seems. I'm paying attention here to all of the times. It puts me on edge, splits me into fragments held together by these flimsy words, by the act of bashing imaginary ink into shapes and arranging them into more elaborate shapes and silent sounds you can decipher. A clue: the beginning is not the beginning. This is not just about rape, or *my* rape. It's about the big rape: patriarchy, with its endemic traumata.

Patriarchy seems like an old-fashioned word, a twentieth-century word. I feel I'm showing my age in invoking it, but there is no other word that gets at it. The Ancient Greek word *patriarkhes* denoted a society where power was maintained and passed down through elder males. In modern parlance, a 'patriarchal society' generally refers to one in which men are predominantly represented in positions of power as head of the family unit, bosses in the workplace and leaders in government. Though some like to think 'the patriarchy is dead' (Hanna Rosin in *Slate*), and others view patriarchy as 'a term used by feminists, to blame men for all their problems' (*Urban Dictionary*), many feminist thinkers still use the word patriarchy to 'describe the society in which we live today, characterised by current and historic unequal power relations between women and men whereby women are systematically disadvantaged and oppressed' (London Feminist Network). In this rendering, the political, economic and social systems established over millennia function as a structural reinscribing of patriarchy, so that, for example, even when women are admitted into roles of responsibility and representation, including high-level leadership – such as Theresa May as Prime Minister of Britain or Hillary Clinton as US Secretary of State and presidential candidate – they are bound to, and by, the institutions and attitudes established by patriarchy, which continue to disadvantage women (and others on the lower realms in patriarchy social orders).

What do I mean, then, when I say this is a book about patriarchy and its endemic traumata? I mean I'm going to make the case that patriarchy is inherently traumatic, and that we might coin a new word – *traumarchy* – to denote the intersection of the two. Why, then, am I talking, in the next breath, of myself, my life? I have to speak from the inside out because patriarchy isn't 'out there'. Our skin is not an impenetrable barrier against its effects. It infiltrates our beings and shapes our lives – first from the outside in, then from the inside out.

The word memoir comes from the Latin *memoria*, recast into French, *mémoire*, during the fifteenth century. People think you have to be special to write memoir, but I, for one, am a cliché. This book exists not because trauma and shit going down in childhood is exceptional or inherently interesting, but because it's chronic, commonplace, sometimes dramatic and often tedious in its stranglehold of repetitions, daily struggles, and predictable and unpredictable outcomes, and no one gets out alive. And then there's the question of my unreliable memory, my damaged brain. What does it mean to communicate a fractured, faded memory?

If I told you I've heard thousands of stories and witnessed the ravages in the lives of countless friends, acquaintances and passing strangers in detoxes, rehabs, support and therapy groups, you'd think I was exaggerating, but there it is, everywhere we turn: in news headlines and advertisements, on the street, behind every closed door. Course, not everyone lives in the slipstream of a familial clusterfuck of trauma, but even the most well-adjusted and loving of families aren't immune to tragedy, freak accidents and diabolical developments, and we draw generational straws in cultural clusterfucks such as fascistic, oppressive regimes, unjust systemic structures, economic depressions, and wars (military, psychological, domestic). Not all unfortunate events or even extreme sufferings are traumatic, but many are.

Some live with unimaginable clusterfucks. Syrian refugees rejected at every border. Survivors of concentration camps. First Nations people torn from family and country. In any event, clusterfuck is the turf we're on. We're on the trail of religious imperialism, notepads at the ready. We're investigating its misogynies and carnage. We're tracking the shadows of liberalism, that project of modernity and the Enlightenment. We're taking down the statistics, and plotting revolution. There are those who appear to come out unscathed, but few really are. A lot of people lie. You want to know what kind of book this will be. It will slip between viral shimmerings like photographs out of focus with ghostly figures in the background (they mean us no harm), part manifesto, part epic poem, part library, part love letter, always a conversation. Are you listening?

A note from my mother: 'I carried you in fear because I had two miscarriages before. I tried not to, but in the trying was the fear. You were born sucking your thumb. It was a very easy birth as births go. You whimpered like a baby puppy for about three weeks. It used to break my heart. You would only open your eyes in the early night morning hours. It was three weeks before your dad saw them. I just loved you so much and always will. I was twenty-nine and my first Saturn return was happening. My own lack of nurturing was just emerging and we both suffered. There was love and fun also, and the process goes on ...'

When I was twenty-six and two years sober, one of the many self-help books I resorted to in desperation suggested gathering together photos of early childhood with a view to reconnecting with the 'inner child'. I had no baby photos so I wrote my mother, whom I rarely saw during those years due to my tendency to freeze in a constellation of encrypted, overwhelming emotion in her presence, a state that expressed itself in less than loving behaviour. The overexposed black and white photo she sent, along with this note, written in her lilting hand on powder blue paper, shows a baby not long in the world swaddled in soft cotton blankets in a latticed, frilly cot with an enormous bow on the side. Only a head of black hair is visible and a three-quarter profile of a small sleeping face with eyes closed tight.

This is the gestation story my mother told me when I was a child. She'd already had two miscarriages by the time I was conceived. They were trying for a girl and had just about given up; while contemplating adoption my mother fell pregnant again towards the end of 1962. When I was six months in the womb, some drama, the details of which died along with my mother's body, sent her to the hospital. Doctors listened for a heartbeat and could hear none. They thought the foetus was dead and prepared to remove it, but my mother grew agitated and refused to let them. In order to placate her they agreed to leave it until morning. When they came back the next day there was a strong heartbeat. A miracle! They ordered her to rest for the remainder of her pregnancy. I can't be sure the bit about the miracle is true. That might be the embellishment of a fanciful child's imagination, but one thing is certain, because one of her oldest and closest friends confirms it: my mother spent many months of the pregnancy confined to bed, reading, as she had done throughout her sickly childhood, fearful of losing me, fearful, as she had been for as long as she could remember. There are times I've wondered if I whimpered because I had some pre-verbal sixth sense that the world into which I had arrived was a deeply troubled one, and that I was in for a hell of a ride.

A big blonde moon sits high in the night sky and hundred-k gusts take another power line down. I sit in the dark.

When I came to in that Bondi hotel, I was groggy and disoriented, and being fucked by a guy who wouldn't stop when I struggled to get out from under him. I said I wanted to go and he said no. After, I lay on my back, rigid, looking at the ceiling, him lying beside me. I remembered being on the roof with him and his friends, then following him to his room, just the two of us. I remembered sitting on the edge of the bed next to him, talking. Then nothing – blank – till I woke up to the pounding. I didn't know what else he might do, and his not letting me go terrified me. I didn't know where my clothes were, but I was frantic to leave. I leapt up, made a break for the door and ran. At least I think that's what happened going by flash-bulb grabs of memory.

Those images dissolve as I reach for them. One moment I make out shapes as if viewing quivering, faded old film; the next they are gone – poof.

As a child I got swept up in the drama of Barbra Streisand crooning about memories illuminating the corners of the mind in her 1970s hit 'The Way We Were'. Research, however, suggests that memories don't just occupy or light up a given region of the mind, they *are* the mind. Reporting on emerging findings, Nick Stockton writes that 'sensory experience triggers changes in the molecules of your neurons, reshaping the way they connect to one another. That means your brain is literally made of memories, and memories constantly remake your brain.' Another way to describe it: the brain is 'plastic' – dynamic and capable of modifying itself. Stockton quotes neuroscientist Nikolay Kukushkin explaining that remembering a given memory involves reactivating previous connections between parts of the brain. These connections are fine-tuned at synapses, which are sensitive to the strength or weakness of signals. Kukushkin emphasises that memories haven't been stored in a system, as if static or fixed in place – rather, memory, which helps us learn from the past with the aim of improving function in the future, is 'the system itself'.

Light bounces off a face and its rays sharpen to a point on your retina. Your cornea focuses through the eye's internal lens, converting the image to electrical impulses that speed along your optic nerve like a superhighway to the visual cortex in the brain; as if a camera has been clicked, the image is caught. Someone speaks, their voice making sound waves that travel through the canals of your ears. When the waves hit the eardrum it vibrates and a trio of tiny bones in the middle ear hammer the vibrations towards the snail-like cochlea in the inner ear, where they are transformed into electrical impulses by tiny hair cells and carried to the brain. You smell and chemicals in the air make their way through your nose, sending a message to the brain by means of sensory nerves. You eat and your taste buds detect the chemicals in the food; they transport that sensory input to the brain, resulting in the perception of taste. You are touched and receptors in your skin and muscles race signals up your spinal cord to the brain. Your nervous system shoots impulses along a network of cells and fibres in complex conversations between brain and body. Hormones circulate in your blood and work your nerve cells, making you hungry or horny. This elaborate symphony and the way it makes you *feel* is in constant play with the environment and the beings and objects you encounter, registering information in more detail than can be consciously acknowledged. Your brain collects and connects it all via neurons and synapses, creating 'mosaics from these milliseconds-long impressions', as Stockton puts it. This is the basic process of how each and every memory is made. What's particularly revolutionary about Kukushkin's findings is that they suggest 'your brain's molecules, cells, and synapses can tell time'. His study concludes that the relation between neurons, molecules and synapses encode these combined sensations as imprints 'in terms of the relative time they occurred', packaging the memory into 'a so-called time window'. It's obvious how the making of memories might be disrupted or confused by excessive alcohol consumption, but what about trauma?

Trauma theorist Cathy Caruth says the problem of traumatic memory comes down to the inability to fully witness the traumatic event. A gap 'carries the force of the event and does so precisely at the expense of simple knowledge and memory. The force of this experience would appear to arise precisely, in other words, in the collapse of its understanding.' This reads like a cryptic puzzle. It feels like a cryptic puzzle, this living with gap-like memories undone by the force of what incites them. Caruth explains that the event, not being registered and integrated in the normal way, cannot become, as Freud's contemporary Janet called it, 'narrative memory'. *The event cannot become the past.* It never settles into its 'time window'.

People think of memory as being about the past, but that's a mistake. As Thomas J. Gross writes, citing neuropsychiatrist Daniel J. Siegel, it's more accurate to say it's about 'how the past affects future outcomes'. Biologically, this function of memory is, Gross says, the way in which we construct our reality based on factual knowledge of the world, the way we come to know ourselves as a self. Traumatic memory is a kind of past in the present that informs the future. Those who are significantly affected by it are trapped in a temporal whirl they can neither comprehend nor control. And those of us grappling with its mystifying workings need to heed caution.

Elizabeth Loftus, a researcher of 'false memory', says in a TED talk that most people erroneously think of memory like a recording device, but that in reality it is constructed and continually reconstructed. It is as vulnerable as a Chinese whisper. This is murky territory. We want to rewind memory, like tape, to imagine it as mediatised, captured certainty. We want it to be true or false, sound or silence, but either way to be solid. We need to know we're not mad (or even if we are, that something really happened). Instead memory slides around inside us like blood and between us like a sticky mutating membrane.

As a child I coped with life in a 'dysfunctional' addiction-addled family by dancing. My parents separated when I was four, the same age I started ballet. I danced all through my childhood, rocking myself to sleep with fantasies of being a prima ballerina. Then, at the age of twelve, following several harrowing years of domestic violence between my mother and her defacto partner Albert, and in my final year of primary school, I started going to school early and, by special arrangement, writing a novel in the staff room before the teachers arrived.

Though I had no way of knowing it at the time, this childhood attempt at novel writing was a kind of trauma testimony. The story told of a young girl lost alone in the bush, negotiating a host of scary trials and tribulations and triumphing against the odds. There was a fire in the summer and to survive it my heroine jumped into a creek and lay underwater holding her breath for a magic-realist length of time until the fire passed over her. There was a grisly old hermit, stern and distant, and it seems obvious to me now that he was my father. The project marked a shift from dancing and towards language and literature. This is how I became a writer. Unintentionally, while I was busy chasing other leads, pursuing other goals, imagining other lives.

I've been published widely and I've earned three writing degrees and I teach writing in universities, but I remain humbled by language and writing. In *Shadowlands*, the film based on the life of writer and scholar C.S. Lewis, a student recounts his father's adage that 'we read to know we're not alone'. And Jonathan Safran Foer once observed, in an interview promoting his debut novel, *Everything Is Illuminated*, that writing is an attempt to not be alone. When I think back to the motivation of my twelve-year-old self, rising early to write a novel in an empty staff room, it is her loneliness that comes to mind – a loneliness born of the maddening disconnect of trauma.

Psychiatrist and Holocaust survivor Dori Laub cites massive psychic trauma as 'a record that has yet to be made'. This is his way of describing an experience that occurs too quickly or suddenly to be processed, that fails to leave a mark in thought and language but whose presence is felt and expressed in delayed symptomology. Caruth puts it this way: 'In its most general definition, trauma describes an overwhelming experience of sudden or catastrophic events in which the response to the event occurs in the often delayed, uncontrolled repetitive appearance of hallucinations and other intrusive phenomena.' It lurks, transmitting down the line, rearranging cells and relationships. When it resurfaces (surprise!) it may or may not appear pathological. Some traumatised individuals are jailed (the addicts, crims and socioeconomically disadvantaged) while others are rewarded (the shame-driven high-achievers).

When it causes havoc we withstand it like bad weather, nursing child-like fantasies (imperceptible sometimes) of rescue by *deus ex machina*, that magic moment in a play, novel or film where some divine force descends on a seemingly hopeless situation, saving the day. In Ancient Greek theatre this God was literally lowered from the heavens via a device or 'machine', which is why it translates from Latin as 'God out of the machine'. I don't mean to sound defeatist when I say I have given up waiting for the God out of the machine and that I think the machine is swallowing us all up. It's true that like Nick Cave I don't hold with the notion of an interventionist God, but if I did it would be writing. In writing and reading, a touch of salvation is possible, a loosening from the machine, some kind of rising out of it, some kind of not being lonely, the balm of world-making words.

This book had its unwitting beginnings back in 2007 when I wrote about my experience of growing up with violence in a memoir essay titled 'The Exiled Child' for *Divided Nation*, the fifteenth edition of *Griffith Review*. It was later reprinted in *The Age*, where some tasteless sub-editor had rebranded it with the punny, cringeworthy title: 'Home Is Where the Pain Is'. It was shortlisted for the Alfred Deakin Prize for an Essay Advancing Public Debate in the 2007 Victorian Premier's Literary Awards, up against Frank Moorhouse, Amanda Lohrey and Noel Pearson (Moorhouse won). I had never before had this kind of response to a published piece. I lost count of the number of people who tracked down my email address and wrote to me. And several years later it proved the catalyst for my return to university to undertake a PhD on transgenerational trauma and its literary testimony. I'd already spent years coming to terms with how trauma played out in my own life, and I wanted to understand more about how it worked socially.

In other words, I had been writing a long time before I realised trauma was a grand theme. It's not a particularly original grand theme since most books, at least so far as poetry, fiction and creative non-fiction are concerned, deal with trauma one way or another. I have no unique claim to it. As trauma tales go there are far worse than mine: in many ways my traumatic experiences have taken place in a privileged context. I'm a white woman from a western, working-middle-class family. I'm not moneyed or financially secure, working as a sessional academic and teacher, one of the many anxious labourers in the rising new class of the precariat, but I am rich in social capital, and have benefited from good fortune. I write about trauma because I don't know how else to live with it, because I'm still coming to terms with it, still searching for connections, and because I know many others are too.

During my research and reading across continental philosophy, cultural psychoanalytic theory and poststructuralism, one of the works I found most compelling was a book of collected essays by Hungarian–French analysts Nicolas Abraham and Mária Török. Edited and elaborated on by Nicholas Rand, the essays emphasise transgenerational trauma by way of strikingly gothic conceptions. They speak of the 'crypt', the 'phantom' and 'psychic tombs'. Abraham and Török's thinking and writing about trauma are so poetic that reading them inspired a poem in homage:

Writing a Dear John letter while reading Abraham and Török

Dear [insert name here],
You have eaten me

(a me that stands in for another that is).
They call it incorporation.

You swallowed me deep in your belly of
unsobbable sobs, of
unsayable to-be-saids
in your belly of rotting sugar.

You kept me on a chain
like a pet
      you starve
at the door of the crypt (of your child mother).

They call you a cryptophore, a poem, a poet.
They dare to rewrite *Hamlet* and I dare to rewrite you.

Of course the secret,
not just any secret,
not just *a* secret,
but a tomb, an enclave, a haunting …
your grandmother God in her cardigans
giving you the gaps, giving you the fear,
the wordless passing of the baton
of shame, of shame
and the silence of corpses screaming.
They call it the phantom.

I want out your belly love,
to stand with Hamlet in an ending ined,
in an ending where
only the dead
      are buried.

'Poetry has always been able to utter the will of free will, coming back to the memory of words and extracting its sense and time,' says Julia Kristeva, the philosopher, literary critic, feminist theorist and psychoanalyst. What does the free will want but to be free, to live? Abraham and Török speak of working-through/mourning/ healing as a mysterious but affirming force of psychic life, the result of processing everything from whatever's in your field of vision (wind-shivery leaves) to your worst nightmare. It can be facilitated by therapy but is by no means limited to it. Reading and writing are among the many currencies in which it moves. This force has worked overtime on my anxiety and panic attacks, addictions, agoraphobia, and many-headed compulsions, which are never only mine. It does what it can under the circumstances and the circumstances aren't always conducive. It's alive and pumping, but it gets tired. In short, it's chalked up some wins and some losses, though neither is absolute.

I spent hours that night at the police station, where I gradually sobered up. There were tests at the hospital, and my father appeared in the hallway, taking his place beside me on one of those hard plastic waiting-room chairs, with a sad, drained look on his face. His presence pained and intimidated me at the best of times, but I was grateful for his way of going quiet, of underplaying, in dramatic situations. What happened that weekend spooked me for months; there was an odd emotional hangover. There were drawn-out legal proceedings. I remember a series of long phone calls with my old friend Renee, talking it through from the Manly flat I was then sharing with my older brother.

I'd first met Renee when I was around twelve or thirteen through my friend Heidi. Heidi was a big-boned, pink-skinned blonde who befriended me on my first day at Glebe Primary School. She was a diabolical child and a treasure, and against the odds she grew up to be – so far as I am able to observe – a functional and accomplished woman. Heidi lived around the corner in a rundown one-bedroom flat, little more than a bedsit, with a drunkard dad who worked in a factory and who, she told me once, was not her real father. It was hard to know what to believe with Heidi, but she didn't seem to be lying when she said that her mother had committed suicide when Heidi was a baby (the man she grew up with was, apparently, her mother's partner at the time) and that the bossy old battle-axe who lived down the road was her grandmother. There were a couple of half-sisters around. One was dour and dark-haired with a sour cast of mouth who would have been at home in a Chekhov play; the other was blonde, livelier, and worked in an office somewhere. Heidi had the bedroom, and when he wasn't at the factory or the pub Heidi's father, a child-sized elf-like man, slept it off on a filthy-sheeted single mattress in the lounge room with a small black and white TV blaring from the foot of the bed. On Thursdays, payday, he would come home extra-soused and pass out on the bed with five-, ten-, twenty-dollar bills falling out of his trouser pockets. We'd light-finger them out then take off up to Broadway shops for a Thursday evening shopping spree of whatever took our fancy.

I never did work out how Heidi got to know so many Glebe eccentrics and outsiders, but I mostly got to know them through her. When I was around thirteen or fourteen she took me to a plain double-storeyed house up around Cowper Street. I didn't know then (or rather I knew in that way of knowing and not understanding) that it was a Sydney 'colony' of the Californian cult The Children of God, later renamed The Family. A decade or so later the sect came to public attention amid accusations of serious misconduct, including child abuse and financial mismanagement. I don't recall being subjected to overt sexual abuse there, but I do remember the promotion and practice of a bizarre evangelistic method called Flirty Fishing, which involved members, often young women, using flirtation and sex to lure new members into the cult.

Heidi also took me to a dilapidated house up on Derwent Street where she introduced me to an old Bukowski lookalike named Jim, who wore Buddy Holly glasses and shuffled around, potbelly protruding from dull-white singlet, long curly grey hairs growing out of his flabby upper arms. Random young women – mostly lesbians or sex workers (or both) – came and went from Jim's at all hours. I took it at face value, grateful to have somewhere to enjoy Vegemite toast on white bread (not available at my house), bludge smokes for hours on end, kill time, and sometimes con Jim or one of the women into giving us money. There was plenty of sexual innuendo, rumours of porno film screenings at night after we'd gone home, and jokey suggestions that some of the women might have serviced Jim. Still, we viewed it, perversely, as a safe place where we could hang out, smoke and talk freely, away from home. It was there at Jim's that I first met Renee, though I had no way of knowing then that several years later she'd come back into my life and be my only friend at a time when I desperately needed one.

I was lonely then in a way I'm not lonely now. That's how I came to be at the bar of a quaint ye olde pub on George Street on a Saturday afternoon drinking with strangers. I'd not long returned to Sydney having fled to London in 1980 at sixteen, determined never to come back to Australia, eager to escape its provincialism, to have a bigger life, to be *there* rather than *here*. I had fantasies of becoming an 'actress' but that was really my mother's dream. She'd grown up in the age of the silver screen and had an encyclopaedic knowledge of old Hollywood. Greta Garbo, Vivien Leigh and Marilyn Monroe were her favourites and though she dabbled, appearing on *Beauty and the Beast* during the '60s, doing small-time theatre shows and working as an extra in '70s TV shows and films, if she had a missed boat a serious acting career was it. I had fantasies of being someone else, somewhere else, as if being in the glitzy capital at the heart of a dying empire would somehow make me more substantial, more important.

How do I explain the circumstances in which an unaccompanied minor moves 10,560 miles across the planet alone? I can feel myself wanting to protect my dead mother, wanting to explain how headstrong I was, how persuasive I could be, wanting to stress that my pushing wore her down, but the fact is she let me go and she shouldn't have. Sometimes, when I see fifteen- and sixteen-year-olds – young people the age I was then – I am overcome with sorrow for my young self. As sophisticated as they may appear, whatever their adult veneers, they strike me as child-like and incredibly vulnerable, and I struggle to comprehend how the adults in my life failed to see me that way. To understand something of my mother's decision, you'd have to understand a mother–daughter dynamic in which on some vital level the tables were turned.

There were several contributing factors to my mother's poor parental decision-making. She had been stifled by an over-protective mother and longed all her life for freedom from those oppressive demands, so her permissiveness with me was, at least in part, the result of an extreme pendulum swing. She suffered terrible guilt about my childhood, about what I lived through in service to her addiction to pills and troubled men. I knew how to work that guilt to get my way. And despite her feistiness, she was never too far away from a crippling self-doubt that led her to hand over power to those around her, even her own children. This bred in me a sense of false empowerment and gave rise to a deeply ingrained over-responsibility that clashed with wanton irresponsibility in my youthful precociousness. I assumed a position of authority and leadership, especially so far as my destiny and liberties were concerned. As a Cold War baby, I was convinced that nuclear fallout would wipe Europe out in my lifetime and that I needed to get there sooner rather than later, but mostly I went because I had to keep moving, because an imagined somewhere else was always better than the actuality of where I was. And I went because of my first cousin Jake, with whom I was besotted.

A debonair extrovert, Jake had moved to London to pursue a career in film. He seemed so cosmopolitan, even though he was only a few years older than me. His larger-than-life demeanour was a direct consequence of being the son of my Uncle Hugh, my father's elder brother and a renowned author in his day, and Hugh's second wife, Phoebe, an Elizabeth Taylor–esque beauty from the Macarthur-Onslow dynasty. Jake was warm and wild and had a to-the-manor-born air about him, but even the glorious Macarthur-Onslow birthright had its roots in a traumatic defeat.

The Macarthurs (historically known by various other spellings) were a distinguished clan in the Scottish Highlands and some make controversial claims that they were descended from King Arthur. The clan reached their zenith of power around the fourteenth and fifteenth centuries, boasting significant land holdings as the keepers of Dunstaffnage Castle until King James I had the Macarthur clan chief beheaded to keep their influence in check. The execution served its purpose, weakening the clan's political power base, but the Macarthurs refused to be snuffed out. Come 1746, John Macarthur of Strachur and his seven sons fought as soldiers in the Jacobite army in the ferocious civil war showdown at Culloden Moor. John and one of his brood were slain on the bloody battlefield. The surviving sons scattered in fear for their lives; Alexander Macarthur fled to the West Indies along with numerous other Jacobites, eventually returning to settle in England where his son John – named after Alexander's fallen father – was born.

John Macarthur grew up to immigrate to Australia with his wife, Elizabeth, who gave birth at sea only to lose the child before nursing John through life-threatening illness aboard the Second Fleet. Thanks to a generous land grant, and on the back of convict labour and amid frontier wars, the Macarthurs became colonial aristocracy after pioneering a world-famous merino wool industry (John Macarthur's image appeared alongside a ram's head on the old two-dollar note, and the district is still named after him). Having made his fortune, Macarthur built a majestic Georgian manor called Camden Park House on the traditional lands of the Dharawal people, south of Sydney.

The story of Jake's forebears is a saga worthy of a melodramatic mini-series, and Alan Atkinson (no relation) has detailed it, at least so far as the public record in Australia is concerned, in a book titled *Camden*. Suffice to say that Macarthur's charms, ambition and successes were matched by flourishing flaws, turmoil and scandals; he was instrumental in the infamous Rum Rebellion, an attempted military coup, which resulted in his exile, and in his absence Elizabeth – considered by many, including some within the family, to be the real pioneer – managed the estate and expanded its business interests. After establishing his little empire, John Macarthur died insane and was buried in a family vault shaded by Chinese elms on a humble hill west of the mansion.

Five generations later, Phoebe, the youngest of Lieutenant-Colonel Edward Macarthur-Onslow's three daughters, became a local celebrity. In a 1950s spread in *The Sun-Herald* she stands in trousers and lipstick beside her father's Hornet Moth, wearing an expression of intelligent determination. She's only seventeen, already a successful model, and she's busy taking acting and flying lessons (she went on to become the youngest licensed female pilot in New South Wales). She tells the reporter about her plans to head to Hollywood before she turns eighteen. A 'Lord Strathallan' – a Cambridge graduate in Australia to 'learn the shipping business' – is noted as her 'constant escort'. But the film-star plans and hinted marriage to Lord Strathallan don't come to pass. Instead she meets my uncle, the dashing writer Hugh Atkinson, already married with two children, Damien and Aram. The rest, to twist the adage in on itself, is family history.

Trauma is tenacious in its tendency to transmit inter-generationally, and neither success nor beauty nor money can stop it. My toffy-voiced aunt Phoebe may have seemed to readers of yesteryear gossip columns the personification of Australian faux-royalty, but beneath her socialite glamour, renowned generosity and impressive hosting skills, the brutal losses of Culloden Moor continued to reverberate. And like the son of John Macarthur of Strachur who died at the hands of Hanoverian loyalist troops, Jake lost his battle too young.

I can count the number of times I've been to Camden on my fingers, mostly because my father and Hugh lived in different countries for much of my childhood, though they were close all their lives. I do remember a couple of family outings to what was then certified countryside and Jake coming to stay with us for a weekend when I was very young, before my parents divorced. After Hugh's career as an author took off, the charming couple jetted to the Northern Hemisphere, raising Jake and his sister, Rachael, in Malta, Majorca, Guernsey and London, hobnobbing with luminaries like Peter Finch and Phillip Knightley. (Hugh once warned me off becoming a writer by evoking a memory of watching a tortured Dylan Thomas labouring over troublesome words, though I'm not sure if this bears up: my father says that like all good fiction writers my uncle could be creative with the truth.) In the absence of this worldly branch of the family I heard occasional stories and saw the odd photograph in Mediterranean technicolour.

On Sunday visits to Seaforth, my grandmother waxed lyrical about the winning ways of the golden couple and their children, and I understood that they lent a kind of distant nobility to the family. A proud Scotswoman, she had looked down her nose at Australia ever since she had been forced to emigrate as a teenager with a fondness for the poetry of Robert Burns. She never quite recovered from being ejected from Great Britain – still the centre of the universe at the turn of the twentieth century – only to find herself in a dusty one-horse town in central-west New South Wales. And though her own breeding was working-class, and she had willingly accepted the hand of my grandfather Clarence, a mild-mannered and handsome fellow from a family of Trundle master butchers, she believed herself married beneath her intellectual station. It was as if she saw her firstborn as her rightful heir, hobnobbing with the gentry in the opulent hotspots of 1960s Europe. I couldn't hope to compete with my pedigree cousins for her affection; I was inferior, a Sydney girl, the second child of her second son.

It wasn't until they returned to live in Leura, during my first or second year of high school, that I got to know Hugh, Phoebe and my cousins. Hugh and Phoebe separated not long after their homecoming, and shortly afterwards I woke up one morning to find Hugh passed out on our sofa. He and my mother began a relationship and over time I grew close to him, viewing him as something of a father figure. It may be more accurate to say my mother and Hugh resumed the relationship they began when I was a small child. My brother, many years older than me, swears he saw them kissing passionately in our childhood home before my parents' divorce, and one of my mother's closest friends confirms their affair, adding that Hugh, a suave author on the rise at the time, had bought my mother a car. Uncle Hugh was alcoholic, gifted, clever, cultivated and witty, which was a lot of fun so long as it stayed on the right side of acerbic and wasn't directed at you. I was mostly spared his withering gaze and vicious tongue, but not entirely, and my mother copped it plenty. His nickname for her was 'pygmy' on account of her being short and petite and, though many might take that as a slight, it demonstrated the more tolerable, affectionately mocking side of his verbal abuse. One of my mother's close friends says she once complained that he called her a cockroach, a term clearly intended to be demeaning and humiliating. Even so, both my mother and I loved him madly, and after she died in 1997, only a few years following his death, I found a bundle of adoring love letters from Hugh to my mother. I read only the first lines of a few letters – enough to know it was not my place to read more – and in those words their admiration and desire for each other was palpable.

It was during the early years of my mother and Hugh's on-again-off-again defacto relationship, when I was fifteen or sixteen, that my crush on cousin Jake took hold. My mother and Hugh were shacked up in a humble weatherboard house just outside of Woy Woy and I was staying with them. I spent my days writing in a journal and riding my bike around Brisbane Waters, and sometimes Jake would visit. Bored with satellite-city living I moved back to Sydney just after my sixteenth birthday, and into the Glebe studio apartment my mother had acquired, the better to be closer to Jake, who was living in a house in Surry Hills owned by Phoebe. I passed the days of a Sydney summer listening to Double J radio and Neil Young's *Harvest* over and over, drinking with friends, daydreaming about Jake and finding excuses to make contact.

One day Hugh showed up on my doorstep, having been turfed out by my mother. We went on a bender around town with Jeremy, an ex-boyfriend of mine Hugh was partial to, and a couple of other friends, during which we were refused entry at the infamous Journalists' Club, despite Hugh's longstanding association, probably because Jeremy got around barefoot in an op-shop suit in breach of the dress code. It lasted for days, and somewhere in my timeworn, booze-soaked memories is a clear replay of lying next to Hugh on the floor, both of us drunk, half-asleep or both, and him groping me. I struggle to write those words, and to leave them be once written. I make myself write them against a force field of prohibition and shame. I imagine my aunts and my surviving cousins reading them and dread sets in the gut. I am ashamed for him yet it is not *my* shame.

It only happened that once. I want you to understand (hear the rising panic in my voice?) that I do not believe he would have done it sober. At no other time in our relationship did I experience him as sleazy, or did I feel sexually sized up by him. I want to say these things. I want to make excuses. To be sure you understand the conditions. Shame is part of what drives alcoholism, addiction and abuse, and in so doing it reproduces and is transmitted. And shame is often transmitted, paradoxically, by shameless acts, acts in which one person's avoidance of shame demands another carry it. As Teresa Brennan points out, feminine beings – those who do not exhibit the valued, westernised signs of masculinity, whether because of their gender identity, youth, race or even species – are required to carry a disproportionate amount of shame, fear and other punishing affects. It is the way of patriarchy.

We feminine beings learn early on to take this load, to wear it as ours, to do the work, day in and day out, of enabling silence, denial, minimisation, unless we make a conscious decision not to, and learn how not to (and of course, children have a very limited capacity to do either). I force myself to write that one time my only uncle sexualised me and fondled me, tried to kiss me like a lover, when I was not yet the age of consent and he knew how much I looked up to him, because this is a story that plays out the world over. A 'good' man, a 'drunk' man, a 'talented' man, a 'trusted family member' or 'friend', a man whose family and community assume to be above it, objectifies and abuses a child in his care or a young woman in his presence. When it comes to light we ponder, discuss and engage in argy-bargy about what causes men in such numbers to do these things. There are many possible devils in the detail, but the bottom line is that when men do this they do it because they can, because they've been enabled and trained by aeons of patriarchy to do it, because deep down they've been imprinted with the notion that they are masters of all they survey since the day they were born with a penis and thus bequeathed a gendered privilege (are we at risk of overusing that word; are we too preoccupied with identity point scoring?). And too often we protect men, protect ourselves and each other, from the truth of what they do and from our collective duty to examine how and why it is men reach that moment, and how best to intervene on this structural (there can be no other word for it) abuse. When my mother showed up unannounced shortly after the drunken fumble she found the studio trashed and empty and added me to her growing list of evictees. I did not tell her about the unseemly moment that had passed between her partner and me.

As a mature, educated woman, as a known feminist, I am expected to be the kind of woman who does not struggle to say that my long-dead uncle crossed the line, yet here I am: wanting to retract, to stay silent for my father's sake, my aunt's sake, my cousins' sake, my dead mother's sake, wanting to whitewash the memory of a man I revered and who has some bearing on my becoming 'a person whose most absorbed and passionate hours are spent arranging words on pieces of paper' – a writer – as Joan Didion once put it. Why do I imagine that what I seek to protect them from is theirs or ours alone? Why does it feel so personal, so singular, as if it's about an individual (him, me) when I know that what I protect against belongs to society, shameful and shameless by turns, to a history well beyond that of my family?

What I unwittingly, instinctively want to protect against is the shame that permeates patriarchy. It's what I've been trained to do. It's what we've all been trained to do, but protecting against this shame means protecting, colluding with, its shamefulness *and* its shamelessness, with patriarchy itself. 'I was very struck by all the passages in Primo Levi where he explains that Nazi camps have given us "a shame at being human"', says the French philosopher Gilles Deleuze in an interview with Antonio Negri. 'Not, he says, that we're all responsible for Nazism, as some would have us believe, but that we've all been tainted by it: even the survivors of the camps had to make compromises with it, if only to survive.' So it is that we make compromises, from the start, in order to survive, except that many don't, or do so wretchedly. We've been brought to a critical point in which the future of humanity and the planet itself is less certain than ever. Having reached the twenty-first century, we're on our knees with climate change, financial crises of false economies, unprecedented instability in western political leadership, and global terrorism operating in a context in which many countries have nuclear capability. There is no time left for decorum. One must say the words that need to be said, exposing the circulating shame that in hiding propagates.

The windows rattle and the wind howls. I try to sleep, surrounded by ghosts.

I can't remember how Renee and I reconnected in the aftermath of the seedy Bondi rape, but somehow she appeared in my world, no longer working as a sex worker, and we'd talk on the phone and occasionally I'd go visit her in her nice little flat and we'd sit around drinking green ginger wine and listening to Rodriguez singing about sugar men. What I remember most distinctly is the sound of her voice, on the other end of the phone, telling me that my problem was I saw two sides of everything. I didn't understand what she meant, and that bothered me. It felt like I was missing something important.

So I continued angsting over my feelings of guilt and responsibility, convinced I'd 'brought it upon myself'. At a bar on my own for hours on end; flirting outrageously; going off in a taxi with people I didn't know to I wasn't sure where; changing my mind about fucking mid-coitus (if I'd even made up my mind to start with); panicking and bolting; making a public, pathetic spectacle of myself. I would have dropped the charges, but they weren't mine to drop: the cops had pressed them and now I had no choice but to have a court case hanging over me. I counted my lucky stars that I was not required to be present and I had no hesitation in electing not to attend.

The nagging guilt came with another feeling I had no words for. It had preceded the rape, which produced yet more of it. I'm not talking about the energetic movement of a necessary, transient humbling designed to regulate unchecked interest or hubris. I'm talking about the chronic presence of a noxious, transmissible traumatic shame. American psychologist and affect theorist Silvan Tomkins conceived of nine affects: shame-humiliation (inherently punishing), anger-rage (inherently punishing), fear-terror (inherently punishing), distress-anguish (inherently punishing), interest-excitement (inherently rewarding), enjoyment-joy (inherently rewarding), surprise-startle (inherently neutral), disgust (inherently punishing) and dissmell (a biological response of revulsion, to putrid meat for example – inherently punishing).

These are, according to Tomkins and his adherents, hardwired and present from birth, and in combination with life experiences they form an emotional memory that becomes the scaffolding on which much of the personality is built. Our less than fully conscious attempts to regulate affect (to maximise those we experience as positive and minimise those we experience as negative) results in what he calls 'life scripts', psychic and behavioural patterns that inform the way our lives play out. Tomkins viewed shame as the most pernicious of the affects. 'If distress is the affect of suffering,' he pronounced, 'shame is the affect of indignity, of defeat, of transgression, and of alienation. Though terror speaks to life and death and distress makes of the world a vale of tears, yet shame strikes deepest into the heart of man.' It struck deep in my heart back then though I didn't know its name.

I was relieved when the guy didn't show for court and I got on with it, putting the sordid business behind me.

Fast-forward thirty-plus years to 2016. One of the sorry tales that circulated around social media was that of the Stanford rape case. Brock Turner, a twenty-year-old former Stanford University student and star athlete, was sentenced to jail for the attempted rape of an unconscious twenty-two-year-old woman behind a dumpster at a frat party in January 2015. The woman understandably chose to remain anonymous. Two documents generated reactions from around the world: a letter from Turner's father in defence of his disgraced son, and a victim impact statement of over 7,000 words addressed to Brock and read out by the woman during his sentencing hearing.

The outpourings by Turner's family are toxic examples of how the rotten apple falls close to the poisoned tree of delusional, closed-hearted, sexist entitlement. The words of the young woman whom Turner violated – not only in the initial assault but also in wilfully dragging her through a trial and attempting to shift the blame in self-serving denial – reminded me of that night in Bondi and its aftermath. I read her statement, cheering from the sidelines. I exulted in its length and strength. In its clarity and her capacity for articulation in the face of layers of abuse. She was everything I was not in the wake of that ill-fated bender. This was a young woman standing her ground against a society and a legal system that had failed her and claiming her right to a voice, to speak, to be heard (I want to think this signifies some kind of progress, but the power of her words is undercut by the fact that they exist in order to call out a culture that still produces and enables men like Turner).

A Brock Turner Family Support page was set up on Facebook, seeking donations and spreading propaganda and slander. While it was active it launched a #brockinallofus campaign that featured posts protesting, 'We've all made mistakes. Whether it's failing to drive in the winning run in your little league game or oversleeping and missing an important test, or, like Brock and his companion, drinking too much and getting a bit too touchy-feely.' Whoa. Wait up. We're comparing a childhood sporting disappointment and a malfunctioning alarm clock to rape and blatant victim-blaming? Next to this text a black and white cartoon depicted three female figures each holding a placard marked by one of the following words: *We / Are / Brock*. The troubled Turner family ended this post by thanking supporters for their prayers. Jesus wept. Following persistent complaints, the page was eventually shut down, but not long afterwards Turner was released, having served only three months of his already lenient six-month sentence (the prosecutor had argued for six years). It's an insufferable and seemingly circular crisis in which we live, an asylum run by lunatics, and we do our best to juggle in a mania of 'isms' and stress, soothed only by love and voices of support binding against the micro-aggressions and micro-transgressions that build to these horrendous moments made public spectacle.

Another petition in my feed that week protested the banning of Melbourne comedian and feminist commentator Catherine Deveny. Facebook had slapped a thirty-day lockout on her for an 'offensive' status, which read: 'Here are the top ten causes of violence. 1. Men. 2. Men. 3. Men. 4. Men. 5. Men. 6. Men. 7. Men. 8. Men. 9. Men. 10. Men.' It appeared Facebook moderators did not consider the Brock Turner Family Support page to be 'violating community standards' while a simply stated opinion by a lone woman was promptly deemed 'inappropriate' and penalised. When the World Health Organization announced in 2015 that the leading cause of death for young women aged fifteen to nineteen was suicide (the leading causes of death for young men of the same age were road injury and interpersonal violence), Professor Vikram Patel, an internationally recognised psychiatrist and expert in global mental health, cited gender discrimination as the probable cause. 'Misogyny kills,' writes Jessica Valenti, the young (female) journalist discussing the finding. Valenti, an outspoken feminist commentator for *The Guardian,* withdrew from social media platforms in July 2016 after the rape and death threats usually directed to her were extended to her five-year-old daughter.

Controversial American academic and social critic Camille Paglia defends patriarchy, suggesting that second- and third-wave feminists (such as Deveny and Valenti) who call men out for sexism and misogyny are puritanical, punitive and demonising. 'History must be seen clearly and fairly: obstructive traditions arose not from men's hatred or enslavement of women but from the natural division of labor that had developed over thousands of years during the agrarian period and that once immensely benefited and protected women, permitting them to remain at the hearth to care for helpless infants and children,' insists Paglia. Yet US-based historian Dr Amanda Foreman, in her four-part BBC documentary, *The Ascent of Woman*, states there is evidence suggesting that the development of patriarchy was not based on the 'natural division of labour' and nor was it as beneficial to women as Paglia claims. It was, Foreman asserts, surplus agriculture, as well as the development of a military to protect and expand it, that seems to have led to the advent of rigid patriarchal practices and attitudes, manifesting in a variety of ways across distinct cultures.

Donald J. Trump and his henchmen at the helm of the so-called free world demonstrate more starkly than ever before that government all too readily becomes less a system of democratic representation and more a corporatised, masculinist oligarchy, unhinged in its loveless lust for domination, and, as if poisoned by the fumes of their own toxicity, corrupted by the patriarchy it desperately seeks to reassert. Feeling their patriarchal power base slipping, they refuse to go down without a gaslighting-us-on-the-way-south fight. In the aftermath of Trump's election to the US presidency, those who saw the rise to power of an ill-prepared demagogue as a devastating coup debated about which ushered in the unfortunate outcome: was it down to class, race or gender? Foreman's reading of patriarchy's beginnings would seem to support Marx's view of class as the dominant organising principle of society, in that production of surplus for profit gave rise to both early capitalism and patriarchy, but since sexist, racist and speciesist principles now dominate economic and socio-political operations in such an entwined way, arguing the toss is a waste of valuable time. This is why many are now adopting an intersectional approach as our best hope of making substantial and sustainable change. As Patricia Hill Collins puts it, class, race and gender (and I would add species) form interlocking axes of oppression within a matrix of domination; it is less useful, then, to determine which packs the biggest punch (the answer will always depend on who is answering anyway) than to understand the ways in which patriarchy drives the entire operation.

Even if Paglia is right to acknowledge the once-productive foundation of patriarchy and a biologically influenced 'natural division of labour' that enabled the survival of the human species in ancient civilisations, she glosses over the fact that the productive–destructive balance tipped towards the latter as modernity ramped up, and that, for all of patriarchy's achievements, women and the lower classes, the workers and slaves, have paid an unspeakably high price for those gains. Patriarchy was profoundly traumatising from the start, with its inequities and focus on war, devastating for men as well as for women, children and non-human animals. Paglia also protests that patriarchy didn't start out motivated by significant numbers of men hating, enslaving, exploiting, oppressing, or otherwise victimising women and girls, but according to Foreman it took almost no time before laws came into being that amounted to, or paved the way for, just that. And despite many of those laws having been rewritten in light of challenges to the patriarchal worldview, it's hard to conceive of the kind of treatment received by the likes of Valenti as anything less than downright hateful.

It's difficult to reconcile statistics on violence towards women with Paglia's selective thinking on the glories of patriarchy and the shortcomings of modern-day feminists. Her logic comes across as one-eyed. For example, when she observes that 'it was labor-saving appliances, invented by men and spread by capitalism, that liberated women from daily drudgery', she disregards the pesky detail that men dominated the field because humankind evolved over aeons in which women were not generally permitted into public life and disciplines such as science and engineering. She also fails to acknowledge the many damaging inventions by men, and the threat of catastrophic climate change that many scientists link directly to the Industrial Revolution and the rise of consumerism and capitalist mass production dating from the mid-twentieth century.

There's another irony inherent to Paglia's argument: if patriarchy was a reasonable arrangement for much of human history, the very same advances she celebrates men for having made have also rendered it largely redundant, or have at least transformed the cultural landscape to such a degree that a process of re-negotiation has long been in order and in play. In her positive spin on patriarchy, Paglia makes no mention of the high price men themselves pay for the stubborn remains of patriarchy: according to the Australian Bureau of Statistics' 2016 *Causes of Death* report, the number of deaths by suicide is three times higher for men than women, and the ABC's Siobhan Fogarty reported that the suicide rate of young Indigenous men in Australia is the highest in the world.

Fast-forward to October 2017. The Harvey Weinstein shitstorm hit the internet after *New York Times* investigative reporters Jodi Kantor and Megan Twohey broke the 'open secret' of his decades-long systematic and serial sexual harassment of women (reports estimate at least fifty women have come forth to accuse him). While Weinstein, one of the most powerful film producers in Hollywood and co-founder of Miramax, denied allegations, played with semantics, and faffed about with a joke one-week stint of sex addiction outpatient treatment for show, the #MeToo movement went viral. Tarana Burke, an African-American activist, had initiated the grassroots Me Too movement in 2007 to help underprivileged, unrepresented or otherwise marginalised survivors of sexual violence feel less alone. The hashtag was introduced on 16 October when actor Alyssa Milano tweeted encouragement for women who had experienced sexual harassment or assault to follow suit.

Millions of #MeToos flooded feeds in the days and weeks that followed. And then the responses rolled in: #MenToo (men joining in), #ItWasMe (men owning up), #IWill (people vowing to take specific actions to combat sexualised abuse), but there were boycotters too. Amy Gray sent public love to those participating but declared to the world at large, 'You don't get to read my #metoo.' Jacking up against disclosing her trauma 'on social media platforms that continually silence women and protect their attackers' for the passive consumption of many who 'won't read the articles, won't look at the statistics, won't physically campaign for reform', Gray pulled no punches. 'We've given you the evidence whether it's through the courts, police, articles, or research papers. Either no one listened or we were censured for saying it. Some of the people who weren't heard aren't here any more.'

I found myself strangely conflicted. I was moved as woman after woman posted #MeToo; I felt obliged to stand with the womenfolk (and others who joined in), but I was torn between wanting to be counted and a complex configuration of sympathy with Gray's unyielding, uncompromising stance and several perplexing reservations. It was not a question of eligibility. My inner cynic was wary of tokenism, suspecting this would be yet another temporary viral solidarity that failed to dismantle the hierarchical structures set in place by patriarchy. And there was also some other, harder-to-pin-down cause for pause, in which my innumerable lived experiences of sexual abuse, coercion and harassment resisted being contained to a six-character badge. In the end I identified as someone who qualified for #MeToo in the context of airing my reservations, which was either the honest thing to do or the coward's way out, depending on your view.

As the days and weeks wore on, I witnessed the value in terms of collective solace and it became clear that, far from being the flash-in-the-pan trend I feared it might be, #MeToo opened a floodgate, though to what ultimate effects and ends remains unclear. Beyond its social media moment, the testimonies kept coming from within industry after industry. Abusers were named, and stories were told that often included aftermaths featuring bribery and intimidation. Some of those named faced real-world consequences. A handful issued tricksy image-control statements. Yet more hid under rocks. And the odd fellow fessed up with an actual apology. Penning the foreword for my academic book, *The Poetics of Transgenerational Trauma*, in October 2016, days before the US election, American affect theorist Gregory J. Seigworth wrote about the women 'taking to social media to share the details of their personal encounters with male sexual aggressors' in light of Trump's 'sexually predatory behavior'. It turns out that was just a warm-up for the post-Weinstein explosion of what Seigworth described as women's voices reverberating 'across an already charged public atmosphere, forcefully speaking back against sexual intimidation, assault, and patriarchal power' (and yes, I know it's not just women, but women have been, and continue to be, the drivers of this phenomenon). The eruption of #MeToo demonstrated that people abused by those who benefit most from patriarchy aren't just angry when they speak out: it takes courage to express that anger in a culture that protects your perpetrator/s.

But if we're talking courage we also need to talk class. In 'The People #MeToo Leaves Behind', published in *Reveal* some weeks after peak #MeToo, Bernice Yeung pointed out that the ability to participate is somewhat predicated upon privilege. Many of those who did so faced possible negative consequences, but those consequences didn't likely come down to not being able to feed the children. Working-class women, Yeung reminds us, such as those who clean hotel rooms or pick crops in relative isolation, are especially vulnerable to sexual assault, and usually aren't in a position to take action or publicly out perpetrators, either due to financial dependence on the employment with precious few alternatives, or because they don't realise they have a right to complain. Recognising that not everyone is 'empowered' enough to be a 'silence breaker', Tarana Burke and Alyssa Milano joined forces with Unicef USA to launch #HerToo. In a *Guardian* article dated 21 December 2017, Burke and Milano described #HerToo as a commitment to supporting Unicef's efforts to 'end discrimination and violence against girls and women – and against all children suffering violence and harassment – worldwide, through education, protection and policy reform', though there were no details proffered as to what that might mean in practical terms.

Some wrestled with confusion, while others took their place on one side or another of starkly illuminated social schisms. The women of Hollywood turned out in black in symbolic protest, bringing to mind the wonderful line in Chekhov's *The Seagull*, in which Masha declares that she wears black because she is in mourning for her life. Several non-English-speaking countries started their own versions of #MeToo. I wasn't a fan of the French phrasing, #BalanceTonPorc ('Expose Your Pig'), disliking its shift in focus and speciesist conflating of pigs – known for being highly intelligent and sensitive, and not given to inappropriate displays of sexual acting out – with abusive men. In January 2018, a hundred Frenchwomen, including Catherine Millet and Catherine Deneuve, signed off on an open letter published in *Le Monde*, which managed to make a couple of fair points amid a series of extremely problematic statements. Announcing that #MeToo had gone too far, and decrying a lack of distinction between rape and persistent or clumsy 'flirting', the women expressed concerns about trial-by-social-media public prosecutions and mob-justice mentality, according to the *New York Times* translation. The letter focused on #MeToo almost entirely in terms of sex (rather than relations of power or structural and historical gender politics), casting #MeToo as a puritanical relapse harking back to the Victorian era and accusing participants of enacting a 'witch-hunt', an unsavoury and horribly ironic metaphor given the literal meaning and history of the term. Reprisal columns were dashed off and promptly published, and the media reported 'counterblasts' charging the signatories with being apologists for rape and rape culture.

The deafening noise of the perpetual opinion wars can make it hard to hear yourself think, but the one thing that does not appear to be debatable is that almost all women (and many others) encounter the predatory behaviour and (often sexualised) aggressions of those men who most manifest the ugly underbelly of patriarchy's teachings, and many do so routinely. Sometimes even the strongest and healthiest among us find it's seeped in and done damage. Those chronically traumatised as children, by whatever means, become extra absorbent and vulnerable to deforming adaptations. Some become teenagers and adults who unwittingly soak up everyday abuses like sexual harassment and coercion, internalising pain and confusion that then seeps out in an array of paradoxical behaviours. Others shut up shop, building a wall of defence such that none can get through, not to sex, not to heart, not to help. I turned it all inwards, became self-destructive and self-defeating, keeping company with people many years older and men with few scruples.

The winds calm to a hard whisper then pick back up to a tree roar. There are rumours of coming snow. Upon waking I open the curtains with anticipation, but the rumours disappoint and I go on with my day. During the afternoon a freak snowstorm hits. White flakes fall from all directions. I'm in the shaken winter fairyland of a snow globe, the kind I loved as a little girl.

The worst thing about getting a new therapist is having to tell your story all over again.

I followed Jake to London, aged sixteen, leaving the Sydney summer for the northern winter, arriving with an overcoat that was pitifully unequal to the cold. When I landed at Heathrow I was scrutinised at customs, where officials deliberated about whether to let a visa-less Australian teenager enter the country on her own. Men. Uniforms. Fast talk. I was accustomed to talking my way through hairy situations on the spot, working the system. I'd already crossed the Nullarbor and back alone, and hitched rides in semitrailers on the desolate stretch between Darwin and Cairns, scamming charities and collecting social security 'counter cheques' from town to town. I knew how to handle a couple of confused guys at a border.

Waved through, I caught a bus to the city and made my way to the YMCA. I slept the jet-lag off for the better part of two days before pulling out the scrap of paper with Jake's phone number and dialling it from a phone booth in the YMCA lobby. He was living in Chelsea, it was 1980, and London was at the tail end of punk and swinging into New Romance. I did a lot of smoking and drinking at the kitchen table, depressed and overweight, and no competition for Giselle, the lithe and lovely dancer Jake held a torch for (they had been sweethearts back in Australia). That didn't stop Jake and me having an affair, and though I remember very little of it (I don't recall most of the sex I had as a teenager), I do remember a certain tenderness, and how painful it was for a girl already despondent and exhausted, wracked by acute feelings of inadequacy, and bewildered in a new land.

I pause to look up the definition of memory: the process in which information is encoded, stored and retrieved (where did all those fucks go?). The behavioural neuroscientist Jee Hyun Kim defines memory as 'a past that has become part of me'. Attention, she says, is critical for initiating memory formation. Short-term memories are made by neurons connecting, chemically and electrically charged, while for a long-term memory to develop the neurons need to talk enough to forge a protein pathway that makes a physical change in the brain (non-present, neuron-mute fucks).

When I left the Chelsea flat, having been outshone by Gigi, I moved into a shared bedsit in a boarding house in Islington I'd circled in the paper. My roommate was a Canadian punk called Bernie who spent most of her time working on her look in preparation for weekends at the Hope & Anchor. I got a job cleaning tables at the National Gallery, drank cups of Earl Grey tea, and established a network of doner kebab takeaways where I could get credit in exchange for flirtation when needed. There was an American boyfriend called Randy, who must have been in his thirties, but mostly I nursed a series of unrequited infatuations that dissipated upon the first sign of reciprocation. My paternal grandmother was born in Bishopbriggs, just outside Glasgow, and in those days an Australian could claim permanent residence if they had a British grandparent, so I stayed in London for close to two years, being one of the more forgettable students in an Alexander Technique class, working shit jobs and drinking hard.

'I've broken myself,' Jake told me decades later, swinging between his brokenness and what was left of his boozy bravado during the time I spent with him as he lay dying of alcoholism at the age of forty-nine in a cottage on the Macarthur-Onslow estate. He gave me one of his rings and told me I'd helped him become a man (I've never understood what he meant, unless he was suggesting that he wasn't as experienced back then as I had assumed). He knew I understood the compulsion that drives a person to drink destructively, and that I didn't judge him. He knew I'd long stopped, but he didn't want sobriety. Few alcoholics readily do: giving up drinking is generally a dreaded prospect to a problem drinker, and without some desire for freedom from enslavement there's no hope of achieving it. Jake never got there. Even then, at the end, perspicuous and poignant integrity swung into defensive arcing up: he had received a letter from my father and objected to my father's casting of him as an alcoholic. I left with a heavy heart. Jake had said during the visit that he was sorry, he should have protected me in London, but there was no protecting me from myself, just as there was no protecting him, or my other cousin Damien, who died from an overdose of sleeping pills in his twenties.

I wake up to find the sun melting the carpet of snow on the lawn. The moon is high in the finally blue sky and four wild cockatoos screech to a halt in the foliage of the now-sedate eucalypts.

I left London deflated, my delusions of international grandeur in ruins. I stayed with my mother in a flat in Kirribilli where I ate too much and moped around and felt like I'd failed and I didn't know why. On the morning of the Saturday when I ended up at the quaint ye olde pub on George Street, my brother had mentioned his band were rehearsing in the city. Bored, I had set out to go watch them when I got lost and found myself in one bar and then another.

I was lost and I didn't know why.

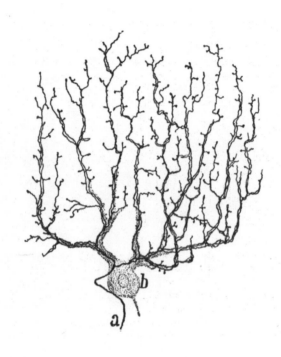

The twenty-one-year-old party girl in the apartment next door had her techno playing at top volume again. My then-husband and I had tried politely requesting she bear us in mind. We remembered being young and tried to be patient. We didn't want to be *those people*, people who call the cops on someone outside an emergency, but, exasperated and impatient for respite from her late-night good times, we resorted to drastic measures. We made the call and waited, hoping a verbal warning would give her cause to reflect.

As the officers appeared in the hallway we took turns watching through the peephole and listened from behind our door, exchanging triumphant smiles. This, we hoped, would sort it out once and for all. But when the cop who arrived that fateful night, and who had heard the doof-doof blast from downstairs, skipped the warning and took it upon himself to issue a twenty-eight-day summons to cease and desist, our smiles quickly sank. It had gone further than we intended already. He pulled out his pad and all hell broke loose. We opened the door as our neighbour, dressed up for a night on the town, tried frantically to shut the door on the cop with the pad. He stood firm, one leg holding the door ajar, demanding the information he needed for the summons. When she realised she had no retreat, she grew wild, kicked at his shins and threw a live cigarette at him, her eyes wide in confusion, rage and terror. He warned her to cooperate or he'd arrest her for assaulting a police officer. I appealed to her to calm down. Suddenly his back-ups burst forth from the blinking lift; six or seven officers surrounded her in the narrow hallway. She flailed like a trapped animal. Her breast fell out of her dress. She cried out: she couldn't breathe; she was having a panic attack, a heart attack; she wanted her doctor, her mother; she couldn't believe this was happening; she had a party to go to. As the cops descended to make their arrest, her heels made skid marks on the cream hallway walls. It was clear they thought her a random loose cannon or, worse, a cop-hater. But for the first time since she'd moved in, I felt an empathic connection with her.

I've lost count of the times in my life when people came to negative conclusions about me: I've been branded a juvenile delinquent, an alcoholic, a drug addict, self-destructive, depressive, anxious, controlling, obsessive-compulsive, overly sensitive, phobic, highly strung, and a hypochondriac, and not always unjustly. Around the time of this unfortunate event I discovered a new descriptor, and according to the literature it may be at the heart of all the others: chronic trauma survivor.

My body aches in lament as my eyes scan the headline: 'Murdered Queensland Toddler Beaten from "Head to Toe"'. Mason Jet Lee, not yet two years old, is found dead with horrific injuries. His mother goes to the media, appealing for help. She doesn't understand. He was so beautiful, so gentle. The mother's ex-boyfriend, who was with Mason the night he died, was arrested and questioned for eighteen hours, but not charged, and he steadfastly protests his innocence. Following a post-mortem whose findings suggest the boy was abused over an extended period of time, the police launch a homicide investigation. A journalist interviews the ex-boyfriend. He looks like he hasn't slept for a year and his eyes don't make contact with the camera or journalist as he describes, in a shaking voice, the night he called the ambulance. 'You did nothing to hurt him?' asks the journalist evenly. 'Of course not,' he says, crying with no visible tears, 'I love him.' Months later the three people who were living in the house the night Mason died, including his mother and the ex-boyfriend, are charged with manslaughter. I feel sick as I read about the injuries Mason suffered and the 'excruciating pain' he endured. I'm torn between tears and a furious scream.

I realised many years ago I was a messed-up person, but it wasn't until I read *Trauma and Recovery* by Judith Herman – a book my therapist at the time referred to as 'the Bible in the field of trauma studies' – that I came across the phrase 'chronic trauma survivor'. Many who grow up in an environment of family violence, where trauma has become the norm, come to the realisation that they are profoundly traumatised only after decades of suffering. Some never connect the dots. Most, like me, will have collected a hefty sack of labels along the way, labels that all too often only succeed in describing symptoms and snowballing shame. One of the hardest things about being a chronic trauma survivor (and it has no end of hardships) is the crushing loneliness of being misunderstood, even by oneself.

Elizabeth Waites provides the simplest definition of trauma I've yet encountered: 'injury to mind or body that requires structural repair'. How do you *structurally repair* memory? I have known for the best part of two decades that growing up with violence damaged me, but I used to think of that damage as a vague, amorphous influence on my equally vague and amorphous emotional life. It wasn't until I was in my forties that I learned this damage occurs at a concrete level, changing the structure and wiring of the brain, and that this structural damage explains why the process of recovery for those chronically traumatised as children is such an enormous and gruelling challenge.

In a report titled *Children and Domestic Violence*, researchers Dale Bagshaw, Alan Campbell and Lena Jelinek describe children as 'the "silent", "forgotten" or "invisible" victims of family violence'. They outline the problem of the traditional division between domestic violence and child protection. When child abuse is viewed as a health and welfare matter and domestic violence is referred to the police, courts and women's refuges, children fall through the cracks. The researchers conclude that domestic violence *is* a child protection issue: 'There is now increasing recognition that these are not separate phenomena and that children's exposure to domestic violence is a form of child abuse.' Blah blah blah. I can't hear you over the roar of the machinery of endgame capitalism and Mason's unheeded cries. Governments are busy with the economy. Policy proves itself unequal. The seething violence breaks loose daily, hourly, even as we speak.

Is Julia Kristeva right? Is grand-scale social revolution no longer possible in the information-saturated, mediatised spectacle of present-day culture? Must the thirst for justice be satisfied only with these 'intimate revolts', this act of writing and reading, in the face of so much suffering? Memory is constructed and reconstructed. Each and every memory is a representation of a representation of a representation (multiplied by as many times as the memory has been 'remembered'). Each remembered moment is a constellation of moments that passed in waves of energy and particles, of moving matter and light and colour, of inanimate objects – tables, lamps, plates – that seem real. Language constructs with its brick-words, its grammatical electricity. The heart beats fast. I want answers. Perhaps you do too.

My parents had divorced by the time I was five. Their separation was as undramatic as their marriage, and my memories of my early years as the youngest member of a nuclear family are relatively tranquil. The most damning thing I can recall about my father was that he seemed forbidding, and was often absent, commuting long hours to and from work. I don't remember any *scenes*, just that he disappeared one day. Sydney was one of those big-town-small-cities when my parents met as baby beatniks, hanging around the Theosophical Society in the city with an assortment of esoteric pre–New Age types. When my father took a trip to India in 1952, aged twenty-two, sponsored by the Society, a group of them went down to the docks to see him off. In a photo of my smiling father about to set sail, looking like a young Sinatra, he wears a dapper hat and suit, and my mother, not yet twenty and chubby-cheeked, stands next to him with a wool coat hanging around her shoulders, her hands in short, white gloves. Her expression is hard to read.

After my father returned from his exotic sojourn, he married my mother, and my brother, Marc, was born a year later. By the time I came along eight years down the track, the marriage was faltering. In my father's telling, my mother, who was not suited to be a 1960s housewife, had affairs and swanned around, doing as she pleased instead of doing the housework, endlessly indulged by my enabling grandparents. All of which, he said in so many words, served to make a man feel a stranger in his own home. He didn't like the way my grandparents spoiled my brother and me, and he felt under-appreciated as a husband and father. I lived for my grandparents' visits and of course welcomed the spoiling, and though I felt the loss of my father when he went I had no idea who he was.

After he left the family home my mother had an affair with a model called Catherine. There is a photograph of Catherine in one of my mother's disintegrating albums now stacked on a shelf in my office. She has a square, angular face and sports a mod aesthetic: structural dress, white cap, false eyelashes and frosted lipstick. We moved from Frenchs Forest back to the inner west, where my mother's people came from, first staying with my Aunty Nance and Uncle Alf in the Lilyfield house Nancy had been born in. She lived in that house every day of her life (I don't even recall her ever going on holiday) until she went to hospital to die from surgical complications.

My mother was suddenly out a lot – looking for a house and a job, being newly single and socialising – and I somehow got it in my head that my mother was a 'prostitute' and judged her harshly for it. Children are sponges. I was too young to realise how troubled and upset I was by the separation and the move, to comprehend that I felt unmoored and confused and alone. It seemed to me that my father had disappeared without a trace and that in a way my mother had too. Looking back now, I find it remarkable that I came up with the prostitute story at such a young age. I didn't know (or at least I don't remember knowing) about my mother's affairs until several years later when I started asking questions, and yet I seem to have sensed something about my mother's sexuality, a libertine predilection, and the shame society ascribed it.

Aunty Nance was a devout Catholic who wore a cross around her neck, had a set menu for every night of the week, attended church on Sundays, and tried to teach me the Biblical creation story by way of a beautifully illustrated children's book. She couldn't have children of her own and she was kind to me, and I'm sure she would have liked to love me, but though I remember her as my primary carer during that period, we never did meet heart to heart. I later learned that it was during this time my mother met Stuart Jones, a narcissistic, alcoholic baby-man who played clarinet in the Sydney Symphony Orchestra and who became a thorn in my side for the next few years.

For a long time after my parents' divorce, I clung to the hope that they would reunite. I interrogated my mother about why they'd parted. I was an inquisitive child and to my mother's credit she didn't try to shut that down, but there are certain details a child of six, seven, nine, eleven, doesn't need to hear. I learned all about the affair that proved to be the final straw for my father, and that her lover had tried to persuade her to elope, but she refused to leave my brother and me (read: I felt responsible for my mother's happiness, or lack thereof, and became convinced it was my fault she had missed the chance to be with the love of her life). There was an obvious fondness between my parents and whatever drove them apart had not stopped them enjoying a certain kind of friendship, but, as she explained patiently over and over again, it was not likely they would reunite.

Divorce was not common during the '60s and I keenly felt the stigma of being from 'a broken family'. I absorbed the images of happy television families, and suffered from a constant sense of bewilderment and inferiority for failing to belong to one. I was eight or nine when my mother finally got rid of Stuart and we moved into a brand new apartment in Glebe. At my new school, Stacey was one of the children I befriended. She was an athletic redhead around my age and the daughter of a single father. It didn't take us long to hatch a *Brady Bunch* plan: Stacey would come to my place after school one afternoon and stay too late to walk home. Her father would come to pick her up. We would introduce him to my mother. They would fall in love. And we would all live happily ever after. In between the idea and its execution, we each primed our respective parents about the availability and charms of the other. Al arrived at the appointed hour and lingered late into the evening, talking with my mother on the velveteen sofa while we girls giggled excitedly in my bedroom, plotting our deliriously fun future as sisters.

Al and Stacey moved in shortly thereafter and the four of us enjoyed a blissful faux-nuclear family honeymoon. My mother, an indoorsy person and an avid reader, was thrillingly lured out of doors on a string of adventures. We took boats out on the water, went bush, and enjoyed long country drives on Sundays looking for buggies (Al's hobby), stopping for afternoon teas of scones with cream and jam at rustic cafes. Not long after I'd started calling Al 'Dad' and Stacey started calling my mother 'Mum', my newfound joy gave way to powerlessness amid the mayhem of adult traumas clashing. Home became a place of increasing dread and secrecy. Unlike with Stuart, I had dared to love Al, only to come to fear him from a reservoir of disappointed grief, partly because he was violent and probably sociopathic, and partly because he let me down so badly. I had desperately wanted him to be a loving partner for my mother and a father figure to me. I had handpicked him for the role. 'If the idea of "home" implies physical and psychological safety and security as well as shelter,' writes Jill Astbury, 'then a child, adult or older person affected by domestic violence experiences a hidden "homelessness".' For a child – who is inherently dependent and who needs a safe environment to develop a sense of sure-footedness in the world – this homelessness can be a kind of lifelong exile. Is exile, then, a matter of degree? How many children can truly have a home in a society in which gender- and race-based discrimination and violence are routine?

Stories about those languishing in every kind of exile, imprisoned in 'processing centres' like Nauru, Manus and Christmas Island, fill my Facebook feed year after year, successive governments signing off on their trauma, even though experts have likened Australia's offshore detention centres to the torture 'black sites' used by the US in the 'war on terror'. I sadface this world. The war on terror is a war of trauma. My weaponised trauma versus your weaponised trauma. *The Guardian* runs a story about Paul Stevenson, a 'psychologist and traumatologist' who has 'spent forty years helping people make sense of their lives in the aftermath of disaster, of terrorist attacks, bombings and mass murders, of landslides, fires and tsunamis'. Stevenson made fourteen deployments to Nauru and Manus during 2014 and 2015. 'In my entire career of forty-three years,' he tells journalists Ben Doherty and David Marr, 'I have never seen more atrocity than I have seen in the incarcerated situations of Manus Island and Nauru.' Child suicide. Mismanaged rapes. Self-harm. Child sexual assault. My body beneath the weight of their tortured bodies. *No way: you will not make Australia home. Australia first. Rise up. One Nation. Heil Hitler.* Are you an 'economic migrant', a 'queue jumper'? Never mind. If you're not sufficiently traumatised when you get here, you soon will be. 'Make a whistle from my throat,' begins an anonymous poem penned by a refugee held in Baxter Detention Centre in 2005, 'I do not know what will happen after I die. I do not want to know. But I would like the Potter to make a whistle from the clay of my throat. May this whistle fall into the hands of a cheeky and naughty child and the child to blow hard on the whistle continuously with the suppressed and silent air of his lungs and disrupt the sleep of those who seem deaf to my cries.'

Those deaf to these cries count the votes in their blue ties.

There can be no poetry after Auschwitz. This unsettling misquote is attributed to the philosopher Theodor Adorno, writing in the wake of the Holocaust, but according to a translation by Samuel Weber what he actually said was more along the lines of 'it is barbaric to write poetry after Auschwitz', which offers little more reassurance. Adorno later softened and qualified his position stating that 'Perennial suffering has as much right to expression as a tortured man has to scream' and he clarified that what he meant to raise was the difficult question of whether after Auschwitz one can go on living. What he was getting at, then, was that culture, including language, had been so twisted by the Nazis as to have stripped human civilisation of meaning. To continue reproducing culture in the wake of that and in the context of 'the open-air prison which the world is becoming' is ethically unjust. That is to say that to keep doing culture in the ways that produced the conditions that led to monstrosities such as Auschwitz (and Guantanamo and Manus and Don Dale) is barbaric. I wonder if Adorno realised he was calling for a feminist revolution in its sincerest sense, if he was aware that patriarchy lays the foundation from which hellholes like these rise up. The great Chilean poet Pablo Neruda once declared that 'poetry is an act of peace'. In light of this it would be more accurate to say that *after Auschwitz there should be only poetry.* The question is how to go on living.

Even after years of therapy, I am unable to map out a reliable and linear timeline of events, or to articulate a cohesive account of the disintegration of the relationship between my mother and Al. All I know is that one day they seemed content and we were playing happy families, and the next they were fighting. I have no idea whether I witnessed ten, fifty or one hundred and fifty episodes of violence. All I have is a patchwork of random recollections without their broader context. The experts assure me this is completely normal for someone with post-traumatic stress disorder. Judith

Herman describes how it works: 'Traumatic memories lack verbal narrative and context; rather, they are encoded in the form of vivid sensations and images. Robert Jay Lifton, who studied survivors of Hiroshima, civilian disasters and combat, describes the traumatic memory as an "indelible image" or "death imprint".'

A fight has started on our way home from a wedding. Al is in the driver's seat and he has pulled over so that he can strangle my mother. I'm sitting behind him in the back seat, leaning out the window, screaming for help so hard my throat hurts. It's a Saturday night and three or four people in a jovial mood pass by and look at us, but they keep walking and do not help. I'm watching my mother gag and I reach out and pull on Al's hair with all my might. His hands release my mother's throat. He turns around and belts me in the side of the head.

My mother lies on the floor in the kitchen. I think she is dead.

We're camping in a tent pitched at the top of a hill. They've been fighting all day and Al and Stacey appear to have abandoned my mother and me at the campsite. Michael, one of the boys from school who accompanied us on the trip, has gone with Al and Stacey, and the other, Tony, is with my mother and me. The three of us are sitting in the tent and the air is thick with apprehension and tension. We hear a car revving up the hill. We emerge from the tent, blinded by the headlights coming towards us at full speed. We run.

My mother and I arrive home to find slurs scrawled all over the walls in huge, mad red letters.

Some of my 'indelible images' feel realer than others. I feel certain the scene in the car took place. I know I didn't imagine or false-memory our return to our apartment that day to ugly sexist vandalism, and I know I often feared for my mother's safety. I am less sure about events at the camping site, though I do know something threatening took place because I distinctly remember my mother and Tony and me fleeing to the local police station and being put on a train back to Sydney. They blend, these memories, into each other in a timeless soup. Elizabeth Waites explains why they still feel like a bad dream from which I can't quite wake, rather than reality: 'The shock of trauma produces states that are so different from ordinary waking life that they are not easily integrated with more normal experience. As a result of this discontinuity, the traumatic state may be lost to memory or remembered as a dream is sometimes remembered, as something vague and unreal.'

My mother's lifelong dream of being a working actor came to the fore during her time with Al. In her forties, with one child living independently and the other nearing adolescence, she was finally free to pursue her goal; to take classes, sign up with an agent, and take extra jobs and parts in local theatre productions. Together we conjured up the notion that I too had acting talent and she called on an old family friend to take photos of us – individually and together – that might be useful in landing us gigs. A few years back the wife of that photographer contacted me on Facebook. She had come across the contact sheet from that session and asked if I would like her to send it. When it arrived I stared at the small square black and white images, going from one to the next, fascinated by our performances of femininity. In the top corner photo my mother is lovely, arms crossed, smiling gently and awash with light beaming through a nearby window. In another my mother appears to be deranged, eyes bulging, shoulders hitched high and hands on hips. I don't remember the photos being taken so I have no context for this, but I imagine she is 'acting' mad. I note that it seems to be pre–boob job. In the image beneath we stand together before a white wall. She looks to camera, unsmiling, arms crossed again. My eyes are cast down and off to the side; I have my finger in my mouth. I am spellbound by this image in particular. It seems to capture us both in our respective and related traumas. We stand apart and there's a symbolic tear in the wall behind us, between us. My mother is drawn, more brittle than beautiful. There's something about her direct gaze. She resembles a trapped animal, her eyes ghosted by pain. Her mouth is open slightly, as if she wants to speak. I seem lost, spaced out, sad. I'm old enough to have conscious thoughts about my fraught home life, but I never speak of it. I don't know how to.

The younger a child is, the less easily they articulate trauma, but it is a mistake to equate this with a lack of, or a reduction in, impact. Herman reports that among twenty children with documented histories of early trauma studied by psychiatrist Lenore Terr, none of the children could verbally describe traumatic events that took place before the age of two-and-a-half. Even so, these experiences were indelibly encoded, if not in 'indexical' memory, as Ernst van Alphen calls it, in some less traceable form of memory that encompasses bodily and affective imprints. Eighteen of the twenty children showed evidence of traumatic memory in their behaviour. They exhibited specific fears related to the traumatic events, and they were able to re-enact these events in their play with extraordinary accuracy. But convincing as such studies are, the law, relational expectations and familial harmony often depend on coherent indexical memory.

Apart from being disorienting, perplexing and problematic in legal contexts, patchy and contested traumatic memory can cause more familial problems down the track. My brother has gone through stages of feeling the need to help me understand, to set me straight, to fill me in on details of aspects of our shared history I was too young to have been aware of. During these periods he has sent emails explaining my past to me, certain that what he sees as the facts in his possession are essential to my process and progress. When it comes to events I was old enough to remember, though, there remain unresolvable discrepancies between our perceptions of what took place. In one of his emails he spoke of being witness to the violence between my mother and Al, though I had no recollection of his presence. I sent Stacey a message asking if she remembered him staying with us or being there for much of the fighting (we had connected on Facebook through our old school page some years back). I told her that I did remember the rare visit from my brother, and maybe the odd overnight stay, but that when the fights came back to me, all I got was two little girls stuck in the middle. She said she only remembered him visiting occasionally, and couldn't recall him sleeping over. 'I remember the same as you,' she added, 'two little girls. We have survived and are doing okay.'

Herman describes the difference between people who experience a one-off traumatic event and those subjected to repeated and inescapable trauma: 'People in captivity become adept practitioners of the arts of altered consciousness. Through the practice of dissociation, voluntary thought suppression, minimisation, and sometimes outright denial, they learn to alter an unbearable reality.' The adult who experiences a one-off trauma from the basis of an already stable personality suffers differently from someone whose selfhood has formed in the chronic presence of trauma. Terr says that people subjected to prolonged trauma develop 'an insidious, progressive form of post-traumatic stress disorder that invades and erodes the personality'. At the same time, as Silvan Tomkins would have it, chronic trauma paradoxically generates a script of punishing affects that shape its expression throughout a life. Chronic trauma survivors do not fit the classic description of 'simple' post-traumatic stress disorder. Their symptomology cannot simply be understood in terms of nightmares or flashbacks.

How do you describe not just dreaming, but becoming the nightmare, the flashback, cognitively stunned and in thrall to overwhelming panic? Herman has campaigned (so far unsuccessfully) for the term 'complex post-traumatic stress disorder' (CPTSD) to be included in the *DSM* (*Diagnostic and Statistical Manual of Mental Disorders*), arguing that it more accurately describes the complicated picture with which chronic trauma survivors often present. Chronic trauma is, literally, unacceptable. Even now, after all these years, an image will flash up – me jumping onto Al's back and clawing at his giant shoulders to pull him off my mother, say – and I tell myself I must be mistaken, this cannot have happened. These visions cannot possibly belong to me and my life. And while trauma is trauma and, as Herman says, 'the severity of traumatic events cannot be measured on any single dimension', certain 'identifiable experiences' increase the probability of harm, including 'being taken by surprise, trapped, or exposed to the point of exhaustion'. Each of these is typical for the child reared amid family violence. Days that started out as exciting excursions, whose sunniness seemed sure to continue, would, in a splitting second, cloud over before breaking in a publicly humiliating thunderstorm.

An echo of Tomkins' statement that shame 'strikes deepest into the heart of man' surrounds me, and I remember the way these public blow-ups struck shame deep into the heart of my child-body. In these moments, every other family seems normal. Other children seem to deserve more, be more. The shame and fear, unleashed, flies around, sticking to everyone in its midst, but most of all to those most vulnerable and most porous: children, non-human animals and those already severely traumatised. There's a saying that warns against comparing one's own 'insides' with the 'outsides' of others, but for children, whose brains have not yet developed the capacity for reasoned, insightful self-reflection, this is gibberish. The surfaces matter a great deal. The family at the next table who seem to be happy and carefree irrefutably are, and are the better for it, and a rupture there, at the surface, at the table of *your* family, before the judging eyes of others, is nothing less than mortifying.

The most common time for fights to erupt was late at night after I'd gone to bed. I would lie awake stilling myself so that my breath was almost inaudible, the better to monitor the sounds from outside my door for any sign of discord. Once started, the fights went on for hours. Adrenaline kept me from feeling tired, but I passed countless sleepless school nights tracking intensity and, if it got bad enough, intervening in an attempt to referee. No one is more trapped than a child who cannot survive without the adults they depend on. When those adults are also their prime threat, they are trapped in a double bind. Tenderness and terror. Need and helplessness. No moment was exempt from the potential for that sudden sour turn. In some ways it might have been easier if the conflict had been constant, the abuse daily. The contrasts were extreme and the unpredictability crazy-making: the highs were the highest I'd known – our home was wonderful when the adults were happy and I had never felt safer than when our blended home was harmonious – but the lows were intolerable, crushing, the hysteria of high drama followed by a collective emotional hangover that lasted days. At some point, this state of caution slipped into the past and I'd dare to relax into pleasure and security again, only to be jolted out of it, sooner or later, by the all-too-familiar signs of a fight.

Children in violent families are strapped into the seat of an endless rollercoaster ride: when you sense a big dip coming, the feeling is much the same as that stage when you've been on a ride too long but can't get off. Everyone is familiar with the cliché of the woman with the bruised face softening at the sight of a repentant abuser. Without the benefit of a fully developed brain and life experience, children are particularly susceptible to the magical thinking that the cycle of family abuse demands. My mother didn't fit the mousy-victim stereotype. She was an attractive, outgoing, modern working woman who owned her own apartment and was not financially reliant on Al. She was smart and politically aware, and she could be very assertive. Yet she stayed in a relationship in which control, possessiveness and intimidation were routine, vulnerable time after time to the sweet words of remorse and promises.

If at first I too believed these words, I soon grew familiar with the devastation of fairy-tale faith giving way to bitter disappointment and despair. In the shadows of this devastation, a child develops certain beliefs in an attempt to make sense of cyclical trauma. Waites explains: 'Trauma is not merely experienced but interpreted … A child's perception of *what* happened is frequently quite accurate, and vivid veridical memories often persist long after a terrible event, but understanding *why* is harder.' Irrational interpretations can themselves distort developmental processes and complicate recovery, says Herman, and I've uncovered a number of the core beliefs that crystallised in my formative years, including Don't Hope For The Best Because The Worst Will Always Happen;

Don't Trust Happiness Because The Rug Will Always Be Pulled Out From Under You When You Least Expect It; and, most detrimentally, a belief that is so deeply embedded as to almost evade consciousness: The World Is Not Safe And You Will Be Annihilated Any Minute Now. This is the belief most resistant to re-framing, the belief that even now on a bad day stops me taking walks where and when I want to, that has me scanning figures (calculating gender, size, affective aura = assessment of risk) from five hundred feet away as if my life depended on it, that stops me getting on a plane to take up my friend's tempting offer of staying for free in a farmhouse in south-west France, that makes me want to avoid tunnels, that sparks so deep in my cells as to arrange my muscles into painful knots so set that even deep massage only touches the top layers. These are the thought patterns that trigger the mood disorders and syndromes so endemic among chronic trauma survivors, and they inform a dazzling array of symptoms and behaviours, most of which have eluded correct diagnosis for centuries.

It's commonly noted, perhaps most famously by Oprah, that abuse *changes who you are*. It paradoxically erodes *and* shapes you. It changes who you might have been to who you become in its aftermath. Neuroscientists now confirm that this is exactly what happens to a developing mind exposed to abuse and trauma. Louis Cozolino, professor of psychology at Pepperdine University in Malibu and author of *The Neuroscience of Psychotherapy*, describes how the systems of the brain link up to create experience: 'When we reach a certain level of traumatic experience our brain does a number of things that don't enhance our ability to integrate experience. And that really is what dissociation is, it's a cutting off, it's a disconnection of different neural networks.' In other words, trauma causes a profound split between the language-producing conscious part of the brain and the non-verbal, more primitive regions. This is the reason trauma theorists consider trauma *unrepresentable*, unspeakable in the conventional sense.

Even when the trauma story is known and can be told, in therapy for example, a disconnect remains between this linguistic capacity and the hardwired traumatic writing of the brain. In a 'war zone', change takes place at the structural/neuronal level as an adaptation to relentless stress. When the 'war' is over, the brain doesn't shift out of its now-programmed, full-tilt limbic response – it gets stuck there, like a vinyl record with the needle caught in a groove, firing up even at minimal stimulation – real, metaphoric and metonymic. Therapy aims to heal this split between thoughts, feelings and words by encouraging speech connected to the traumatic event, using various techniques for activating cortical areas that allow a person to reintegrate neural networks dissociated by trauma.

My body is at the ready for flight. I can't switch my nervous system off. It scans and calculates tirelessly, antennae out for threats. I avoid going out on Friday and Saturday nights because the energy 'triggers' me. I experience the revved-up speeding down suburban streets, the big bodies spilling out of doorways, the loud lubrications, as threatening and unsettling. What others consider 'fun' I might well find menacing. I feel the micro-aggressions as macro. The body remembers.

In a report titled *The Neuroscience of Traumatic Memory*, Bessel van der Kolk and Ruth Buczynski describe how the thalamus malfunctions in the overwhelmed brain, which results in traumatised people often remembering images, sights, sounds and physical sensations without context, without a coherent 'story' of the traumatic event. So it is that certain sensations or sensory stimuli can trigger a traumatic reaction. Apparently, the brain

forms maps of territories marked dangerous and safe. The brain
of an abused child can become wired to believe, 'I'm a person
to whom terrible things happen, and I'd better be on the alert
for who's going to hurt me now.' This can't be fixed by talking
about the event in the past, which is not in the past at all, but in
the present, in the very sensations of the now. 'The past,' they say,
'is only relevant in as far as it stirs up current sensations, feelings,
emotions and thoughts. The story about the past is just a story that
people tell to explain how bad the trauma was, or why they have
certain behaviors.' All the talking, all the therapy, all the writing,
all the putting the pieces of the puzzle together don't quell that
indefatigable fear that I'm a person to whom terrible things
happen, but they have helped lessen the stranglehold of that fear.
They've given me resources to draw on in dealing with it, and
have enabled me to meet myself with compassion more often in
those moments in which I disappoint and frustrate myself. I don't
see myself as cured. It's not black and white. I don't graduate from
grief; it comes in waves and layers and varying intensities. It laces
my days, never too far away, keeping my heart soft and pulsing.

Trauma gets lodged in the tissues. The breath stops, catches,
flows shallow, mimicking trauma's deathliness. I remind myself to
breathe, guide the breath down into the belly, remind my breath
that it lives, that I live, that I deserve to live, to claim the life in my
body. I remember the body in yoga; remember the breath, stretch
through pain to release, calming the lizard brain. These zones
of reconnection and sacrosanct relief recharge me, help soothe
the fractious fight-or-flight switch that is always tripping on, the
shimmering not-quite-here thoughts-of-danger that can escalate
in a heartbeat to sounding alarm, the stabs of fear. Sometimes,
in meditation, there is a moment that opens up into an ebbing
oneness that, like the sea, can't be broken.

Herman cites three symptomological categories of CPTSD:
hyper-arousal, intrusion and constriction. Hyper-arousal manifests
as irritability and restlessness, a quickening to anger, impulsive and

risk-taking behaviours, hyper-vigilance, sleep disturbances, and psychosomatic complaints. Intrusion includes the flashbacks and nightmares most typically associated with war veterans and PTSD. And constriction, which flies under the radar more than the others, entails various avoidance strategies – shutting down or out, surrender and psychic retreat, fantasy, numbing, trances and dissociation – in which the traumatic experience, and any experience thereafter, may 'lose its quality of ordinary reality'. This usually happens to me in the most mundane of circumstances – at dinner, in a crowded shopping centre or under the glare of merciless fluorescent lights.

I recall a surreal sense of detachment during fights. They felt like film, not quite of this world. In its most extreme form, this detachment presents as dissociative disorder. Most people who dissociate do so in terms of amnesia for certain memories, absent-mindedness and a lack of clarity around certain events or their childhood in general. As a teenager and young adult, I experienced almost complete amnesia regarding the violence and abuse during my childhood. When a drug counsellor in a detox once asked me about my early life, I told him I'd had a 'happy childhood'. I wasn't lying – I believed it; I couldn't remember.

There *were* good times. When I was growing up, my world was peopled by characters, eccentrics and artists. There was colour and laughter and affection. I was one of the fortunate ones. For all the madness, I was wanted and well cared for in many respects, but the amnesiac erasure of the dark side left me with the belief that I'd been raised by bohemians who were above and beyond ordinary accountability, and who, in any event, had nothing to account for. Consequently, while I carried the burden of transgenerational trauma more visibly than anyone else in my immediate family, I had no idea why I was so screwed up. Had I understood my history earlier, I might not have felt so ashamed, so singular in my failure to live well, so alone.

My hyper-arousal symptoms included 'psychosomatic' asthma attacks during our time with Al. They stopped as soon as he left and have never returned. Traumatised people are also prone to 'real' illness and impaired immune function as a result of ongoing inescapable stress. Waites cites several studies in which the experience of trauma 'has been found to be associated with increased susceptibility to infectious diseases, autoimmune disorders, and cancer'. In September 2014 I was diagnosed with endometrial (uterine) cancer and had a radical hysterectomy six days later. A subsequent test result suggested a condition called Lynch syndrome, which puts carriers of a defective gene at high risk of various cancers, most especially colon and endometrial. I was referred to a cancer genetics clinic for further screening and a specialist test that would give a more definitive, if not conclusive, result.

Debating whether or not to undergo the test, I phoned my brother, who has sired five sons, to discuss it with him and let him know the outcome might have implications for him and my nephews. He determined from the outset that he would not take the test himself even if it showed I had the defective gene, nor would he raise it with his sons. 'We're traumatised people,' he said plainly. 'It's going to come out one way or another. I'll take my chances and deal with it if it comes to pass.' I ended up testing negative for the unfortunate gene, but the idea of trauma being somatically expressed as physical illness is a compelling one. As Matt Haig writes in *The Guardian*, 'You can't draw a line between a body and a mind any more than you can draw a line between oceans.' Beyond the established associations between trauma and certain mental illnesses such as depression and anxiety, and the physical toll of trauma-related addictions, it's impossible to measure the extent of lived, embodied sufferings or the collective economic cost of chronic trauma.

But for all trauma's symptomological expressions, its silences and absences can be just as lethal, and its more covert operations are hard to pin down. Even though I still struggle with an ingrained sense of unsafety from living with violence, that type of florid dysfunction in my family has been, in some ways, easier to come to terms with than other, less overt violations. Like neglect. Like the daily familial and cultural abandonments that send the message: you are lesser, you don't matter, you don't exist.

Even (or maybe especially) in an amnesiac person, CPTSD can manifest as eating disorders, self-cutting, and substance and process addictions including workaholism, compulsive sexual behaviour, anxiety and/or panic disorder, phobias, obsessive–compulsive behaviour, perfectionism and over-achieving. Exhibiting lots of symptoms is no guarantee of diagnosis, though. Survivors suffer first from the condition, and second from a lack of understanding of it. As Herman notes, 'Because post-traumatic systems are so persistent and so wide-ranging, they may be mistaken for enduring characteristics of the victim's personality. This is a costly error, for the person with unrecognized post-traumatic stress disorder is condemned to a diminished life, tormented by memory and bounded by helplessness and fear.'

People often lose patience with survivors and counsel them to 'let go' of their anger or fear, failing to realise that survivors are not experiencing a 'normal' order of emotion. Rather, Herman explains, the survivor is 'continually buffeted by terror and rage. These emotions are qualitatively different from ordinary fear and anger. They are outside the range of ordinary emotional experience, and they overwhelm the ordinary capacity to bear feelings.' Though it's broadly believed that people are generally more attuned to emotional complexity and more aware of mental health issues now than in previous decades and centuries, there are few places in the technologised, corporatised contemporary age equipped to recognise and accommodate complicated and problematic beings like these, and yet we are everywhere, even if we don't all wear our trauma on our sleeves.

Perfectionism commonly masks traumatic shame among those
with CPTSD. Domestic violence has an undeniable effect on a
child's self-esteem. In order to preserve faith in their caregivers,
children often reject the obvious conclusion that something
is wrong with unbalanced or abusing adults. Instead, the child
assumes responsibility – and a belief in 'innate badness' or
'wrongness' is born. In an attempt to 'construct some system of
meaning that justifies it', Herman continues, the child 'seizes upon
this explanation early and clings to it tenaciously, for it enables
her to preserve a sense of meaning, hope, and power'. My sense
of culpability was heightened by my regret at having brought
my mother and Al together. Poor self-esteem can manifest as
anti-social behaviour or it can be masked by an abused child's
'persistent attempts to be good'.

I was not an outstanding student at school, but I did excel
at ballet. During the Al years, I threw myself into dancing
with unprecedented zeal. I went to classes after school and all
day Saturdays. I pushed myself to the limit in one class after
another – classical, jazz ballet, acrobatics – and it wasn't long
before I was chosen to be part of the Keane Kids, an elite group
of students who performed professionally on television and in
shopping-centre showcases during school holidays. I embodied
the showbiz ethic 'the show must go on'. By early adolescence,
however, I had given up both dancing and trying to be good.
I took up running (metaphorically speaking), fast and hard. The
stereotypes are entrenched. I was considered a problem when I
cut loose with drink and drugs and men, but the frenzied dancing
was admired. Success means you've licked it, at least until the
early-age coronary, or the collapse of an intimate partnership, or
the discovery that your kid is hooked on ice.

Interestingly, the most notable and visible backlash to trauma-
related stereotyping comes from men who object to men being

cast as perpetrators of violence. A younger generation of vocal feminist commentators like Clementine Ford and Amy Gray are regularly flamed and trolled by the 'not all men' brigade, mostly men's rights activists or sour lefty-lightweights keen to distance themselves from the dirty deeds of the patriarchy. I know women aren't the only victims of violence, and men aren't always the perpetrators, and even when they are it's not always as clear-cut as many would like to think. My mother often provoked Al and at times it seemed she thrived on the chaos. To my child's mind my mother was 'asking for it'. I could never understand why, just when Al seemed to be settling down, she would slam doors, throw objects and revive the drama. Now myself a woman older than my mother was during the years she lived with domestic violence, I understand that people are complex, and that Al and my mother were driven by feelings more powerful than reason – triggers not only stronger than their regard for each other, but stronger too than their love for their children. My mother was physically tiny. She was fierce at times, but beyond occasionally taking aim with a handy objet d'art she was no physical threat to any man. He, on the other hand, was a beef-caked hulk, a man of muscle and fury, yet the cowardly mismatch gave him no pause in a heated moment.

Having spent a great deal of time in recent years reading and writing about trauma, with a focus on the ways it is transmitted across generations and written about, I have little doubt that trauma – along with attitudes born of aeons of religiously sanctioned patriarchy – had a bearing on Al becoming the man he was. The question of accountability is a vexing one for those of us who view transgenerational trauma as undeniable, not only within our own families but across culture at large. But however driven by polluted passion, whatever the dark traumatic secrets of his own past might have been, I hold Al responsible for not taking whatever steps were necessary to prevent his passing his trauma on and to protect his partner and the children in his care. *Not all men*. Not all men act out violence, but most raised as boys inherit the entitlements or imagined entitlements that inform it. And many engage in the micro-denials that enable it. Not all men are dangerous and not all men require so little of themselves in the face of it if they are. #alllivesmatter; #notallmen; #ffssake: *focus*.

A worldwide movement of feminist collectives have been 'counting dead women' since 2012. Karen Ingala Smith began the first count in the United Kingdom. This project, Femicide Census: Profiles of Women Killed by Men, features vignettes that tell the story, as much as is known, about each woman who died as a result of a man's violence. Head shots of the murdered women appear in a grid-like visual memorial. They are all ages, from all cultural backgrounds, smiling, captured in happier moments unseeing their brutal ends. 'I want us to stop seeing the killings of women by men as isolated incidents, to put them together and to see the connections and patterns,' says Smith. 'The murders of some women barely cause a ripple, some don't make it into the national media.' And even when they do, the slippery language of journalese, which usually fails to ground the event in social and political terms, rarely does them justice and rarely acknowledges aeons of patriarchy as the setup. Gabriele Schwab gets to the heart of the whitewashed matter when she says, 'The collective or communal silencing of violent histories leads to the transgenerational transmission of trauma and the specter of an involuntary repetition of cycles of violence.'

When people talk about family violence they often speak of 'women and children', as if they were equal in their capacity to confront their circumstances. I understand enough about trans-generational trauma to know my mother had no choice in having been wounded and that she was compelled to act out her woundedness the way she did, but I do hold her accountable for failing to seek help, though it must be said 'help' was not as readily available then as it is now and, even when sought, not all sources of help are up to the task. However economically, emotionally or otherwise trapped an adult may be by their abuser, whatever fears they hold for safety, they have power, options and abilities that a child does not. Perhaps this is what remains of my rage towards my mother, the part of me that says, 'I don't care how much he broke you down; you were the mother and you should have protected me.'

According to Herman, the psychological control of the victim is not completed until they are forced to violate their own moral principles and betray their basic human attachments. The moment Al succeeded in forcing my mother to betray me is burned in my being. He made no secret of the fact that he beat his own daughter, probably from a very young age. He believed whipping Stacey with a belt was an acceptable form of parental control. My mother had never hit me nor allowed anyone else to do so, but there came a day when Al decided that Stacey and I should both be punished for some childish wrongdoing with 'the strap'.

Stacey could take the beatings, in the sense of not being surprised by them, and she rarely cried, but I went into shock: I cowered and pleaded with my mother not to let him hit me. As the strap came down on the flesh of my buttocks and thighs, blow after blow, I screamed in anguish. She sat on the sofa and watched, her face twisted into a grimace of pain and guilt. I could see in her eyes that she knew she was violating us both, and my howling as she looked on is my 'indelible image' of her betrayal of us both to this day. We later lost many years to estrangement when my belated ire made it impossible for me to be in the same room as her and be civil, and we reconciled only shortly before her death.

Watching a parent suffer and die is hard: you're gripped by a confusion of love and grief and guilt. A sickly woman for much of her life, my mother took ill suddenly in a new and mysterious way and was sent to hospital for tests. I was living interstate and after a prophetic dream in which she died I rushed back to Sydney. Two days later I was holding her hand in intensive care. I was demented with fatigue and sorrow the night she died. I hadn't slept and had barely eaten for days. My partner had come to join me, and when I finally drifted off I dreamed she was holding me, comforting me. In the eulogy I penned in those first days after her death I wrote: 'In reflecting on and celebrating her life, I think she would want us to acknowledge the enormous physical and emotional pain she experienced at times.' She was not always honest when I needed her to be – such is the cunning of denial, the convoluted mental manoeuvres of rationalisation, justification, minimisation, and their working to twist reality inside out, shaping it to hallucinations of convenience and preference – but at least she had a welcome capacity for it, which aided my process of facing our history. I wonder, sometimes, how she would feel about this book. I think she would find it painful and understand what Schwab speaks of when she says: 'Writing from within the core of trauma is a constant struggle between the colonizing power of words and the revolt of what is being rejected, silenced. Trauma kills the pulsing of desire, the embodied self. Trauma attacks and sometimes kills language. In order for trauma to heal, body and self must be reborn and words must be disentangled from the dead bodies they are trying to hide.'

My already troubled relationship with my father and my friendship with Stacey were also collateral damage. In my child's mind, I reasoned that if my father loved me, he would have known and done something about the violence with Al. I longed for his protection all through my childhood and never felt it. As for my relationship with Stacey, it was shattered. Not only were we no longer sisters; we weren't even on speaking terms. Stacey mimicked her father's abuse of my mother by writing 'slut' and other slurs on our belongings. I sought to protect my mother and hardened against Al and Stacey.

A deep rift formed between Stacey and me. As the situation declined I sided with my mother, Stacey with her father. Stacey slept through the fights; I rushed out of our bedroom fearing for my mother's life. Stacey had lived with violence all her life and accepted it as normal, having known no other reality, but to me it felt life-threatening every time. I had lost my friend and I had no one with whom to share the terror. This is the kind of mind-fuckery that happens in an abusive, oppressive situation; even allies and those who share injustices can turn on each other like rats in a cage. When it's not safe to challenge or be angry with perpetrators, or when those people seem all-powerful, untouchable or unreachable, it's tempting to take it out on someone safer. This plays out in homes and boardrooms and factory floors: people pitted against the patriarchy turning against each other while the abuse of power continues unchecked.

Not long after I found my mother sleeping on the sofa with a knife under her pillow, it ended – not with a bang but with the whimper of my exhausted ultimatum. I gave my mother a choice: him or me. She took out an apprehended violence order and Al and Stacey left. I felt responsible for bringing Al into our lives, and I had a distorted sense of my power to influence events, as if she wouldn't have ended up in yet another questionable relationship with a different troubled man had she been left to her own devices. The false sense of empowerment I exhibited in taking off for London when most girls my age were studying for exams and playing team sports had its roots in moments like these, moments in which I imagined myself both the creator of worlds, a little God, and the bearer of them, the one on whose shoulders they must be carried.

I thought Al's exit and the reign of peace that set in as I geared up to start high school was the end of the story, but it was just the beginning of my life as a traumatised teenager. I started smoking, drinking and experimenting with drugs at thirteen, and by fifteen I was drinking heavily and consuming drugs recklessly. I overate and was depressive as a teenager. As a young adult I had a volatile relationship that featured occasional violence, followed by others that kept my stress levels sky-high. I was a poly-addict: I'd take anything that would get me high and preferably oblivious, in any combination, but I had my favourites. I liked barbiturates and benzodiazepines and drank alcoholically as a baseline, started mainlining speed at twenty, and then when that burned me out, leaving me in a state of underweight paranoia, I turned to heroin. I was never tough and I was never cool. I was self-obsessed, chaotic and sloppy.

Sometimes, traumatised people are suicidal. I remember waking up from yet another heroin overdose and realising with a quiet clarity that I was toying with suicide, which brought with it a sense of eerie comfort. But when I continued to survive overdose after overdose, I decided it was time to find a better way to live. Being on the planet in a non-self-destructive way was not something I knew how to do, and quitting mood-altering substances was only the first of a series of necessary major changes. In those early years 'clean and sober', I lived on mania, coffee, cigarettes and sexualised highs. After the shock of adjusting to sobriety subsided, the trauma surfaced in new ways, mostly in painful sexual relationships and pronounced anxiety, which Herman describes as a 'major symptom of post-traumatic stress disorder'.

I was afraid of many things, including the night and physical attack, and I arranged my world so that these fears were rarely confronted. In other words, I became a deft practitioner of what's known in the mental health sector as 'avoidance strategies'. Over the years, I developed new phobias: I was afraid of storms and became claustrophobic and agoraphobic. At one stage, I developed an obsessive fear of illness and drug reactions, proving Herman's assertion that chronically traumatised people often 'perceive their bodies as having turned against them'. The more I cleaned up my life, the more self-destructive habits I addressed, the more anxious I became. I grew more controlling in response, both in my relationships and in my environment, where I developed OCD tendencies. Unmedicated, my brain was maladapted to 'peace time'.

Most of my friends considered me acceptably neurotic, but my lovers and partners struggled to accommodate my relentless array of phobias, internal dislocations and demands. Everyone who ever loved me has suffered by association. My friends could not have failed to notice my extreme self-absorption, although few had the insight to discern its roots in CPTSD. Being mistaken for plain self-centred is one of many misunderstandings. Even if survivors finally see the connection between their past and present symptoms, it doesn't guarantee that others will extend the compassion they crave. If we ignore our past, no one knows and we inadvertently alienate those around us. If we discuss it, we risk being seen as malingerers, as people who live in the past – which is, in a sense, exactly what we do, if not consciously or by choice. 'Traumatised people feel utterly abandoned, utterly alone, cast out of the human and divine systems of care and protection that sustain life. Thereafter a sense of alienation, of disconnection, pervades every relationship, from the most intimate familial bonds to the most abstract affiliations of religion and community.' This passage from Herman's book might sound melodramatic, but it perfectly describes the non-trusting chronically traumatised psyche.

Once, years ago, I phoned my father in a state when I was awaiting nerve-wracking test results. He reasoned with me, pointing out possible benign explanations for my symptoms and counselled me to be patient, not to jump to dire conclusions. I was not consoled and he grew exasperated. His voice rose as he demanded to know why I was the way I was, why I always assumed the worst. In reply, I surprised myself by making, for the first time, a direct connection between my traumatised past and my anxious present. I told him that I never assumed everything would be all right, that I was always braced for the worst and on guard, the better to be ready for it when it came. I told him what it felt like never feeling safe. I told him how, in the wake of violence, a child hopes madly that it will not happen again and when it does, time after time, they learn to expect the shock, the startling tear in the fabric of 'normal'. I told him the worst felt to me surer, more trustworthy, more reliable and more likely than any other possibility. My father listened in stunned silence and his voice, when he spoke, was shaken. It stayed that way for weeks.

It must have weighed on his mind because a couple of months later he emailed asking why I had never spoken of the violence. If only you'd told me, he said. I tried to explain the cone of silence that descends on chronic violence and abuse. If my father had asked the right questions, if anyone had, I probably would have told, but it's too much to expect a child carrying the weight of her own and her mother's pain and shame to confide in those by whom she feels abandoned. Even after many years of therapy, publicly breaking the silence is uncomfortable. I grapple with feelings of disloyalty to my mother's memory, with the fear of being viewed a whinger. But my desire to reach other traumatised people is stronger. I want to speak for those who grew up with family violence or dysfunction and don't find a way out of the maze of substance addiction, those who are diminished and die in trauma's long shadow, those who never find the words. Elie Wiesel, Holocaust survivor, Nobel peace laureate and author of almost sixty books, including *Night*, a memoir about the murder of his family and his survival in a Nazi concentration camp as a teenager, writes: 'For the survivor who chooses to testify, it is clear: his duty is to bear witness for the dead *and* for the living.'

Despite the catalogue of woes, trauma is not all bad news. Its psychological effects do have an upside. Survivors often have a remarkable empathetic capacity and many work in the helping professions. Some days I think I'd trade my freakish antennae and super-sensitivity for a non-traumatised childhood and peace of mind in a heartbeat, but we don't get to rewrite the past, only our interpretations of it. When a series of debilitating panic attacks took me back to therapy in my forties, I focused for the first time on my anxiety and panic disorder and its roots in trauma. I was told that recovery from chronic trauma is possible, but it's a slow and arduous process, frustratingly nonlinear and vulnerable to relapse, and it resists the neatly tied-up-with-a-bow endpoint. At the heart of a panic attack is an utterly overwhelmed child, saying: 'I can't cope. Help!' Recovery means facing the fact that no one is coming. One must learn to soothe oneself. Even well into recovery, the chronic trauma survivor may face setbacks due to high stress levels and inadequate time for the activities that help (yoga, meditation, friendship, etc.) and fresh trauma can set off a relapse.

Herman describes three stages of recovery: establishing safety and support; remembrance, mourning, reconstructing and telling the trauma story; and reconnection with ordinary life. While I've successfully negotiated each of these stages I cannot claim to be free from the negative effects of my history. I've turned many corners, but sometimes I feel like I'm circling within a spiral. My life is transformed. Richer, deeper, better in many ways than I imagined possible, but I am continually brought undone. I still, for example, experience occasional panic attacks, and there are phobias I've not yet overcome or mustered sufficient desire to challenge. Avoidance is a drug. Maybe I'm selling myself short. Maybe I'm exhausted after decades of expending energy and effort. Maybe I've matured and relaxed my perfectionistic impulses. I've reached some kind of acceptance, some kind of inhabiting who I am.

The night my hysterical neighbour was wrestled to the ground and handcuffed by a team of policemen in the hallway outside my door, my ex-husband did what most people would do: he backed off and watched from a distance, ready to help if called on. As for me, the scene activated some ingrained neural pathway and I entered the fray at the speed of light, just like I had back in the day. There I was in an instant, trying to placate my irrational and frantic mother, begging her to be reasonable and stop 'making it worse', imploring her all-powerful assailant mismanaging her overreaction to back off and let her go. When my neighbour was dragged off to St Vincent's psychiatric unit for an assessment, I called three times to plead her case against committal. And when she was released and taken to the station to be charged with resisting arrest and assaulting a police officer, we were outside at two o'clock in the morning, in the cold, waiting for her. When she emerged, she looked straight at me and said, 'I'm broken.' She stopped under a lamppost and lit a cigarette with shaking hands before walking off into the night.

I worried nervously about her the next day. Ancient neurons were sparking and I found it hard to separate my neighbour from my mother and myself. When she knocked on the door and apologised, hiding her face in disgraced tears, I told her I too had panic attacks and that I understood. I suggested she get a letter from a psychiatrist explaining that her behaviour was the result of the fight switch being activated in the fight-or-flight response of a severe anxiety attack, as it might help her defence. I lent her a book called *Power over Panic* by Bronwyn Fox. She said she wanted to find a therapist and I mentioned gingerly that the majority of people with panic disorder have experienced trauma or profound neglect, and that if this was the case she should look for a trauma therapist. She disclosed that she had grown up with domestic violence. Me too, I said.

I don't know what became of her. I do remember her parents came to see us, and asked us to write a letter for her court hearing, which we did. The mother, all pinched features and wiry body, sat leaning forwards and bending over backwards. The father sat stolid, manspreading, tightly coiled and hyper-masculine. My heart ached for their daughter, but I couldn't offer her friendship. We were worlds apart, she didn't seem ready to face down her trauma and wouldn't likely have accepted it, and we lost contact when I moved out after my ex-husband and I separated. I hope she got ready and found good company along the way. In the test of endurance that is the post–chronically traumatised life, friendship is both the gold and the canary in the mine. It has been, all along, my saving grace.

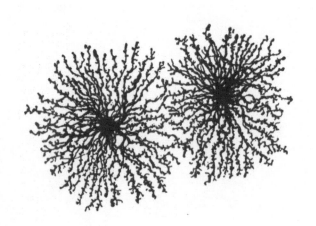

In 1977, on a windy summer day, my childhood best friend, Emma, and I walked into a milk bar on Sydney's Broadway and, as we often did, struck up a conversation with a complete stranger about Sherbet, the Australian pop phenomenon du jour, and star act of an outdoor concert held that day across the road at Victoria Park. The stranger turned out to be Mike Meade, host of *Flashez*, an ABC TV afternoon music show. Captivated by our fervour, he asked if he could interview us. In the park, before the camera, poised between childhood and adolescence, we poured our hearts out. This slice of film is now a time-capsule testimony for a generation of Sherbet worshippers, an eternal reminder of the crazed and vivacious, bold and unspeakably vulnerable thirteen-year-old girls we were. Baby-faced virginal groupies, we both wore our dark hair long and parted in the middle. I'm wearing a white cotton dress and I have a spattering of pimples on my forehead, an early crop of what would become a distressing teenage propensity towards acne breakouts. In honour of Sherbet's guitarist, I have *Harvey* written up the length of my arm and I'm holding a stuffed bear I've named after him, in confusion between amour and childish homage.

Harvey James was my one true love back when Emma and I happened upon Mike Meade. When Harvey died of lung cancer, in Melbourne in 2011, aged just fifty-eight, the internet was momentarily awash with Sherbet: I saw photos I had mooned over when they covered my bedroom wall, photos that once

77

went everywhere I went, images imprinted deep in the still-reverberating pubescent region of my psyche. I phoned Emma to see if she'd heard the news. Though Harvey was the object of my fanatical affections, it was my devotion to Emma that got me through the troubling years following my parents' divorce.

Emma and I met when we were six, after my mother and I left Aunty Nance's and moved into the house across from Emma's in Annandale. It was the early 1970s and we lived opposite each other on a quiet, wide street in a laid-back urban neighbourhood, made more interesting by the mysterious 'Abbey' around the corner, a fifty-room gothic mansion rumoured to be haunted. Emma and I bonded swiftly and ardently. When I was with her it felt like I had a compass that I lacked alone. Our friendship was characterised by a mutual commitment to fun and outrageous pranks. We packed our mothers' bras with tissues, stuffed small pillows under our clothes and wandered around talking up the trials of our pretend-pregnancies.

We stole flowers from gardens with plans to start a guerrilla florist business. We made up unflattering ditties about our nemesis, Stephen 'Dick' Stark, who lived down the road, a rude, bespectacled bullyboy who tortured animals. We choreographed elaborate routines to popular songs of the day and performed them for our families and schoolmates. We planned detailed escapades on family outings, undertaking all manner of orchestrated and spontaneous adventures.

We shared beds during countless sleepovers and traded 'goosies' – back ticklings used as a private currency. I might, say, negotiate being allowed to borrow her blue floral maxidress in exchange for a hundred goosies, which I would deliver in full on the next sleepover (you had to count out loud as you were doing it to ensure you reached the quota – skiving was not permitted). We were the daughters of divorced parents and neurotic, self-absorbed mothers, and we took refuge in each other, but there was one significant difference: Emma was close to, and clearly loved by, her seafaring navy-officer birth father and her gentle sailing-obsessed stepfather, while I mourned the absence and apparent disinterest of my father without knowing it and suffered my mother's childish, whiskey-addled boyfriend, Stuart, whom I held in undisguised contempt (he was as needy and reckless as Al was later rageful and dangerous). Emma was both my escape and my succour. When we were grounded, as punishment for some dastardly transgression (such as the theft of flowers from surrounding gardens), life felt sunless and unbearable, and I watched the front of her house desperately, longingly, for signs of Emma, living for the day I could be with her again.

What does it mean to 'survive' chronic and/or extreme trauma? It means one goes on living, against the odds. There are those who do this alone, as islands, singular in their survival, but I could not have been one of them. Were it not for friendship, for the company of similarly afflicted others, I would not have had the will to carry on. I would not have known how. Friendship was, for me, a lifeline from an early age. My brother came and went, disappearing into teenaged surfiedom on the northern beaches across the bridge. I more or less grew up, after a certain age, as an only child, and my need for the companionship of peers drove me to form ardent alliances. I once wrote a poem called 'Circle', in which I tried to get to the bottom of connectedness (an ambition begging to be humbled).

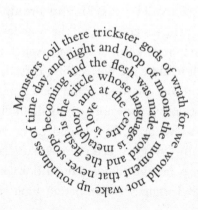

Friendship was refuge from a home in which a balding man fought me for air. Conflicts between my mother and Stuart could be explosive, but they were not as violent and fearful as those to come in the AI years. Pasty, unfit and flabby, Stuart was physically inept, but that didn't stop him indulging his infantile overreactions in distraught displays, upending chessboards if my mother was winning and exhibiting a pitiful jealousy of anyone or anything that demanded my mother's attention, including me. Years later, when I was in my teens, I bumped into him in a pub in Balmain and we got soused in the beer garden and he tried to fondle me. Later still, in my mid-twenties, I saw him at an AA meeting and this time, newly sober, I suffered the ninety minutes in an uncomfortable state of nameless, churning emotion, greeting him with a subdued hello when it ended.

Sometimes when there was friction my mother called in the cavalry: my grandparents, Glady (short for Gladys) and Johnny (my grandmother's second husband and the man most present throughout my childhood). Johnny was not my mother's father, but he loved us and we loved him – at least I know I did, and with a mighty trust I lent to few others. A gentle man, an immigrant who looked like an Asian Elvis, Johnny had been a boxer in his youth. One night, during a particularly nasty fight, they arrived and Johnny surprised us all by punching an already legless Stuart, blow by blow under the street lights, all the way down Annandale Street while I stood in my nightie at the gate, watching and silently cheering him on. It felt like the protection I craved, like someone was on our side, righting a wrong, doing something to help.

When the relationship deteriorated to the point where my mother asked Stuart to leave, he pleaded to be allowed to say goodbye to me, came into my bedroom while I lay in bed, put his hand down my pants and fingered me. I don't know how my mother found out – I vaguely remember an adult conversation in which she said I'd told her right after it happened, but one of her closest friends, whom I think of as an aunt and with whom I'm still in touch, says my mother caught him in the act. In any event, my mother knew about it very soon after it happened, and it was the beginning of a saga that took months to play out. She was predictably upset and my 'aunt' says it was the turning point, the death knell for the relationship, but here's the thing: she didn't walk right away. In the immediate aftermath my mother took him back, and I count this as one of her most damaging betrayals. I cannot imagine a process in which she could even partially reconcile herself to this deranged act, and yet I understand all too well how readily a traumatised mind and wounded being can rationalise the unacceptable. It was, as child sexual assault goes, relatively harmless. He was no doubt drunk and would use that as a defence, and he was clearly not thinking straight, but even as a child I knew some sacred relational seal had been broken. I was devastated when my mother not only let him back into our lives, but also made me move in with him in between the sale of our old house and the purchase of the flat in Glebe. It took decades to forgive her. Despite knowing what he was made of, and to my crestfallen bitterness, she uprooted us to the dank sandstone house Stuart owned in alien Waverley. Losing easy access to Emma was a catastrophe. My loneliness surrounded me and seemed to echo in the damp isolation of Stuart's lair.

I started at a school where I didn't fit in and where the charmless teacher took an immediate dislike to me. Miserable, I was sent to a child psychiatrist. It was at least in part an attempt to help me deal with the abuse, but after several sessions the doctor apparently declared that there was nothing wrong with me other than the fact that I hated Stuart (which I could have told my mother for free), and that was the end of that. I missed Annandale, and remembered my days at Annandale North Public School adoringly, often crying myself to sleep and upon waking, begging not to go to school. But even knowing Emma existed, that I had a Best Friend out there, afforded some comfort.

It's a guess, since I have no clear recall of the timeline, but I suspect the night we were expelled from his house might have been the end that stuck. A fight erupted and built to a crescendo in which Stuart gathered up armfuls of our belongings in a drunken frenzy and turfed them onto the street before booting us out after them. Ordinarily, we'd call my grandparents, but they worked nights and it wasn't always possible to reach them, or even to make a phone call. So we sat on the street with clothes and sundry items strewn around us until a gang of bikers came to our rescue. They asked my mother if she wanted them to sort Stuart out and I was disappointed when she said no.

In Glebe, life began all over again: I was at a new school I liked with a wonderful teacher. My happiness grew daily, but my mother, single and without her first drug of choice, was deeply depressed. I was about nine when I took it upon myself to look for a suitable partner for her, going so far as to perform the old asking-for-a-cup-of-sugar trick on an unwitting upstairs neighbour. I felt responsible for my mother's well-being in a way no child should, and, like the kid who brings booze to the alcoholic parent, I was in a co-dependent relationship with my mother's addiction. I needed her to be okay, so I had to make her okay. I was also frustrated and bored by her depressive state. I disliked her dispirited, downcast mood around the apartment. Just when I was beginning to give up hope, I befriended Stacey and the mutual matchmaking began.

Emma's family had also left Annandale, moving further west, and we had few opportunities to meet. Our friendship was forced to fallow until I was twelve going on thirteen, right on that cusp of childhood and adolescence. In a photo my father took of me in my paternal grandmother's Seaforth sunroom, which overlooked her glorious garden, I am that mythical creature: the girl-child about to bloom into womanhood.

Fast becoming a wilful force to be reckoned with, I finally commanded enough impatient autonomy to pursue my wishes and started travelling by train to Emma's on weekends. We resumed regular contact as if the years between had never intervened.

Coming back to Emma was like a paradoxical homecoming to escape. Home to a shared sympathy that did not require understanding of our respective histories, home to fun and lightness and adventure, home to relief from what experts in the field refer to as 'cumulative childhood stress'. The Adverse Childhood Experiences (ACE) Study, conducted by Vincent J. Felitti et al., sought to understand the impact in terms of disease, both physical and mental, and concluded that the higher the score of cumulative childhood stresses, the greater the risk of substance abuse, depression, suicide attempts, heart disease and a host of other negative outcomes. The researchers 'found a strong graded relationship between the breadth of exposure to abuse or household dysfunction during childhood and multiple risk factors for several of the leading causes of death in adults'. It doesn't take an expert to see that chronic trauma presents challenges to establishing and maintaining healthy friendships, and that children who grow up in abusive environments are likely to find it difficult to trust others, may either have trouble forming bonds or form highly dependent attachments (as I did with Emma), and are prone to having trouble regulating emotions.

But what about the positive influence of friendship, camaraderie and survivor alliances? In another study that explored the protective role of friendship on the effects of childhood abuse and depression, psychologist Abigail Powers and her colleagues noted the 'importance of understanding the effects that emotional abuse and neglect have on adult depression and how perceived friendship support may provide a buffer for women with a history of early life stress who are at risk to develop adult depression'. Emma and I were too young to 'support' each other in the adult ways I now benefit from, but our shared pop

cacoethes was a life-sustaining buffer against stresses and feelings
that lurked deeper than my conscious child mind could fathom.

Our fondness for Sherbet reached peak hysteria one summer while
we were holidaying at my grandparents' council flat in Maroubra.
Somewhere between excursions to the beach to flirt with surfers
several years our senior, lusty binges on lollies and junk food, and
night-time break-and-enters into my grandmother's miniature-
liqueurs cabinet, we got serious about Sherbet. Emma had already
declared Daryl Braithwaite her one true love and another friend,
Allison, had laid claim to Garth Porter. It was time for me to
choose from the remaining three. Alan Sandow, the drummer, was
too thickset and bare-chested for my pubescent liking while the
dark curls of Tony Mitchell, the bassist, weren't to my fledgling
taste. I settled on Harvey, the replacement for founding member
Clive Shakespeare. He was tall and lean, with blue eyes, feathery
honey-brown hair and an impish grin, so I set my sights on him
as we launched our Project Pop Paradise.

We enlisted my grandmother to sew satin bomber jackets for
us, the kind the band sported, with *Daryl* and *Harvey* embroidered
on the back. We wore the jackets constantly and, in the time-
honoured tradition of fandom, we pasted posters all over our
bedroom walls, listening to Sherbet songs on repeat. When
school resumed we spent every weekend together daydreaming,
strategising and pining. It wasn't just about the music, though
we did like the songs. It wasn't so much about Harvey himself,
though he was, it turns out, a good musician and a good man. It
was the instigation of adult desire, a ritual in girls' tribal life: the
teen celebrity crush. Sherbet offered a thrilling diversion.

Conversations with Emma over recent years have revealed
conflicting perceptions of who was the leader and who was the
follower in our friendship. I maintain I followed her lead and she is
convinced she followed mine. Even so, I am certain it was Emma

who instituted two key rites of passage: smoking and Sherbet. Emma's influence on me is irrefutably captured in mimesis; in the *Flashez* clip I copy her manner of speech, which is so notable that Chris James, Harvey's girlfriend back in the day, and later his wife and the mother of his children, asked on Facebook if I still had 'that unique accent'. I replied no, I didn't, because it had never been mine.

The year after we started high school – suburbs apart – Emma and I ramped up our campaign. It was no longer enough to listen to records and gaze on Sherbet's backlit, big-haired, semi-nude form in glossy pictures. We had to meet them, to demonstrate our devotion. 'The amorous gift is a solemn one,' writes Barthes in *A Lover's Discourse*, 'swept away by the devouring metonymy which governs the life of the imagination, I transfer myself inside it altogether.' We swooned, delirious, enraptured, held by the force of our symbiotic projections. It was not about sex. I experienced the inevitable sensual stirrings and sexual curiosities of adolescence but those stirrings and curiosities hadn't yet matured into a full-bodied physical desire for another. My desire was about romance fused to the fetishisation of absence, the man-sized space left by my father supercharged with an unruly mix of need and void in which I could only want what wasn't possible to have, a man who wasn't there.

At the start of our die-hard pursuit, Sherbet was the biggest band in the country and you couldn't get near them. But Emma and I were not your average fans. We not only crossed the line to obsession, we raced right over it, screaming to a faint. When Mike Meade interviewed us that day at Victoria Park we were at the threshold of stalker status:

> *Do you go to all their concerts?*
> Me: Yeah, most of them.
> Emma: All that we can.
> *Do you follow them around?*

Me: If we know where they're going we do.

In what way do you try and catch up with them?

Emma: Find out where they live.

Do you know where they live?

Me: Yeah. We know where Harvey lives. We know where Garth lives. We know half of Garth's phone number.

So, you know where they live. Have you been around there?

Me: No, not yet.

Towards the end of the interview, when asked how we hoped to meet them, I reply with a determined, 'Any way we can. I've just got a feeling we're going to meet them.' Mike Meade replies wryly, 'I still feel that way about the Beatles.' Emma nudges me and whispers for me to tell him what Harvey said. I respond obediently: 'Harvey says in this little book we've got – Sherbet or Harvey, I don't know – your dreams can always come true if you believe your mind.' 'And we believe our minds,' Emma declares.

We were painfully earnest open books, spilling over with affect; or rather we were conduits for a complex current of affect that whipped around the park that day. Affect: to be affected, to affect another. The philosopher Brian Massumi uses the word 'intensity' for affect, defining emotion as 'intensity owned and recognized' and affect as 'intensity unqualified, not ownable or recognizable'. Feelings, says Teresa Brennan, in her exploration of the transmission of affect, are 'sensations that have found the right match in words'.

Brennan puts forth a swath of suggestions about how affect moves between us, stressing that her understanding of affective transmission is of a 'process that is social in origin but biological and physical in effect', meaning that our experience of affect is, from the start and throughout our lives, relational, fluid and contagious, even if our experience of it is felt as distinctly bodily and subjective. If the idea of affective transmission rubs liberal ideology up the wrong way, we need only to view footage of a Beatles concert circa 1964 or consult the history books for examples of wildfire contagions. The Dancing Plague of 1518 began with a lone woman dancing on a Strasbourg street. By the end of the first week there were thirty-five dancers, and by the end of the first month their numbers had grown to around four hundred. The plague proved fatal: some died from heart attack, stroke or exhaustion. Physicians at the time said the plague was caused by 'hot blood', a rather poetic evocation of affect. Another example, centuries later in 1962: the journal *American Scientist* reported an outbreak of contagious laughter in a small town in Tanzania. What began as an isolated fit of laughter (and sometimes crying) in a group of twelve- to eighteen-year-old schoolgirls rapidly rose to epidemic proportions, eventually infecting nearby communities, closing schools and continuing for six months. These epidemics are rare extremes, but they demonstrate the way in which 'bodies can catch feelings as easily as catch fire: affect leaps from one body to another, evoking tenderness, inciting shame, igniting rage, exciting fear – in short, communicable affect can inflame nerves and muscles in a conflagration of every conceivable kind of passion', as writer and theorist Anna Gibbs so eloquently puts it.

Emma and I were caught up in a collective hysteria, one to which young girls are particularly, and culturally, susceptible. It was a gendered performance of heteronormative desire. Gender, Judith Butler maintains, involves a social performance in which 'individual bodies' enact a repetition of meanings already socially established, and thus gender is 'real only to the extent that it is performed'. Significantly, she stresses the importance of the collective dimension and the public nature of this performance. There we were, performing het-femininity on the brink of burgeoning womanhood, being interviewed as 'Sherbet fans'. As I look back now, what seems most real, most true, of that scene of two girls on the grass, in the wind, on that cloudy grey day, answering questions from one man about other men who literally took centre stage that day, is the profound love between Emma and me.

'Love,' says Brennan, 'directs positive feelings toward the other by attending to the specificity of the other (rather than seeing the other through idealizing or demonizing projections).' Our fandom was a heady idealising shape-shifting projection, but our bond was made of heart-glue and grounded in the lived reality of incalculable hours of shared time and space.

Decades ago, when we were children, I gave Emma a toy duck. She kept it into adulthood, even through the many years in which we'd lost contact. In my mid-twenties, I tracked her down and she invited me to dinner. My boyfriend at the time and I were sitting around talking to her and her husband when she disappeared into her bedroom and emerged with the duck. The white of the fur had greyed and it was missing clumps of hair. I hardly knew where to look, certain I would not have kept such an ugly object whatever the sentimental value. These days she remembers my birthday every year before I do: a card turns up in the mail, despite the fact that we rarely see each other. This bond is strong and deeply rooted.

Her card arrived several days ago with a crayon-drawn heart on the envelope. It's almost as if she can sense I'm writing about her and our Sherbet days, because in it she reminisces about the *Flashez* clip, and how cute we were, adding: 'Thank you for being my childhood friend. I don't know what I would have done without you.' And I don't know what I would have done without her. Though I am a lesser friend, remiss when it comes to birthday and Christmas cards, Emma is, as Barthes puts it, a friend in that she can 'leave for a while' without her 'image crumbling'. When you live in a post-traumatic state you live with an absence of solidity. Those who help you keep form by recognising you and affirming your existence, and those who maintain their form, who most stay alive, within you, become precious.

After the *Flashez* interview, we intensified our mission and ramped up our determination. We began hanging around EMI when we knew the band was recording. We got autographs, though Daryl managed to evade us. We started spending every weekend staking out their houses, but the weekends were crowded with other fans who, like us, had done their homework and had the moxie to loiter. Emma maintains we were friendly to the other fans and enjoyed a sense of camaraderie with them, but not without petty bitchiness and jealousies. I recall a sense of competition, a drive to prove ourselves the biggest Sherbet fans ever. Before long we were forging our mother's signatures on sick notes and wagging school to stalk our idols without being fettered by our weekend rivals. We'd meet at Central Station, then catch buses or hitchhike around Sydney in chase. There were various getting-high experiments in the nooks and crannies of the station, the aspirin and Coke failure soon followed by the smoking-nutmeg disappointment. Eventually I managed to source a supply of joints from the women at Jim's and we'd get stoned and giggle irrepressibly for hours at everything and anything, till our tummies hurt, up the back of buses, collapsing with laughter as we walked along the street, set off by minor oddities. There were times when our giggling was so extreme we were incapable of speaking. That special language, those unique signs and shorthands that every close friendship develops. The joke you tell each other over and over again (that no one else laughs at). The way you can read a chapter of mood from a glimpse of the face and hear a song of stress in the tone of a lone-voiced word, the way you both instantly know what's fun and funny.

So many names. So many hours held by others. So many stories told and heard. The cups of tea and cigarettes and meals and films and books and conversations and plans and moments of unbearable sanity and death-defying madness. Maggie: watching you cut up in beer gardens, playing games of pool doubles, decades later coming across a story, while waiting in a supermarket queue, that you sold to the tabloid *That's Life*, detailing sexual abuse by your brother. Pauly: driving the coast at night listening to The Beach Boys. Astrid: that rainy day in New York, having haircuts side by side then running, laughing, up Fifth Avenue without umbrellas, our little failures, you loving me as I am, singing The B-52s' 'Give Me Back My Man' at your family's holiday house with my new lover, sitting with you as you lay dying, stroking your forehead, thanking you for thirty years of friendship and for keeping me company in those first crazy years of sobriety. Katie: you holding my hand in the oncologist's office the night before the operation after that wrenching week when we didn't know how bad it was, when they'd told me it was 'rare and aggressive', the squeeze of hands and our teary relief when she said the scan showed it hadn't spread and a second opinion indicated it might not be 'the worst kind' after all, but a more merciful malignancy that promised, once treated, to let me live well and long. Mal: passing time with you in the waiting room ahead of enduring my prescribed 'brachytherapy' radioactive dildo. Kris: that time years ago when I was frightened of a dire outcome and you said, 'we'll deal with it'; the power of that 'we' and the way it settled me into a knowing of care and calm. Days of hours on the phone. Seasons, reasons, lifetimes. I carry these uncrumbled images there where nothing dies.

During those days of carefree truancy, Emma and I passed many hours at Garth's in Watsons Bay, perhaps because it was the nicest location in which to while away a day. There were huge glass windows at the back of his house, which conveniently faced onto a park. We'd take our position on the grass and stare up, watching Garth and his girlfriend, Mary, and sometimes the whole band, hoping they'd notice us – *the biggest Sherbet fans ever* – and reward us with a smile. Harvey lived in Paddington, and we made contact

with him several times over our many stakeouts. He was the
sweetest back then, the one who had the most time for us. Perhaps
he was the least jaded, the least worn down by the pressures of
fame and the constant presence of testy fans, having been the last
to join (he had been with the band less than a year at the time
we commenced Project Pop Paradise). He seemed to see beyond
the fan-girl caricature to the tender young beings we were and
to return a little of our love. The most celebrated of our meetings
with him took place at Garth's. We were out front and the sun was
beginning to set after a slavish day of waiting. Harvey walked out,
saw us, shook his head and said, 'Are you girls still here?' He asked
where we were headed and we told him we had to get to the city.
'Jump in, I'll give you a lift,' he said, opening the door of his Jaguar.
'It was only because he knew us from the *Flashez* clip, and he liked
us and we'd already met him,' Emma says of the remarkable gesture.
'That's the only reason we got the lift. He wasn't going to put just
any Sherbet girls in his car.' I distinctly remember that when 'Don't
Cry for Me Argentina' came on I said, 'I hate this song,' and Harvey
said, 'Me too,' and I swooned. Emma insists Harvey said he loved
the song. 'Whenever I hear it I think of Harvey. I love that song
now,' she proclaims. Memory plays tricks on us.

Emma's quest was arduous, for Daryl was the hardest to pin
down and took the longest to meet. In a photo – now battered
and bent from decades in her wallet – of Emma and Daryl on the
day we cornered him, she is crying and overwrought at finally
meeting her hero. We'd come close before but he had always
proved elusive. 'There was another time he came down with
his German Shepherd, Sebastian, and got in his car,' remembers
Emma. 'You and I ran down the street, jumped in a taxi and said,
"Quick, follow that car!" We followed for a while but the taxi
lost him.'

We laugh now about our shenanigans, the way we'd brazenly
flag a cab and forage with increasing play-acting alarm among
our belongings before confessing that we had no money to pay

the fare. The way we coyly played dumb as we conned our way through the days with bubbly, cheeky charm. Emma says people let us get away with it because we were nice and made their day interesting. Then it comes back to me, the dark side to this rollicking. We recall sharp-edged encounters and close shaves, when we accepted food, money or favours from creepy benefactors before making speedy getaways, laughing with relief and bravado at the tragic potentials we had eluded. 'We put ourselves in such danger, didn't we?' Emma says in hushed tones.

Some order of risk-taking is necessary – and yet. Our unthinking determination to live on our own fledgling terms pleases me – and yet. In a 2012 study, researchers Mohsen Kianpoor and Nour Mohammad Bakhshani from the Zahedan University of Medical Sciences in Iran define 'high-risk' as 'volitional behaviors with an uncertain outcome that entail negative consequences'. They note that though this behaviour can manifest at any age, adolescents, confronted with 'the task of defining their own identities', often express bodily and emotional discomfort by 'enacting risky behaviors that function to release and express aversive emotional distress and tension'. They also point out that numerous researchers have highlighted an association between trauma and risk-taking as a 'repetition of the actions, performed or imagined, that occurred during the traumatic event'. High-risk behaviour, then, can be 'conceptualized as a way of remembering, or as an unconscious attempt to gain mastery over the trauma'. No surprises here: 'a history of maltreatment or other forms of psychological trauma is a precursor to health-risk behaviors in both adolescence and adulthood'. That Emma and I moved about in the world as if it were safe for women and girls, as if we weren't the fantasy stuff of men who would do harm in order to get off, impresses me – and yet. Some unlucky young women who take risks as an unwitting way of regulating painful emotions encounter an unthinkable world of pain and trauma. Others are simply going about their lives when they have horror visited upon them.

In 1913 Ernest Austin rapes and cuts the throat of eleven-year-old Ivy Mitchell in Queensland. Between December 1976 and February 1977 Christopher Worrell rapes and strangles seven young women – Veronica Knight, eighteen; Tania Kenny, fifteen; Juliet Mykyta, sixteen; Sylvia Pittman, sixteen; Vickie Howell, twenty-six; Connie Iordanides, sixteen; Deborah Lamb, twenty – and dumps their bodies in the outskirts of Adelaide, aided by James Miller. John Travers and four others rape and stab twenty-six-year-old Anita Cobby to death in 1986 in the western suburbs of Sydney. In 2003 Kevin John Hender rapes and strangles Samantha O'Reilly, aged fifteen. The years come and go. The names change. The violence cycles on, like a virus infecting hosts in each new generation. Our pipe dream of possessing Australia's pop princes might have cost us dearly.

Roland Barthes writes of that moment in which the lover becomes aware that the 'difficulties of the amorous relationship' stem from the 'ceaseless desire to appropriate the loved being in one way or another'; this realisation results in the decision to 'abandon henceforth all "will-to-possess" in his regard'.

Our year of zealous fandom ended gradually as our 'will-to-possess' our temporary idols petered out. At sixteen, just a few years after our Sherbet summer, Emma started dating Derek, a boy who lived five doors down, and they went on to marry and have two children, now adults. In the decades since, Emma and Derek have lived not far from her childhood home, while I've lived eight of my nine lives in different states and countries, in seven significant intimate-partner relationships. 'Our lives just took a different path, didn't they?' Emma observes.

Our lives also took a different path regarding Sherbet. Emma remained a staunch, lifelong fan, while I disowned my Sherbet roots and forgot my 2SM soft-rock past in Sydney's 1980s post-punk scene. Surrounded by musicians, I was introduced to a wealth of music across decades and cultures and genres. Time can be a harsh but often fair judge: though the satin flares haven't stood its test, the Sherbet catalogue remains undeniably significant in Australian music. It was the soundtrack to an era when the nation was not yet on the world stage, not yet digitised and wired, isolated in its own summery, settler-colonial troubled puberty.

Emma's most vivid memory of those days is of me hamming up 10cc's 'The Things We Do for Love', the theme song for our misadventures. 'If I hear it now,' she says, 'I think of you singing it to me.' My obsession with Sherbet, and all that I did in the name of that obsession, was ultimately about my friendship with Emma. She was my partner in playful crime and she held the space in which I could be what I needed to be – a child, beginning to move in complex ways away from childhood. We still dwell in the archives of the ABC, declaring our undying love for Sherbet as code for our love for each other.

Less than eighteen months later I'd leave school in the middle of my second year of high school, not yet fourteen, having persuaded my mother I had no need of formal education since I was destined to be an artist of some kind, a prediction that proved both true and false. Alice Cooper reportedly wrote his 1972 hit 'School's Out' after someone put a question to him: what's the greatest three minutes of your life? There were two great moments in a young person's life, Cooper decided: Christmas morning anticipation and 'the last three minutes of the last day of school when you're sitting there and it's like a slow fuse burning'. He set out to capture that moment in song, and he succeeded. If at times in my childhood I looked towards school as a haven, it often failed to be one. School, it turns out, can be a hothouse of trauma.

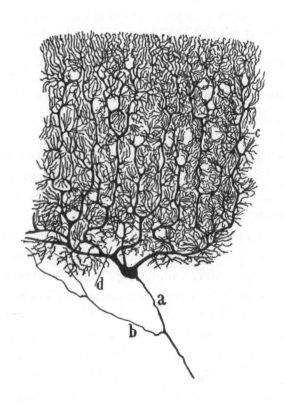

This is how it happens, how trauma snowballs, how it infiltrates and reproduces structurally and institutionally.

The first years of my life, before my parents separated, I lived in Frenchs Forest, on the bushy outskirts of Sydney, in a house opposite a shopping centre and a primary school. My mother was often distracted, caught up in her own concerns, and sometimes there were consequences. Like the time I overdosed on Disprin as a toddler. I'd taken a packet from the kitchen cupboard into the bathroom and eaten the pills one by one, because I liked the taste, while she was enjoying a long phone conversation. I was rushed to hospital with my mother shaking me in the back seat to keep me from losing consciousness.

I spent a lot of time in the backyard, under a willow tree that's no longer there, and sometimes I wandered over to the property of an elderly couple who lived next door. The old man had a shed down the back. I was very young, three or four, and I don't remember what happened there exactly. The vagueness and unreliability of traumatic memory is even more pronounced and precarious when it comes to early childhood, and only a few impressionistic imprints remain. I remember tools on a bench, a concrete floor. I have a flash of light streaming in through a grimy/broken/small window. I don't remember his penis. I remember being surprised/curious/scared. I don't remember touching it. I remember standing in front of him.

I might remember rubbing on my bum. I remember he had an old-woman wife. I don't know what my mother was doing. He said it was a game called trains.

I can only be sure I was sexually abused because my mother told me. This was the story according to family lore: one afternoon, when my grandparents were visiting, as they often did, I tried to get my grandfather Johnny to play 'trains', the 'game' the aged paedophile next door had taught me. Instant commotion and panic ensued. Questions about where I had learned this so-called game. My grandmother Glady was the most affected by this dark surprise, having been sexually assaulted by an uncle over a long period of time as a child (she eventually had a nervous breakdown as a result). There was a family conference about what to do, whether to call the police or not. A decision was reached not to report him or involve the police lest it make this event and the abuse itself more traumatic for me.

Their strategy was to disallow me to visit next door and keep a closer eye on me, to let it fade into the background so that I would not feel that I had been at the centre of a scandal, that I had been bad.

In recent years I learned that not everyone was down with this decision. My brother says he was outraged at their inaction and that at the tender age of twelve he had wanted to leap to my defence and to go next door and give it to the old bastard, but was held back and left to stew in impotent fury. I had 'forgotten' all about the 'game' in the shed and its upsetting revelation in the family living room by the time I reached adulthood. It wasn't until I signed up for a professional development course on child sexual assault in my late twenties, when I was working as a drug and alcohol counsellor in an adolescent rehab, that it resurfaced as a cloud of untraceable, murky affect. By the end of the three-day course I found myself in an odd state: restless, disturbed, as if I was being followed by someone, as if something was brewing. Finally, I had the faintest cluster of recollections of a bespectacled silver-haired predator coaxing me to touch his wrinkled old penis surrounded by his tools. I phoned my mother, who promptly confirmed it. But the unsettling conversation didn't end there. 'There was also that time with Stuart Jones,' she said, in a matter-of-fact way. I had completely forgotten the fingering incident, though its palpable aftermath of misery in Stuart's house had not been dimmed by the passage of time.

Cut.

Fade up on the kindergarten classroom of a suburban primary school. It's a large space with children's art on the walls. Muted daylight pours in through the windows. A group of young children sit on the floor, cross-legged, listening to the teacher who sits up front. There I am, right in the middle among the knot of small bodies, a pretty girl child with shoulder-length dark hair and a fringe. I turn to the girl sitting next to me and whisper, initiating a game of you-show-me-yours-and-I'll-show-you-mine. We take turns pulling the soft cotton crotches of our tiny underpants to the side to reveal our bald-babyish labia in sly-quick flashes while the other leans forward to sneak a glimpse. Stilted giggles and the titillating thrill of naughtiness pass back and forth until we are caught as I'm taking my turn. The class is called back to order and one by one the children dutifully take their places behind their desks. Except for me.

The now-faceless teacher has dragged me out front of the class to reprimand me before a cohort of witnesses. Her words are lost in time, fallen through a crack of consciousness. My developing brain goes into shock and struggles to comprehend what is happening. The only thing that is clear is that I am shameful, shamed, humiliated. I have done wrong and my punishment is to be told so in such a way that the whole world knows. She turns me around and pulls my underpants down, exposing my bare bottom. She makes me stick it out and then she slaps it, hard, several times. When class breaks for little lunch I wander around the playground in a dissociated daze, alone and devastated.

I don't know why I chose that moment for genital peer play. Perhaps I was bored. I don't know if what I did was healthy childhood exploration, an expression of normal curiosity (if inappropriately timed and placed), or whether my behaviour was the kind of typical acting-out identified as commonplace in children who have been sexually abused. When I put the scenario to my friend, sexuality educator Deanne Carson, without identifying myself as one of the children, she said it could be either, but the prior abuse would raise an acting-out flag. What I do know for sure is that the teacher's actions were profoundly traumatic, perhaps more so than the original abuse. The horrible irony of punishing me for exposing myself to a fellow student by exposing my buttocks to the entire class and beating me was apparently lost on her. As was, it seems, the significance of the bum, and the mastery over the anus, for children that age. When my mother found out she stormed up to the school and complained, but the damage was done.

We're all too familiar with tales of hideous abuses by clergy, and my youth was peppered with the horror stories of friends who were sent away to boarding schools. As a teacher of teenagers and young adults, I find the degradation of young people and the abuse of power more unthinkable than ever, and an institutional, educational system that would allow it is unacceptable. 'Corporal punishment', as it's politely referred to, has largely fallen out of favour, but it is still perpetrated in some countries – many schools in the Southern United States, for example, still use 'paddling', the beating of students with an implement shaped like a cricket bat, and it's only recently that the last bastions of institutionalised assault have been laid to rest in Australia. Alan Corbett writes in *New Matilda* that though corporal punishment has been outlawed in many Australian schools for years, some non-government schools have condoned physical punishment until quite recently. Christian Community Ministries Ltd reportedly only gave the directive to its schools to cease the practice in 2016. Australia ratified the United Nations Convention on the Rights of the Child in 1990. That's twenty-six years in between. Why did successive governments turn a blind eye for all that time? Why do they turn a blind eye still?

An exposé of the routine torture of young people in Northern Territory youth detention shocked the nation when images of seventeen-year-old Dylan Voller, shirtless, hooded and strapped to a restraint chair, aired on national television. This and other horrendous abuses took place at Don Dale Youth Detention Centre, a purpose-built maximum-security prison for almost exclusively Indigenous 'juvenile delinquents'. What happened at Don Dale – the stripping, assaulting, gassing and isolating of prisoners without access to running water – is, apparently, not confined to that institution. And it is perfectly legal. Helen Davidson reported in *The Guardian* that Prime Minister Malcolm Turnbull, in calling for a royal commission, asked that the investigation undertake an examination of 'the culture which allowed it to occur' and 'should not be confined to the culture of the detention centre alone'. So, a royal commission into neo-colonial patriarchy then?

There are people, children and adults, who appear to be freakishly unlucky, who seem to attract abuse and misfortune like trauma magnets, apparently destined to it. Many severely or chronically traumatised people are disproportionately subject to seemingly unrelated traumatic events, time after time, so that looking upon them you might be tempted to wonder if the woeful story you're hearing is imagined, or embellished, if they're telling tales to garner sympathy or to procure favour through victimhood, or whether they somehow masochistically bring it upon themselves. The traumatic cycle works in both mysterious and logical ways, gathering speed along various trajectories. New trauma sticks to old trauma like Velcro.

In his exploration of writing trauma in *The New York Times*, Saïd Sayrafiezadeh discloses terrible harassment that occurred during his tertiary studies. Sayrafiezadeh starts out recounting an early major trauma: a neighbour raped him at the age of four or five, and, like mine, his family chose not to report it. Years later, he continues, he was sexually harassed by a male professor at college, who befriended the unwitting young man and insisted Sayrafiezadeh was gay, despite his protestations, and repeatedly attempted to seduce him. The stalking began when Sayrafiezadeh was a freshman and continued throughout his studies, which, unsurprisingly, he did not complete. Reflecting on this experience, Sayrafiezadeh reasons that he did not take appropriate action in the face of relentless harassment because, thanks to the inaction of his family, he had no model for how to assert and protect himself in the face of abuse. He goes even further, stating that 'what was happening between me and the professor had originated some fifteen years earlier' on the afternoon he was brutally raped, concluding he had been playing out a 'fundamental need to be menaced by a predator, and then, in the final moment, to elude that predator's trap'.

My feelings split in two reading this. At one level, I understand exactly what he means, and know all too well the way trauma replays in what seems to be a paradoxical attempt to come to terms with an indigestible reality. I am intimate with the impulse, the compulsion to try to rewrite the script of a film already cast, shot and screened. An old friend of mine calls this baffling and beleaguering attempt to master trauma our 'genius'. When I phoned her once, self-flagellating and reeling in shame over having made a mistake I felt I should have seen coming, thereby repeating an old pattern, she consoled me that all was as it should be. Reaching through my bitter disappointment that my shiny new awareness was not enough to stop me running headlong into yet another rendition of the same old sad tune, she reassured me that – rather than berate myself for failing to prevent a painful situation that mirrored my familial past – I might thank my 'genius' for setting up another opportunity to heal. At another level, though, I'm uncomfortable with the way Sayrafiezadeh seems to take excessive responsibility for the harassment. This is what chronically and severely traumatised people tend to do, what victims of sexual assault and harassment often do. Self-responsibility and understanding = agency. Both are crucial to untangling from trauma's stranglehold, but the repeated patterns of victimisation, the systemic traumatic transmissions, will continue until and unless we sufficiently address the socio-political conditions that create them.

My brain is numb after two solid days of grading. I'm teaching pathway provider college: students who didn't get the ATAR to get into university, and international students funded by parents who pay hefty fees upfront. Many of these students are immigrants from war-torn countries: it's a different ballgame to teaching second-year sandstone English majors at elite varsity. Even those students who do come from money, or at least come across like they've grown up with a sense of entitlement, walk on thin ice here in the lucky country, out of their element, often disadvantaged by a poor grasp of English. I've taught a lot of first-year university. There are students who shine, students who want to learn and are committed to doing their best, but there are those too who flail through semester, half-arsed and half-hearted. I never know how many choose to be in my classroom, how many among them even want the careers they are training for, how many understand that – however slick the university's promotion – there are only so many jobs to go around, how many are resentfully doing what's expected, dragging their feet through one assessment after another.

I was excited about starting school, and, being a sociable child, I liked the concept of school, if not always the daily reality. I open my photo album to find my first formal school photo, in black and white. I'm probably five, and it can't have been long before we moved from Frenchs Forest to the inner west. I don't know if it's the teacher from my kindergarten class or a different one. She stands at the back with mousy brown hair and a benign face. She doesn't look like a woman who would beat the naked flesh of a small child. I'm in the front row, in possession of one of ten pairs of feet neatly pressed together, as directed. The other children have their hands on their knees but, already disobeying orders, I have mine clasped in my lap. My back is ramrod straight and I'm wearing a goofy grin, head held high, hamming it up, over-compensating.

I have few memories from my time there, but I do recall having an early existential crisis in assembly one day, overwhelmed by a feeling of dislocation, of unreality. Heightened experiences of depersonalisation (a feeling of disconnection from one's thoughts, body or emotions) and derealisation (a feeling of disconnection from one's surroundings) are, of course, associated with trauma. I remember the peculiar feeling of finding myself in a body yet not feeling of that body, *in* that body, sat in a sea of other bodies, and none of it making any sense. I don't know whether that particular sensation was trauma-related or the result of one of those eerie existential fractures in time in which one experiences the self as alien in a moment of metaconsciousness. I'm not even sure if there is a difference.

I remember, too, going to the tuckshop and observing the other mothers, the *Leave It to Beaver* mothers, volunteering there. I remember wishing I had that kind of mother. A housewife mother, a TV mother, a mother devoted to her children, a mother who had no visible self, a mother who in demonstrating her devotion by working in the tuckshop would elevate my status in the schoolyard as a Very Loved Daughter, as special. It strikes me as both terrible and frightening that, in just a few short years on earth, I had already been culturally indoctrinated into at some level wanting a Stepford wife as a mother. But there it is. I wanted parents who came to parent–teacher nights (not altogether unreasonable). I wanted to be Lisa who lived round the corner, whose dad just adored her. I thought she was a living doll and I was green with wistful, self-loathing envy. I hated my weird name and sometimes I tried to pass as a Lisa or a Debbie, but my not-quite-like-the-other-childrenness seeped through and sooner or later everyone knew I was not Cindy Brady. Meanwhile, my mother matured and perfected her make-up, all provincial desire, a restless, discontented storm in a B-cup.

I want to think things have changed, that schools are more sympathetic to troubled kids now than they were back in the 1960s. I assume children chronically traumatised at home or by world events (refugee children, for example) are more likely to be met by caring staff who have some understanding of trauma and its tell-tale signs. Many teachers are busy doing a tough job well, and there is growing awareness in the education sector as to the prevalence of trauma. Some schools make concerted efforts to understand the effects of trauma and to explore how the school community can best support affected students. But that's no guarantee a child, already traumatised or not, won't be traumatised at school.

Deanne spends her days travelling around schools in Victoria, delivering comprehensive and progressive sexuality education programs. She says she has seen teachers grab children by the arm and drag them across the room, seen them bully the bullied child. She's encountered 'clip' systems – endorsed by the Department of Education – where a list of behaviours, rewards and punishments are positioned at the front of the classroom, and children's names are moved from one category to another depending on whether they are disruptive or not. It's an improvement on having one's bare butt cheeks publicly slapped, but still.

'Teachers have an incredible privilege of being with students for six hours a day,' says Deanne. 'A teacher who practises positive, mindful leadership can be of emotional benefit to all students but particularly those with trauma backgrounds or unsupportive home lives. Conversely, teachers who use shaming or bullying techniques to control their cohort can compound distress already experienced by some children.' One principal she spoke to informally estimated the number of students who experience trauma to be around 40 per cent. Aside from pressing concerns about the harmful potential of teachers' behaviours, and questions around how teachers manage already troubled students, there is also the matter of how trauma is enacted or transmitted child to child, which happens most often by way of bullying.

Few children schooled in the western world escape experiencing or witnessing bullying. When we think of bullying we think of the traditional scenario: a bigger boy beating up a smaller boy, or the infliction of a 'hazing' initiation rite on a terrified newcomer. We think of boys and we think of the body, or of persistent schoolyard name-calling. We know girls can bully, and most of us recall the 'tough girls' of our childhood, but they were a rarity, an aberration of girlhood. In recent years, there has been an increased focus on the complexities of a girl culture that thrives in the corridors and toilets of schools. Movies such as *Heathers* and *Mean Girls* helped bring the dark side of this secret society to mainstream attention, and revealed it as a breeding ground for a kind of bullying that often evades notice and official consequence.

Dr Ken Rigby from the University of South Australia defines bullying as repeated aggression in which there is an imbalance of power, but while male aggression is usually easy to see, often manifesting in physical assault or intimidation or overt verbal abuse, bullying among female students can be harder to recognise because of its tendency towards psychological mind-games. During our years together at Annandale North Public School, between the ages of six and eight, Emma was relentlessly bullied at school by a freckled strawberry blonde called Cheryl who became our sworn enemy, and over the duration of my schooling I copped my fair share of bullying, but did not suffer any protracted or severe victimisation. I suspect I got off rather lightly. In any event, I want to focus here on my bullying behaviour because the queue of victims is always much longer than the queue of perpetrators, which begs the question of who can possibly be doing all the perpetrating.

Some years ago I received an email from an old school friend of ours, whom I'll refer to as Tom C. Tom had come across some writing of mine and managed to track me down. I had no recollection of him so I asked if he had been among the boys I'd claimed as a boyfriend. He wrote back saying that yes, Emma and I had once given him a heart-shaped cushion with *We Love You Tom* sewn on it, along with a series of gushing notes. He admitted the lingering sentiment of first love was the reason he'd decided to get in touch. I was seized by concern that the gift he had taken as praise might have been one of our mocking pranks and, wracked with guilt, I phoned Emma. She reassured me that Tom C. had not been the butt of a joke – we really did like him. We liked him so much we trapped him in my bedroom and forced him to kiss us, attacking him with hairspray and lipstick at any sign of resistance. I mentioned this to him in an email and jokingly offered to pay his therapy bills, but moments after I sent the message Emma phoned to say that it wasn't Tom we had set upon with the hair product after all. Rather, it was another boy we regularly victimised, who hangs on the blurry edges of my memory. According to the Australian Human Rights Commission, the kissing/hairspray incident qualifies as sexual harassment, which is categorised as a subset of bullying.

Children are, essentially, conformists. A sense of belonging is the appeal of the best friend or clique; they affirm and enhance the self. Belonging to an 'us-world' grants inhabitants a sense of being larger than life. The faith in the other members of the 'us' and their faith in you, the movement of this faith flowing back and forth in an open channel, somehow feeds the self, makes it bigger than it was, gives one a confidence and boldness unachievable alone. For the most part, the 'us-world' Emma and I created was harmless fun – watching Jamie Redfern on *Young Talent Time*, arranging dance routines, looking for oysters around the rocks of the sailing club that Emma's family frequented. But there was a toxic side to our firm friendship, rooted in social traumata and conditioning, carelessness, and cruelty. Bullying, racism, rejection and all their negative consequences are the shadow life of the need to belong, to carve out an 'us' against the 'them'. The very nature of belonging to one friendship, group, school, area or subculture necessitates rejection: some will not be admitted. Belonging is, then, defined in relation to non-belonging others. This is natural and not, the experts assure us, cause for alarm. When does this normal social order become bullying, and how does it relate to trauma?

One day, a boy called Angelo, who lived at the end of our street, threw a birthday party, to which Emma and I were not invited. We scooped a dried-out dog turd off the footpath and wrapped it up in endless sheets of newspaper, finally covering it with gift-wrap. We presented the gift to Angelo at his front door, party balloons bobbing in the rooms behind him, with our smiling wishes for a happy birthday. We also turned on a girl who lived a few doors down, for no good reason. My mother had some innocuous pills that had the peculiar side effect of turning her urine blue. Emma and I stole a few of these and produced some blue piss of our own, then poured it into an empty perfume bottle and gave it to the girl as a present. I have no idea what these children made of our cruelty, but the memories stand as evidence of the unspeakable spite children are capable of in their us-against-them narratives.

I'm ashamed to admit now that if racism wasn't the root of these dastardly deeds it was certainly the fertiliser. At that time, the children of Italian and Greek immigrants were marginalised at school, with their strange-smelling foods and their pierced ears and olive skin. I wasn't raised by my family to be a racist, at least not your average white-supremacist kind of racist. But, as with gender, the learnings seep in from all around from the moment we can make even partial sense of a sound or an image. Even so, there's no denying those wilfully unkind acts expressed a pointed anxiety around difference, and an arrogant assumption of superiority. I have no recollection of our thought processes or if we manufactured justifications, and though researchers, educators and psychologists continue debating exactly why bullying occurs, they do seem to agree on the common theme of power and control. To my mind, shame is key, specifically the kind of shame John Bradshaw calls 'toxic shame', which I refer to as 'traumatic shame'. Direct correlations have also been made between bullying and abuse in the home.

A 2007 survey of seven hundred fifth-grade students indicated that both bullies (youth who bully others but do not tend to be bullied themselves) and bully-victims (youth who both bully and are bullied) report high levels of victimisation in their homes and/or communities (59 per cent for bully-victims, 61 per cent for bullies). Bully-victims also report high levels of child maltreatment (44 per cent) and sexual victimisation (32 per cent). Though researcher Melissa K. Holt and her colleagues stress that victimisation in other domains was not a factor in every case of bullying, the findings underscore the importance of keeping 'the broader victimization context in mind so that the youth who do experience multiple victimization forms can obtain the services that they need'. Other studies discuss a 'blame the victim' and 'pity the perpetrator' mentality among some teachers. Still, everyone agrees that bullying presents a major challenge that involves an incapacity, or unwillingness, to extend respect in the face of difference.

When I mentioned to an Italian-Australian friend over lunch that I was writing about bullying, she told me she had been targeted as a 'wog' because she dared to be attractive, talented and a top student. She explained, 'I wasn't allowed to stand out. As soon as I did, a hate campaign started against me. It began with taunts about my loving myself and thinking I was beautiful.' But many victims of bullying are at the very lowest rung of school's social order: the only student from a particular cultural background, the stutterer, the loner odd child — persecuted not as tall poppies but as worthless weeds. Some children are not just bullied for their difference, but tortured for it.

When we caught up for coffee, Tom C. volunteered the haunting story of an event that took place not long after I'd left North Annandale. A lone Aboriginal girl stands in the playground. A child starts chanting, 'Scaboriginy, scaboriginy ...' Other nearby children join in. Before long she is surrounded by what seems like the entire school chanting and clapping. It's an image befitting a horror movie. I struggle to imagine how this child psychologically survived this ordeal. I can't help wondering where she is now, what her life is like and how she shares her days with this scarring memory.

I wasn't raised to be a racist, at least not your average white-supremacist kind of racist (reprised). My grandfather had emigrated with his family from Myanmar as a young man. Emma was of Pacific Islander and Chinese, as well as Anglo, heritage. Before marrying my mother, my father had fallen in love with and almost married an Indian woman named Meera. My parents were once evicted for having Indian dinner guests in the 1950s. My mother was friends with renowned First Nations actor, filmmaker, activist and teacher Brian Syron and the playwright Bobby Merritt, who had been brought up on Erambie Aboriginal Mission (she later had an affair with Bobby, and years after that, when I was in my late teens, I also had a brief fling with him). When I lived in multicultural Glebe as a child, I had Fijian and Chinese friends and an Italian boyfriend. But for all that I can't claim we were above racism. You're infected before you hit kindy (as young as three, according to professor Mahzarin Banaji, psychologist and prejudice expert at Harvard University). You harbour it like a latent virus for which the only antidote is an educated dose of judicious honesty and corrective humility. I like to think I wouldn't have participated in this schoolyard stuff of nightmares though I can't be sure and – note to self – just not actively participating is not enough in any case.

I think of that girl standing alone in the playground surrounded by jeers and white faces and wonder if I would have had the courage to cry out against them, to stand with her against the hateful humiliation, but if I'm honest with myself I know I wouldn't have. I was a child who took knick-knacks and gifts from my grandparents to school as currency with which to purchase popularity. I was too desperate to be liked, to fit in. Shame circulates, menacing like a ghoul looking for its next feast of flesh. It stopped at that girl because she was Aboriginal in settler-colonial Australia, and her abusers had inherited not only the land their descendants stole from her, but also their attitudes and entrenched sense of superiority.

This collective schoolyard bullying was, of course, symptomatic of the weighty systematic abuses and relentless traumas inflicted on First Nations peoples since Arthur Phillip sailed the First Fleet into 'Port Jackson' in January 1788 on his mission to establish a British penal colony. Over the past two hundred and thirty years, Indigenous Australians have suffered a severity of generational trauma matched by few other peoples on the planet. Professor Judy Atkinson (no relation), a Jiman and Bundjalung woman, and an expert on trauma, violence and healing in Indigenous communities, responded on social media to the news about Don Dale and the torture of youth in correctional facilities. In her post, she expressed dismay at the failure of patriarchal and institutional efforts to contain or correct the effects of transgenerational trauma:

> The 'system' itself is broken and in crisis. Are we willing to look at the Child Protection system that can't cope, a system that is unable to keep children safe, even when they are in their care? Are we willing to question the education system, the one place where all children are supposed to be each school day, at school, yet which suspends kids for a hundred days in two hundred over a year, or expels them? To what? To where? The first suspension is the first step to Juvenile Justice and

prison. Are we willing to question what happens in our educational system when we have known abusers working with kids, and nothing is done? Are we willing to name the fact that in the health workforce, very few workers have trauma informed knowledge let alone trauma specific skills: in the health system, in the child protection system, in the correctional system? Are we willing to acknowledge that some kids are on Ice at seven years of age, and we don't have rehabs that take in kids of that age for detox? Are we willing to look at the unskilled workforce, at every level? And that under[funded] or unfunded workers, who do have skills, have their programs discontinued? Are we willing to look at the fact that when a child or children are removed by the state and placed in a non–Aboriginal family, that family may receive $120,000 or more, as paid foster parents, but if the same child is placed with their grandmother, the grannie receives no financial support?

Well, are we?

But Atkinson is not talking to white people. She knows we're not listening, or not listening nearly hard enough. She knows we're busy fretting about tax cuts, interest rates, crows' feet. She's addressing First Nations people, going on to say: 'what are we going to do? Protest! Yes, that is important. But what about working to put up clear alternatives to this system that is broken. I hear the talk about self-determination, but that means taking responsibility for ensuring our kids are safe. At this time in my life, self-determination means working together to put up programs so we can work with the kids like Dylan Voller, and the many others like him I know. I don't think the state, the system, is going to do it. It is broken.'

I'm sad for the girl surrounded in the playground, now an adult living with that memory if indeed she still lives. Sad for the Dylan Vollers and the kids on ice and for the families and communities so torn by trauma and its web of a/effects that they struggle to keep their children safe, but I'm angry too. The neoliberal neo-colonial capitalist patriarchal system is broken, propped up by government propping up big business with bailouts and offshore tax havens for the rich, chugging on thanks to the hard work of people, either complicit, powerless or oblivious, and defended most heartily by those compromised by conflicts of interest. The ignorance of a nation perpetuates this brokenness, and seems determinedly unequal to the challenges it presents. Those wielding the power and funds don't know how to listen; don't know how to ask the right questions. They lack a comprehensive understanding of the long-term effects of severe and chronic trauma that might inform more effective measures, responses and assistance. Perhaps because there is too much at stake. Land. Resources. Investments in the status quo. And leadership suffers from the same tendency to deny and minimise that afflicts the general populace. Governments disregard or underplay the role of trauma for many reasons (ignorance, yes, but also cynicism, pathological neoliberalism, and ethically bankrupt agenda-setting), and it doesn't help that the notion that trauma can be transmitted across generations is relatively new, contested and difficult to verify.

At the frontier of trauma studies, researchers are seeking to confirm whether trauma can be passed down not only through abuse, neglect, stories and a myriad of trauma-related behaviours but also directly in the form of 'molecular memory'. The suggestion here is that epigenetic changes – or the modification of gene expression – in one generation can be inherited by a subsequent generation. The epigenome, as Kylie Andrews explains for the ABC, is 'a set of instructions that decides which bits of your DNA are activated, or which genes are switched on or off'. It shares our cells with our genome (the double-helix DNA code unique to each and every individual), but it is tailored in different cells to suit specific locations and functions in the body: while your genome can't be altered, your epigenome can.

Dr Rachel Yehuda is professor of psychiatry and neuroscience and the director of the Traumatic Stress Studies Division at the Mount Sinai School of Medicine. In a study of Holocaust survivors and their children, Yehuda and her team claimed to show that the trauma experienced by survivors incarcerated in a Nazi concentration camp, or who experienced or witnessed torture, or were forced to hide during the Second World War, created epigenetic changes that also showed up in their children, proving 'epigenetic inheritance'. In other words, the findings assert the traumatic experience of one person can affect subsequent generations and that trauma can be transmitted biologically.

Such claims remain controversial, and bioinformatics researcher Ewan Birney criticises the paper for being 'riddled with flaws', saying the 'absurdly small' sample group of thirty-two people renders it redundant. Birney has legitimate concerns, but Yehuda is not alone in insisting this research has merit. Amy Bombay, an assistant professor of psychiatry at Dalhousie University in Halifax, has researched epigenetic transmission in relation to the 'Indian residential school system' in Canada, a network of religious assimilationist boarding schools for First Nations peoples akin to the Aboriginal missions in Australia. Bombay, who is Anishinaabe (Rainy River First Nation), was motivated to conduct this research by her own family's extensive history of incarceration in the schools. In a 2015 interview with Rosanna Deerchild on Canada's CBC Radio, Bombay maintains that 'experiences and the environment can basically turn on or off genes so that the function of those genes is changed. In terms of how that is transmitted generationally, we know that if those changes happen to be in the germ line, so in the egg or the sperm, they have the potential to be transmitted across generations.' Bombay adds that this research has been crucial to helping First Nations families and communities understand their legacy of trauma and begin to heal it. It also comes in handy as a riposte to those in the non-indigenous population who wonder why First Nations peoples can't 'just get over it'.

Even if epigenetic transmission cannot be irrefutably established (yet), there is evidence of complex processes of transmission accounting for the way second-generation (and beyond) survivors experience the effects of their forebears' trauma, theoretically argued in literary trauma theory and interdisciplinary research. In other words, science is not the only way this question can be approached. There are also compelling literary testimonies of transgenerational transmissions that bear witness by way of a creative empiricism.

Trauma theorist Marianne Hirsch combines feminist theory and memory studies to argue that the traumatic experiences of one generation can be experienced by the next generation. She refers to this as 'postmemory', which she describes as 'a structure of inter- and trans-generational transmission of traumatic knowledge and experience' and a 'consequence of traumatic recall but (unlike post-traumatic stress disorder) at a generational remove'. Literary studies scholar Ernst van Alphen counter-claims that the transmission of trauma between generations is impossible, because memory is fundamentally individual and 'indexical', and as such the memory of an event cannot be transferred from one being to another. Postmemory, Hirsch qualifies, is not identical to memory: it is 'post'. It is not the same memory as that of the person who experienced the trauma but it 'approximates' that memory in its 'affective force'. Postmemory, then, is:

> not mediated by recall but by imaginative investment, projection, and creation. To grow up with such overwhelming inherited memories, to be dominated by

narratives that preceded one's birth or one's consciousness, is to risk having one's own stories and experiences displaced, even evacuated, by those of a previous generation. It is to be shaped, however indirectly, by traumatic events that defy narrative reconstruction and exceed comprehension. These events happened in the past, but their effects continue into the present. This is, I believe, the experience of postmemory and the process of its generation.

Art Spiegelman's lauded graphic hybrid novel *Maus* is one of the most famed examples of this kind of testimony. 'My father bleeds history' are the first words of this comic masterpiece, penned and drawn by Spiegelman, the American-raised son of two Polish Jews who survived the Nazi concentration camps against the odds. Based on his interviews with his father (Spiegelman's mother died by suicide when he was twenty), *Maus* depicts, in multimodal nuance, the ways trauma is transmitted from one generation to another. In *MetaMaus*, which details the making of *Maus*, Spiegelman describes the book as a 'three-hundred-page *yahrzeit* candle', adding that his 'unconventional way of remembering' was an act of commemoration, 'more meaningful to me, actually, than a tombstone that I don't think I've ever gone to visit in the last twenty years'.

Lily Brett, a German-born, Australian-raised and US-based novelist, essayist and poet, has written profound poetic testimony of her second-generation experience of the Holocaust. Both her parents survived Auschwitz before immigrating to Melbourne. Her poetry collections, *The Auschwitz Poems* and *After the War*, detail the traumatic legacy and daily transmissions of living with survivors of heinous crimes. In one poem, titled 'Everything Looked Normal', Brett recounts the suffering behind the veneer of normality, noting the four locks on the front door, her mother's obsessive cleaning and the curtains hanging 'weighted with banished sadness'.

Weighted with banished sadness, and with the postmemories of ancestors killed in massacres, driven from country, enslaved as domestic labour, stolen from family in keeping with the governmentally orchestrated genocidal assimilation project, the Dylan Vollers in the 'land of the fair go' endure fresh horrors that are designed to set them on the straight and narrow, but that instead add to the mother lode of trauma that gets passed down the line. I wonder about the abusers who work in those facilities, the ones tasked with managing the Vollers. I wonder if they signed on already thugs or whether the system, to some degree, made monsters of them. The systems (read: discourses) that ensnare us also define us, at least if you take Foucault's word for it.

I'm what they call a 'sessional', one of the growing army of casual hired hands recruited by the twenty-first-century university to do teaching grunt-work and save the institutional coffers a packet on sick leave, annual leave and research support. This rise of casualisation is evident across a number of industries, but it's also part of a global trend in which the tertiary education sector, once hailed as a decidedly public project, has become increasingly corporatised and profit-driven; a trend fuelled, at least to some degree, by substantial withdrawals of government funding. I never know where I'm working next, and often my contract isn't confirmed until the week before classes start. I move around, adapting to new systems, new coordinators, new teaching teams, every few months. I'm among the swelling ranks of a new 'precariat' class, forced to work as a short-contract labourer, lurching from semester to semester on a thin-ice foundation of job insecurity. I don't have time to ponder the effects of these conditions, but then again, I don't have to. My body keeps score and presents me with the tally in the form of stress- and fatigue-related behaviours, the flipside of the purposeful pleasures of teaching.

During a *Science Friction* interview on ABC's Radio National, Yehuda cited a study she led investigating epigenetic changes before and after psychotherapy, assuring host Natasha Mitchell that the findings indicated positive outcomes post-therapy. This supports, she said brightly, a conclusion that a beneficial environment and relational influence that facilitates stress reduction can go some way to reversing the effects of trauma. That's cause for optimism, but the converse is also true, unfortunately – many negative, high-tension and insecure environments exacerbate the stress response associated with trauma. And there is no shortage of such environments: the prevalence of questionable enterprise agreements and contract work over job security; the housing affordability crisis; a social safety net full of gaping holes.

Traumata has prepared us well for precarity. Who better to dive and swoop and juggle and change direction at a moment's notice than those who have learned how to master those skills at trauma's heels? For some, though, it leads to breaking point. A newspaper story by George Morgan circulating in my social media feed told the sorry tale of 'John – the "unknown scholar" – philosopher, contrarian, a member of the academic precariat' who taught at a leading university before he killed himself. John, single and with no living relatives, had scraped by on casual tutoring since completing his PhD in philosophy fifteen years prior to his death. He was passed over for numerous faculty positions, as I myself have been, in a fiercely competitive environment where, as one colleague put it, 'luck and politics' often decide who gets the gig. When no offers of work came in during his last semester, John had no means of paying his rent. Facing the increasingly hostile welfare net less than accommodating of precariat workers, and no doubt depressed and disheartened by systematic devaluing, John took a train to the Blue Mountains and jumped off a cliff, his body found by a bushwalker. Given John was one of the more apparently privileged among us – male and white – it bears thinking about the implications for those with fewer advantages. I'm aware that even in precarity I too am relatively fortunate.

I can thank feminism for my three degrees, for the privilege of this precarity, for my being able to pay my rent by teaching university rather than cleaning toilets, but we've got a long way to go, baby. In *Why I Am Not a Feminist: A Feminist Manifesto*, Jessa Crispin argues that feminism has been co-opted by neoliberalism, the New Age and the media in the course of becoming popularised. While some of her claims are, in my view, troubled and others highly debatable, there is some validity to the idea that for a certain kind of comfortable white woman living the individualistic capitalistic dream, feminism has become less a social justice movement and more a 'social justice warrior lite' posture (think Mia Freedman and all those 'You go girl!' memes). Pockets of lively fire-in-the-belly activism aside, has western feminism undergone a kind of pasteurisation process in which its dangerous microorganisms (healthy anger, the capacity to think deeply and critically, collectivism and sisterhood) are no longer present in many contexts in which 'feminism' is evoked or implied?

We've settled for too little, says Crispin, sold ourselves short: we've accepted the promise of mere entry into existing institutional and cultural power structures where we were previously denied access. Apart from the obvious question of who constitutes this 'we', it's worth considering whether the rights and freedoms won by feminist forebears have given way to a red herring, a sleight of hand, a trap for those whose declared feminism goes no further than a focus on selfhood or sisterhood within a particularly raced and classed niche. To the degree that there may be such a thing as the faux-feminism Crispin rails against, it suffers from blinkered whiteness and homologising. And it is not only entirely unequal to the task of dismantling aeons of patriarchy, it actively works against it – padding identity, promoting feel-good delusions, and giving predominantly middle- and upper-class women a sense they're making a positive contribution on behalf of other women when they're really reassuring men who don't deserve reassurance and feathering their own reformist nests.

In any event, it's important to remember that there is a difference between appeasement and taking a stand, between being market-friendly and revolutionary, between ethics committees coming up with ways to make vivisection incrementally less torturous for imprisoned non-human animals and the non-negotiable demand for the abolition of animal experimentation. An understanding of feminism as defined by the *Oxford Dictionary* – 'The advocacy of women's rights on the ground of the equality of the sexes' – is perhaps too simplistic and not visionary enough for the urgent challenges we face (that pesky 'we' again). Does mainstream 'feminism', packaged for safe mass consumption, with its project of equality between men and women, aim too low? Do we need a new word for clear-eyed analysis of the unholy trinity of patriarchy, rabid liberalism and end-stage capitalism, in which not only feminised beings, but many men too, are disadvantaged and suffer – for an advocacy that seeks a complete re-imagining of the social order?

If the term 'feminism' still comes in handy in the meantime it's because of things like this: students constantly call me 'Miss', despite my telling them from day one that my formal title is Dr Atkinson, but they can call me Meera. It's well known that gender bias in the student–teacher relationship is commonplace and numerous studies indicate that male teachers consistently get more glowing student evaluations than female teachers, regardless of actual merit. For example, researchers at North Carolina State University conducted a study in which students in online-only classes were told the tutor they never saw was either male or female, and then were asked to rate the instructors on twelve different traits at the end of courses. 'We found that the instructor whom students thought was male received higher ratings on all

12 traits, regardless of whether the instructor was actually male or female,' said Lillian MacNell, lead author of the subsequent paper, crucially adding that the 'ratings that students give instructors are really important, because they're used to guide higher education decisions related to hiring, promotions and tenure'.

An article by Aviva Shen – titled 'Students See Male Professors As Brilliant Geniuses, Female Professors As Bossy and Annoying' – noted that women 'are far more likely to be called "feisty," especially if they teach humanities classes'.

I teach a subject called Ideas and Society. During a lecture on 'Imperialism and Colonialism: "the west and the rest"', I ask students if they think colonialism is inherently racist. Every semester the majority think it is. Most students today have benefited from a primary and high school education that addresses Australian history with more nuance and clarity than my Anglo-normative formative education ever did, but I wonder if they would have been any more likely to rally around the Aboriginal girl surrounded by jeering bullies.

Racial bullying is not the only kind of bullying. Children are sponges who soak up the bigotries of the society into which they are born and regurgitate them. As such, homophobic, transphobic, ableist and sexualised bullying commonly manifest in schools, though it is, interestingly, girls who are thought to lead the field in sexuality-related bullying. Bullying between girls is held to be less often about strong-arming and shirt-fronting and more often related to sexual status or their perceived attractiveness or promiscuity.

When I think back to those occasions when I found myself on the sharp end of bullying, it is girl bullies that mostly come to mind, though of course this perception is skewed to my own experience. There are bullyboys, and teacher-bullies, like the one who picked on me ceaselessly when we moved to Stuart's

Waverley sandstone house, but girls can turn on girls with a ferociousness that can be especially wounding. According to Rachel Simmons, author of *Odd Girl Out: The Hidden Culture of Aggression in Girls*, the peak bullying phase for girls is between the ages of ten and fourteen. Girls, she says, use 'backbiting, exclusion, rumors, name-calling, and manipulation to inflict psychological pain on victimized targets. Unlike boys, who tend to bully acquaintances or strangers, girls frequently attack within tightly knit networks of friends, making aggression harder to identify and intensifying the damage to the targets.' Simmons writes that in almost every group session she held with girls 'someone volunteered her wish to have been born a boy because boys can "fight and have it be over with"'. Clearly, this doesn't mean bullying by or between boys is any easier for its victims to endure, but it does point to a cultural genesis in the differences between the ways boys and girls bully.

According to the National Coalition Against Bullying (NCAB) website, 27 per cent of Australian students are bullied every few weeks or more often and 13.5 per cent report having lies spread about them at school. Reporting from a 2005 conference on bullying, Paula Beauchamp quoted NCAB spokesperson Dr Michael Carr-Gregg describing girl bullying as hierarchical, with a 'queen bee' (a wonderfully evocative metaphor popularised by Rosalind Wiseman in her book *Queen Bees and Wannabes*) at the top followed by 'sidekicks, bankers, float-ins and targets'. A friend of mine, now retired, was a high school teacher for more than three decades. Having worked at a girls school for many years, she had her own term for girl bullying. 'I called it "ice" bullying,' she says. 'I noticed it all through my career. They just "ice" some poor kid out of existence.' Despite what might be written in policy, bullying was rarely addressed at her school. 'It's much harder to detect as a teacher. You're busy teaching, not busy observing every nuance of every group.' She points out that inadequate communication between teachers is part of the problem. 'There's a cone of silence for the classroom teacher. You could be teaching a kid six times a week and not know they have any issues. You only know there are problems by the look on their face, intuition and academic performance going down.'

It makes broad sense then, that many forms of bullying can be viewed as a feminist issue and many educators see the endemic of sexualised bullying as internalised sexism. Embedded in societal beliefs about femininity are age-old assumptions that relations between girls are trivial and that women and girls are inherently 'bitchy', sly by nature, and prone to gossip and ridicule. But the subtle, backhanded and sideways nature of girl bullying might more accurately be linked to the way in which girls and women are heavily conditioned to be 'nice'. In the film *Mean Girls*, Cady – who has recently started high school back in the United States, having previously lived in Africa – says of one conflict: 'I knew how this would be settled in the animal world, but ... in "girl world" all the fighting had to be sneaky.' Simmons backs the conclusion that girls tend to act anger out via clandestine and abusive behaviours. She focuses on girls' reluctance to talk openly about their feelings of anger towards each other and their resistance to confrontation, suggesting this is fertile ground for bullying.

Russell Meares, professor emeritus of psychiatry at the University of Sydney, explores why some bullied children are more profoundly affected than others, and his work sheds light on how the gendered nature of bullying works. Meares suggests those with traumatic histories are vulnerable to what he calls 'malignant internalisation'. Healthy psychic development, states Meares, depends upon a process of playful imitation, in which the modelling and teachings of the caregiver are internalised by the child in a way that advances their functionality and supports their well-being. In malignant internalisation the positive dualism and play of this process is lost, replaced by 'high anxiety aroused by the traumatic situation', which in turn produces fearful alienation. 'Normal internalisation,' he writes, 'is associated with, and determines, stable forms of relatedness, whereas the traumatic process underlies shifting, oscillating, and discontinuous forms of relatedness.' Which happens to describe girl bullying very nicely. Quite apart from whatever goes on at home, how are girls to develop healthy internalisation when our broader culture habitually casts the female body as objectified and violenced, declares girls and women 'bitches' and 'ball-breakers' if they dare to be assertive or ambitious, and rewards prettiness and sexiness over character?

When organic and more direct expressions of anger are prohibited, girls have little recourse but to react with suppression and stealth, and where malignant internalisation and traumatic shame run high, peer abuse is inevitable. Technology creates an ever-expanding network of opportunities for those inclined towards bullying, and the NCAB reports one in seven children are cyber-bullied regularly. With its potential for multi-pronged and anonymous attack, cyber-bullying has already been the catalyst for numerous youth suicides.

Meares uses the term 'attacks on value' to describe certain kinds of relational trauma. Though his focus is on familial relations, bullying fits neatly into his schema. In his view, reasonably good conditions are required for a child to develop a secure personal reality and solid self-image. Attacks upon a child's sense of well-being are 'major but neglected traumata'. This is trauma related to invalidation. Deprived of affirmation, children who have not sufficiently encountered such recognition are plagued by 'persisting dysphoria, involving emptiness and deadness'. He adds: 'Out of these negative emotional states emerges a negative judgement of value, of low self-worth.'

Whatever goes on in the complex relationships between girls, the threats they face from outside remain both real and formidable. As I write, a federal investigation is underway into an online pornography ring in which adolescent boys and men swap and exchange sexual images of schoolgirls from over seventy schools from around Australia. Over two thousand images have been posted and traded, with men invited to list the names and schools of specific girls they are 'hunting'. These boys and men characteristically contribute identifying information, such as addresses and phone numbers with directives such as 'Go get her, boys.' 'Targets' are declared 'wins' once a nude photo is obtained and posted. Some targets are so highly prized as to come with a 'bounty'.

I'll never forget the first time I was accosted and harassed out of the blue. I was around eleven, with barely budding breasts, and I still had the colt-like legs and narrow hips of a pre-pubescent girl. It was summer. My mother had sent me to the shops, and as I walked back down Glebe Point Road a man sidled up to me and said something aggressively lewd before disappearing again. My relaxed saunter was shattered: I shook all the way home. It was not just that the words and their delivery were disturbing, threatening even, or that I was shocked by the sudden encroachment into my personal space. It was as if the earth had opened up under my feet, exposing the hell of rape culture beneath society's seeming civility. I couldn't have put it into thought and words that way, couldn't articulate my reaction or what I was reacting to, but I momentarily sensed the ground I was walking on was built on a foundation that seethed with darkness and danger.

When the story about the pornography ring broke in an article by Nina Funnell, feminist commentator Clementine Ford weighed in, pointing out that the young men engaging in the ring are members of the communities and schools their 'targets' inhabit. These so-called average boys and men, using predatory and abusive language such as 'tracking' 'bitches' and 'sluts', 'seek to dehumanise and violate the young women among them and, in doing so, elevate their status within the decidedly toxic masculine space in which they operate', wrote Ford. She concluded that the toxic masculinity in question is 'more widespread and dangerous that [sic] many people will allow themselves to believe'. Ford's article was titled, 'The Epidemic of Rape Culture in Schools Can No Longer Be Ignored', yet there seem to be many willing to continue ignoring both it and the festering toxic masculinity – an explosive melange of transgenerational trauma, socialised conditioning, an ingrained attitude of entitlement and gendered privilege – that gives rise to it.

We might just as well speak in terms of 'toxic patriarchy'. Even if there was once a time in which the evolution of humanity depended on patriarchy for survival, as Camille Paglia would have it, even if it need be acknowledged that over its many millennia countless vital and spectacular accomplishments have taken shape, patriarchy has been rendered toxic, fused with powerful institutionalised religions, colonialisms, consumerist capitalism, the military–industrial complex and the medical–pharmaceutical complex.

An article appearing on *Triple J Hack* in the wake of Funnell's report featured one of the girls victimised on the site. She was sixteen, 'young and stupid' (her words) when she texted a nude photo of herself to some guy she doesn't remember anymore. She never expected it to be shared without her consent and traded on a site dedicated to debasing schoolgirls, and when she was made aware of it; she contacted the police to file a complaint. The cop on duty laughed at her and told her that's what she got for taking compromising photos and sending them out to men. 'I just walked out crying,' she said. It's hard to know what's worse: the blatantly sexist, victim-blaming and uncaring response of the cop, or the fact that this young woman automatically shamed and blamed herself, even as she rightly knew something criminal was taking place and appealed to an appropriate, if sorely inadequate and unethical, source of help.

What chance do young women have to deflect this unearned shame and blame when they are told to carry it, not only by male cops but also by high-profile women who identify as feminists? Mia Freedman, founder of *Mamamia*, posted this tweet after Funnell's story broke: 'Taking nude selfies is your absolute right. So is smoking. Both come with massive risks.' Feminist commentator Amy Gray promptly replied with a take-down. Gray tweeted 'Dear Mia' accompanied by a topless selfie with the words 'Fuck off' written on her chest. 'Let's talk about shaming women and marking them as complicit in being abused,' retorted Gray, who elsewhere defended the consensual taking and exchange of nudies (nude selfies) as a 'fun, sexy, liberating and radical act'. Challenging the assumption that nudies are essentially a self-objectifying, attention-seeking feminist fail, Gray continued: 'Every time you tell women how to reduce themselves, how to avoid the act, how they could somehow behave as less than they are in order to avoid the criminal choices of others, you are making it easier for abuse and attacks to happen.'

Sometime after I was raped, a couple of constables drove me down George Street, insisting I show them the pub where I met the man who raped me. When I had trouble identifying it, because I was drunk on the day in question, it was obvious they thought me a soused slut who had put herself in 'harm's way' (note the subtle shift of language, the way in which men who do violence are backgrounded and the woman – her choice of outfit, her degree of inebriation, her location – is foregrounded). The similarity between my story and that of the young woman dismissed by the police is a disheartening reminder that for all the 'post-feminism' rhetoric, and a degree of actual progress, too little has fundamentally changed. Remarkably, the article about the sixteen-year-old included the following update: 'The Queensland Police Service issued a statement this afternoon saying it had so far found no evidence of child exploitation. ACT Police said those posting the images appeared to know the victims.'

Twenty-six years ago I undertook an undergraduate degree in communications. Aged twenty-seven, I was admitted to university as a special-entry, mature-age student. Even so, I was no less bewildered than those fresh out of school. Perhaps more so: I was only a few years 'clean and sober'. Pumped up by cigarettes and caffeine, I was reeling from both a life less medicated and my re-entry into institutional education. I made friends with another mature-age student called Vivian, a lesbian in a live-in relationship, who was in the same first-year Textual Theory class. The tutor was a middle-aged man. It was common knowledge he was married to another faculty staff member, a well-known writer. The tutor often came to the cafe and sat with students during the break. I didn't know then, as I know now that I myself teach tertiary students, that his comments over coffee about how I should take up yoga because it might help settle my manic energy were not entirely appropriate, assuming as they did an uninvited entry into my private life. Although those conversations didn't constitute sexual harassment, other uncomfortable and more overtly sexualised advances followed. The breaking point came when Vivian told me he'd gone to her house (I can't recall the pretext of the visit) and kissed her against the fridge in the kitchen. We decided to take action and filed a complaint. I remember meeting with the head of school at the time, but I blank on what transpired thereafter. I do know the problem of sexual harassment at universities hasn't gone away. Only weeks ago a young woman in my class came to me asking my advice on the behaviour of another (male) lecturer, who initiated private messages on Facebook and who had, on another occasion, chastised her for smoking because it was 'unbecoming of a beautiful young woman'.

A series of articles in *The Guardian* have detailed the prevalence of sexual harassment in Australian universities and sundry shoddy institutional responses (or lack thereof) to it. Melissa Davey wrote about a survey of 1,926 University of Sydney students, published in May 2016, which revealed that one in four students 'reported having experienced an incident of sexual harassment or assault as a student, and 6% of all respondents had experienced an incident on campus or at a university-related event'. An open letter, written by women's officers from the University of Sydney over the past decade, demanded action on sexual harassment and assault on the university's campus. Anna Hush, one of the women's officers responsible for the letter, was among those who welcomed the announcement of a long-overdue national survey on sexual assault and harassment at universities, initiated by Universities Australia and conducted by the Australian Human Rights Commission (AHRC), but stressed the findings must be 'followed up by concrete, well-informed action'. Hush also pointed out that this survey, which confidentially canvassed over 30,000 students from thirty-nine Australian universities, was critical because sexual harassment and assault '[goes] unreported 99% of the time', for understandable and unacceptable reasons.

When the AHRC released *Change the Course: National Report on Sexual Assault and Sexual Harassment at Australian Universities* on 1 August 2017, many who have laboured in universities, long aware of routine sexualised abuses in the not-so-ivory tower, felt momentarily vindicated. The report, which included personal stories and quotes from 1,849 written submissions (the highest number of submissions the AHRC has ever received for a single investigation) confirmed that one in four students – and 63 per cent of women – reported experiencing sexual harassment in a university setting, that women were at least twice as likely as men to be harassed, and that trans and gender-diverse students were more likely to have been harassed. It also states that 83 per cent of students reported the gender of the perpetrator of sexual assault as male, and 94 per cent of students who were sexually harassed and 87 per cent of students who were sexually assaulted did not make a formal report or complaint to their university. Half of the students who reported being sexually assaulted by someone they knew in a university setting identified the perpetrator as another student and, though strangers came in at second place, university staff were also implicated, as evidenced by the passage below based on a written submission:

> Amanda rode the bus to university with a university professor. The professor would sit next to Amanda or gesture at her to sit next to him. During the bus rides, the professor stared at her and complimented her appearance. This behaviour made Amanda feel uncomfortable. They usually walked together from the bus to campus, but one day Amanda told the professor that she was going shopping. As she walked away he put his arm around her and kissed her on the cheek. From that day, Amanda arranged for her sister to call and stay on the phone throughout her 20 minute bus ride to avoid interaction with the professor.

Guardian journalists Sally Weale and David Batty report that experts – including Ann Olivarius, a UK lawyer specialising in the area of sexual harassment; Dr Alison Phipps, director of gender studies at the University of Sussex, who has researched the issue in a score of universities; and Ruth Lewis, sociologist and coordinator of the Universities Against Gender Based Violence network – are calling institutional leadership to account, asserting that the turn-the-other-cheek strategy of university bureaucracies comes down to self-serving whitewashing. For example, non-disclosure agreements essentially provide a loophole for alleged perpetrators by allowing staff to resign without further investigation and to relocate to another institution to potentially offend again, having been granted licence to represent themselves and their departure as they wish. If the abuse in the first instance doesn't completely break the seal of trust between students and educators, these policies are chipping away at whatever remains. Confidentiality clauses in settlements, preventing all parties from discussing the offences publicly, designed to protect the reputation of the faculty and university, ensuring a cloak of silence around abuse, mirror the abuse around abuse that takes place in highly dysfunctional families. This systematic blind eye leaves thousands of students vulnerable and unsupported on this most basic aspect of student safety.

Unsurprisingly, the problem isn't confined to Australia. In May 2016 Sara Ahmed, celebrated scholar and self-declared 'killjoy feminist', announced her resignation from her post as professor of race and cultural studies at Goldsmiths, University of London, in protest at the institution's 'failure to address the problem of sexual harassment'. Ahmed was privy to information about six investigations into allegations involving four members of staff. It was not, Ahmed pointed out in blog posts following her departure, that nothing at all had been done in response to complaints, but that the 'enquiries have not led to a robust and meaningful investigation of the problem of sexual harassment *as* an institutional problem'.

This might well be the central challenge that western, modernised and bureaucratic-driven society faces. Well-meaning and important efforts by pockets of individuals to tackle sexism, racism, homophobia, transphobia and a host of other forms of discrimination are not enough. Good intentions and paper-thin policy cannot guarantee lasting change on a grand scale, because there is an absence of meaningful institutional investigation into, and understanding of, not only these specific manifestations but also their roots in patriarchy and its attendant traumata.

The victims of the 'toxic' and 'hyper' masculinity Clementine

Ford speaks of are not limited to attacks on girls and women, or to the male-on-male 'interpersonal violence' that is the leading cause of death for young men worldwide. Frequent headlines tell of those non-human animals, those other 'feminine beings' who bear the terrible brunt of the toxic masculinist destructive bent, though much of the damage done goes unrecorded. Even when heinous acts do make the news, the systems in place, such as the legal system, prove inadequate and fail to address the core problem.

A lone baby wombat survives a drunken rampage in which a group of men deliberately run over and kill a family of ten wombats one weekend at a Kangaroo Valley camping ground. Elsewhere, in South Australia, another group of men hunt down a kangaroo, torture it to death, then post gloating videos of the torture on Snapchat. In Melbourne, a four-hundred-year-old gum tree dies after two separate ringbarking attacks. 'Who does this?' asks one headline covering the wombat murders. Who indeed. We have at the ready at least part of the answer. Men. Almost always men. #notallmen, but some men, often in groups or pairs. We discuss these as isolated events, random aberrations in an otherwise healthy society, rather than as extremes of a socially constructed norm. We seem, collectively, institutionally, to fall short in the task of focusing on society's complicity as a starting point to investigate how this toxic masculinity – a hardened or hyper-masculinity with an aggressive, violent, sexist edge – comes into being and what we need to do to prevent its circulation. So long as we participate in this collective denial and minimisation, we fail to reach those afflicted by it and encourage them into the fold of a community of care.

'Who does this?' Who gets a sick thrill from a cowardly kill? People demented by internal conflicts, people whose mood has been altered by addictive substances, and whose capacity to empathise has been eroded. Women are not immune to the toxic effects of history and social conditioning, but seem less inclined towards the kind of violent acting-out that men frequently perpetrate. Sugar and spice; everything nice. Gender conditioning goes some way to determining how trauma is transmitted: it's not so much that women do it less, but differently. Feminist author and activist bell hooks calls patriarchy 'the single most life-threatening social disease assaulting the male body', demanding that men 'become and remain emotional cripples'. Patriarchal ideology, she adds, 'brainwashes men to believe that their domination of women [and other feminine beings] is beneficial when it is not'. Women and men need to come together, she insists, in the understanding that the gendered 'normal traumatization' – a term hooks borrows from family therapist Terrence Real – within patriarchal societies wounds everybody, to greater and lesser degrees. Without exception.

Living with a degree of traumatic shame is the norm rather than the exception, but as Joseph Adamson and Hilary Clark note it can take a deadly, deflective form. 'When violations [of privacy or selfness] occur in chronic or traumatic form, then shame becomes the core of severe structures of defense in the traumatized individual or community ...' This shame then manifests as an 'aggressive shamelessness' that Adamson and Clark view as having 'invaded modern life'. Men seem especially prone to violent expressions of it, and feminine beings bear the brunt of it, since they are positioned in patriarchy to be controlled, oppressed, annihilated or exploited by masculine beings.

There is substantial evidence that bullies in our society tend to do well, especially in male-dominated corporate life and the military–industrial complex, both of which, in their specific ways, valorise, support and reward bullying. Bullies are disproportionately represented at the top of business and politics. But what becomes of the bullied, and of those most wounded and victimised by other means? What becomes of all those traumatised by 'attacks on value' or scarred by rape culture? Do any of us come through unscathed? We fill prisons, offices, psych wards, housing commission slums, Buddhist monasteries, what remains of women's crisis accommodation. We become writers, drink in pubs, sleep rough and over-achieve. If we have the means, why we might even end up at a Tony Robbins event (please take note of your reaction: a quiz follows). Did you a) bristle at the mention of his name, b) smirk, c) feel a surge of hope, d) determine, in the beat of a second, to skip over the following section in protest? Stay with me.

Robbins came to prominence along with the likes of Louise Hay during the 1980s pop-psychology/New Age/self-help boom. Joe Berlinger's film *Tony Robbins: I Am Not Your Guru* documents Robbins' seventy-fourth Date with Destiny seminar, which ran for six twelve-hour days in Florida in 2014 and cost each person $4,995 to attend. Robbins, once a Californian kid who grew up with an abusive, alcoholic mother and an absent father, is now a role model and hero to millions worldwide. 'I constructed this Tony Robbins guy. I built this motherfucker,' he declares proudly at the start of the event, seemingly to indicate two things: that the Tony Robbins he was before he built the Tony Robbins he is now was not a Tony Robbins worth being, and that those in the audience could also rebuild themselves into people worth being and he was about to show them how. A voiceover claims that Robbins has helped more than four million (the number of people to have attended his events during their twenty-five-year run at the time the film was made), including luminaries such as Princess Diana, Bill Clinton, Mother Teresa and Mikhail Gorbachev.

Robbins' simple statement, 'If I can discover what beliefs and values control me, I can literally re-design me', describes his central thesis. This poses a challenge to the conventional wisdom of much theoretical and clinical trauma theory, which highlights trauma's resistance to control (or even access) by the conscious mind. It also presents a promise irresistible to the many who are suffering trauma's ill effects, but the $500 million question (Robbins' net worth according to celebritynetworth.com) is this: can he deliver the goods? Can we really change ourselves and our lives regardless of how much of a clusterfuck of trauma we stagger out of?

I first encountered Robbins and Hay decades ago, a few years after I left rehab, when someone suggested I try the positive affirmations espoused by Hay, who claims to have cured herself of cancer through positive thinking. Previously a die-hard cynic, I was trying to practise an open mind. I was desperate to feel better, to live better, so I pushed through my scepticism and, squirming, practised positive affirmations while looking in the mirror, to no obvious avail. While cognitive-based therapies of various kinds can be useful interventions for reframing problematic thought patterns, claims about improving mental and physical health through affirmations are a vexed prospect when it comes to chronic post-traumatic stress symptomology. Experts have established that the parts of the brain most affected by psychic trauma are not necessarily the same part of the brain that practises affirmations.

Neuroscientist Joseph LeDoux describes the amygdala, one of the areas most identified with trauma, as an unconscious processor separate from the conscious system. He states, 'It's like a default unconscious, as opposed to being the Freudian sense of unconscious – something that was conscious, but was too anxiety provoking and therefore shipped to the unconscious. The amygdala gets direct sensory information and learns and stores information on its own, and that information that's stored then controls emotional responses.' The amygdala is associated with 'implicit memory', which doesn't require conscious involvement. The hippocampus, however, another area of the brain closely linked to trauma, is crucial to the process of memory being available to consciousness: neuroscientist Marc Alain Züst calls it the 'place of interaction between unconscious and conscious memories'. Thus, there is doubtless some capacity to engage with this subconscious region through various forms of therapeutic interventions.

Bessel van der Kolk, a leading expert in trauma studies, acknowledges that 'language gives us the power to change ourselves and others' but he does not seem to support the hypothesis that it's as simple as repeating affirmative phrases. In fact, he goes on to say that language offers this potential 'by communicating our experiences, helping us to define what we know, and finding a common sense of meaning', which is a far more complex operation than the repetition of conscious thought and statements deemed 'positive'. This means the claims made by Hay and ilk for 'positive affirmations' are questionable, to say the least, as far as severely or chronically traumatised individuals are concerned. Speaking of the tendency of education systems to focus on cognitive development at the expense of more holistic approaches that integrate the physical with the psycho-emotional, van der Kolk states: 'Despite the well-documented effects of anger, fear, and anxiety on the ability to reason, many programs continue to ignore the need to engage the safety system of the brain before trying to promote new ways of thinking.' This suggests that a post-traumatised psyche, with its involuntary bent towards hyper-vigilance and anxious affect, is especially disadvantaged by any approach that simplistically applies cognitive reprogramming to a much more complex reality.

Another aspect of my reticence regarding methodologies like those of Hay and Robbins relates to their emphasis on personal responsibility in controlling complex processes such as trauma that are largely operative at an unconscious level. Though Robbins distances himself from Hay in rejecting the cast of 'positive thinking', both avoid tackling the question of trauma directly and instead promote an individualistic responsibility over social and political responsibilities, and each of them, in their own way, promotes the idea that a given person is wholly liable for the conditions of their life. My concern is that people might assume the burden of failure if the desired changes and outcomes do not eventuate, compounding guilt and shame to the distress of traumatic symptomology.

Alarm bells go off when I'm told there's an instant cure for what ails me when I feel certain, intuitively and experientially, that the ailment is deeply rooted. Those alarm bells ring even louder when in the next breath I'm told that the cost of accessing this cure comes close to the down payment on a one-bedroom flat. This was my experience when I once attended a free Robbins event run by his underlings. The masculinist hype and evangelistic modus operandi had me hightailing it out the door, rattled, discomfited and suspicious about the claims of overnight transformation. I wrote him off as a charlatan, but now I wonder if it isn't more complicated than that, if his shtick isn't a way of keeping his own trauma at arm's length via a perpetually performed, mood-altering high that also conveniently generates personal mega-wealth.

In Berlinger's documentary, which critic Mike D'Angelo savaged as 'a glorified Tony Robbins commercial' (Berlinger was apparently motivated to make the film after his own positive experience of a Date with Destiny event), Robbins makes his entrance for an expertly pre-hyped crowd amid pulsing party music. He hollers and makes his signature air-punching, jazz-hands gesture, which true believers mirror back ecstatically. He reassures those who have gathered – people of all ages and races from all over the globe, serviced by a team of staff including translators – that the event is not just some 'bullshit positive thinking seminar. I'm not going to tell you to start chanting there's no weeds, there's no weeds, there's no weeds and hope shit isn't there … We look for the weed and we rip it out.' Those fighting words are followed by a self-effacing clarification: 'I am not your guru.' He didn't come to fix what ain't broke; he's just there to guide you to your own mission to self-knowledge. He gets down to business, selecting individuals from the two-thousand-plus attendees to work with one on one in front of the entire audience.

Robbins swears a lot, using what he calls 'the science of taboo language' because 'words have the power to pierce the conscious mind; I'll do whatever it takes to break the pattern, so you can reclaim you really are.' But here's the rub: a great number of those attracted to Robbins' grand claims come from histories of severe or complex/chronic trauma. He doesn't sell his method as a cure for trauma in so many words, but trauma is everywhere at his events: in the subtext, in the audience (extremely troubled and traumatised people are referred to as 'red flag people'), and in Robbins himself. I'm particularly intrigued by an 'intervention' in which he asks people who are suicidal to stand. An attractive young woman is among those who have risen to their feet. Robbins makes a beeline for her and goes to work, teasing out the reason why someone with seemingly so much to live for might want to die.

'No one really knows what's inside me,' she says. 'I'm tired of having so much pain and carrying it for so many years.' Robbins challenges her to stop stalling and spill the beans. Her story comes out in a cascade of running words and tears. She was born in the Children of God cult: 'We had to be soldiers of God, and they believed that God's love was sex.' She goes on to describe a history of experiencing and witnessing abuse, winding up with the admission that her family is a mess, suicidal. She's the 'together' one, she says, the 'solution maker', except she's broken inside. She's hit a wall and can't do it anymore. And now here she is, surrounded by strangers, pouring it all out, red-nosed, grief gushing, and Robbins is *right there*, riveted, teary. He hugs her long and hard. 'You've been trying to make sense of all this, but there's no sense to it … You were in a position where you didn't get to choose. Now you're in a position where you get to choose. You take all the power back today.' There's a flash of hope in her eyes, then a veil of wariness. She had, we later learn, sold everything she owned to attend the seminar on the suggestion of a friend. Can she trust the words she's hearing? Can she trust him? 'Is she on the road to being healed, we wonder, or has she just exchanged one possible cult for another?' asks film reviewer Jeannette Catsoulis. Writing on Berlinger's film in *The New York Times*, Catsoulis soberly notes the 'vampiric' aspect of Robbins' 'public siphoning of hurt'.

Afterwards, backstage, Berlinger interviews a still visibly emotional Robbins. Berlinger digs in, asking what happens for him in that moment in which he witnesses another's pain at such close range. Robbins tears up: 'I just felt her, felt for her,' he says. He tries to describe his process when working with people in distress, talks about how it comes through him, how if people lead with love they'll find a way and if they lead with fear they'll fail and he will not fail someone that raw. He admits it's the memory of his own suffering that makes him want to help others in theirs. Berlinger isn't satisfied, probes deeper, points out that he himself suffered as a child but doesn't have the ability to show up for a random attendee the way Robbins showed up for that young woman. Robbins cracks: 'It's my obsession (crying). It's an obsession to break through, to help. I'm addicted to it. It makes me feel like my life has deep meaning, not just surface meaning. Everybody's got their thing. This is my thing.'

Bingo. In this moment we see that it's not quite as straightforward as Robbins being, as he is oft charged, a con man swindling gullible people out of millions (though he is clearly profit driven and business savvy). I suspect Robbins genuinely believes in what he does in his 'seminars'. He openly admits he's *driven* to do it, thus exposing his own vulnerability and still-throbbing traumata. He may have built the motherfucker that is Tony Robbins, millionaire motivational speaker and life coach to the rich and famous, but the traumatised kid's been with him every step of the way.

The seminar closes with a meditation introduced by feel-good pop psychology hyperbole: 'We brought our desire, our hunger, our love, our caring, and we left our fear, our limitations, our frustrations, and our fucking pasts behind. That's what we did here, ladies and gentlemen.' There's something sad about the passion and force with which he says this and his own desperation to believe it. I know you can leave your past behind or I'd still be in a Darlinghurst bedsit injecting low-grade heroin, but I also know there is no absolute and compartmentalised 'past' when it comes to severe and chronic trauma.

My sociologist friend, Dr Elaine Swan, who has researched therapy culture extensively, says Robbins 'performs a classic charismatic self-help guru body and presence. He reproduces politically problematic psychological ideas. For me, he is the epitome of the US self-help psychologicalisation of the social. Of course, people do get a few tips from self-help. And some claim it helpful. Most respond to it as what Paul Lichterman calls "thin culture", drawing on it along with other resources to try to get through whatever they need to. When people pay so much for a seminar, they tend to claim some road-to-Damascus experience.' Another friend, Professor Zachary Steel, chair of trauma and mental health at the University of New South Wales, says that while he appreciates many of Robbins' sentiments, he doesn't believe PTSD can be treated as readily as his teachings imply.

Despite my concerns and scepticism, I came away from the documentary curiously moved. No doubt, this is its intention and maybe it marks me a sucker. There's something touching about the vulnerability of all those people searching, reaching, even Robbins himself. Something about the struggle of the human spirit and all that collective pain is compelling regardless of the questionability of the show-biz context and hyperbolic claims. At the end of the seminar, Robbins instructs the audience to reflect on three moments in their lives for which they are profoundly grateful and to feel the blessing of those moments. 'Make your life a masterpiece,' he says, by way of a goodbye. What, I'm left wondering, would he say to those who torture a kangaroo and post trophy footage of the unspeakable and avoidable suffering they inflict? How would he help the boys and men trading 'wins' in the pornography ring to make a 'masterpiece' of their lives?

John Bradshaw, my favourite of the pop psychologists who came to prominence in the self-help heyday of the 1980s, was a philosophy-trained educator, counsellor and author, and a gifted, Southern preacher–inspired orator. Bradshaw was one of the few among that generation of grassroots gurus to avoid the 'psychologicalisation of the social' noted by Dr Swan, and to substantially ground his 'recovery' teachings in a socio-political context. Describing patriarchy as characterised by male domination and power, Bradshaw acknowledged the social constructionism of many of today's ills, stating 'patriarchal rules still govern most of the world's religious, school systems, and family systems'. bell hooks echoes Bradshaw: 'Patriarchy is a political-social system that insists that males are inherently dominating, superior to everything and everyone deemed weak, especially females, and endowed with the right to dominate and rule over the weak and to maintain that dominance through various forms of psychological terrorism and violence.' It's not hard, then, to imagine how young men might think nothing of killing a wombat for kicks or posting a nudie of a girl from school with a 'go get her boys' invitation. It is only our routine minimising of patriarchy's daily realities and operations that gives rise to surprise when inevitable persecutions and barbarity transpire.

I grew up in a less mediated time, one in which my childhood prerogatives, whims, experiments and insecurities were confined to the home, the neighbourhood, the schoolyard and the occasional party or group foray in the outside world. I had managed, in my first year of high school, to wheedle my way into the clique of popular kids in my grade, where teasing was relentless and rake-thin girls were called fat. I recall a constant feeling of unease, of niggling duplicity and fear. I dropped out of the clique voluntarily at the start of year eight, instead aligning myself with selected outcasts. Up until then I had identified with mainstream society, longed for my family to be more in step with it, looked to it for role models, and aspired to succeed in its image, but sometime during that second year I began to feel a sense of alienation, fused with a subliminal questioning of societal norms and values. Not only did it no longer seem important to be in with the puerile popular crowd, school itself no longer seemed important, or necessary. I spent much of that year in truancy, my growing boredom and disillusionment gradually incubating a determination to leave school altogether.

At thirteen I went to work on my mother, convincing her that being forced to stay in school sucking up a conventional education would be a waste of my valuable, artsy-oriented time. I was itching to enter the realm of adulthood, to be autonomous, to embark on adventures. I didn't know it then, but my desire to grow up fast was about the fact that in many ways I'd already been forced to. It was a reaction to the pain of powerlessness, to having endured a childhood entrapped by the vicissitudes of adult madness, but if I imagined independence as freedom from all that, it only proved to usher in another set of traps.

So it was that I left school one day, not yet fourteen, simple as that. I showed up at administration with a note saying we were moving to Perth (a bald-faced lie). My mother was busy working her office job, so I took an old English man called Ernest along for company and effect (he posed as my uncle). He lived in the flat below Heidi's, and afterwards we went back to his place, where

I bummed his smokes, drank his beer and passed time playing cards, as Heidi and I frequently did. The condition my mother had set for my leaving was that I was to do a secretarial course at a private college in the city, with fees paid for by my hard-working grandparents. I was then very much like many of my students are now: studying at the behest of family, undisciplined, unready, uncommitted and oblivious to the sacrifices being made by those who loved me. I befriended a girl a few years older and we soon developed a daily ritual of meeting up at a city cafe near the college for a brunch of lemon sugar pancakes before spending the rest of the day skiving at the Hilton Hotel rooftop pool or window shopping. During the evenings and on weekends, I spent time with my new friend's circle: sexually active teenage girls, and young men with acne who drove their panel vans lightning fast. Those young men were products of their gender conditioning and generation, but they were good guys and I remember them fondly. I don't recall being sexually pressured and I was treated with a baseline of respect. I was still a virgin, but when I took one of them as my boyfriend, we passed many evenings heavy petting in my bedroom.

I was underage, but I often spent Saturday nights at Chequers disco, run by Chinese businessmen with underworld connections and rumoured links to the American Mafia. I would dress up in stilettos and jeans so tight I had to lie down on the bed, breathe in and have my mother pull the zip up with the end of a coat hanger hooked through it. The men there were older, leerier, less respectful than my acned buddies, but despite moments of unpleasantness, many reasonably happy hours were passed dancing and drinking before catching a cab home in the small hours. I remember my father's disconcertion when, years later, I told him my mother had allowed me to go out until all hours at this age; while I shared his incredulity, I wanted to ask why he had so little idea about the life I was leading at the time and whether he ever took pause to reflect on the dilemmas faced by a traumatised single mother in raising a headstrong, manipulative and traumatised teen.

After many months at business college I had failed to learn shorthand and Dictaphone, but I did manage to learn touch-typing in the occasional class I bothered to attend, which now serves me well. I drifted from that circle of friends and took up art classes run by an eccentric blowhard in the underground bowels of Haymarket. This experiment was also paid for by my grandparents. Though I had a firm conviction regarding my artistic destiny, I wasn't yet sure what kind of artist I would be. The painting classes were an attempt to explore whether I had any talent in the area of visual arts. I didn't, unmoved by the mixing of paints and the highlighting of trees on stock-standard landscapes. The most exciting thing to happen during my time there was the announcement of an art tour of Italy, Greece and Egypt, which I became instantly obsessed with. I campaigned and nagged my family to fund my place on the tour. My first overseas trip followed and I visited world-famous artistic sites with a small group of sundry Australians, the youngest a decade older than me at twenty-four. In Egypt, I was told to cover up in certain buildings and on the streets. Dressed in my western teen girl attire, I was ogled and taken for a whore. By then, I was used to being noticed by men, but I wasn't used to the unbridled overtness of the smutty stares or the cultural assumptions that amplified the objectification.

After returning from my European sojourn I lost all interest in art classes. I spent days wandering around the streets of Glebe, visualising my possible futures and pondering my seeming stuckness. I don't recall whose idea it was, but before long I had enrolled in a beautician course at Madame Korner's in Potts Point. Yet again, my grandparents footed the bill. For months, I dutifully donned the crisp white uniform and practised my facial massage technique, eyelash tinting and make-up application on the postmenopausal ladies who came for cut-price student treatments. I was learning the tricks of the trade.

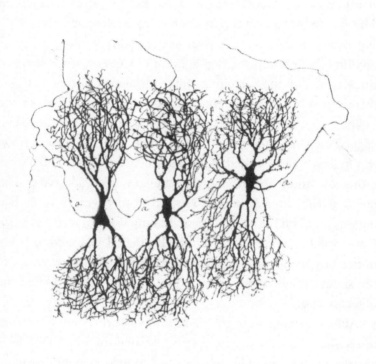

I come from a family of beautiful women.

This short, simple statement raises immediate questions: why am I so sure? How to define this 'beauty' I lay claim to regarding my womenfolk? And most importantly, how does it relate to my exploration of patriarchy and trauma?

I am certain the women in my family are beautiful because I look at photographs of them in their youth and see that they embodied the cultural ideals of beauty in their time: white, evenly featured, clear-skinned, slim to curvaceous, conscious of their sex appeal, stylish. I also observed others' responses to them over decades. I witnessed the dedicated, daily feminine labour of my mother and my grandmother. My aunts have been celebrated for their beauty and my cousins admired for theirs. And I have been an apprentice to the great project and burden of appearing beautiful.

Definitions of beauty are often debatable and socially specific, but if declarations of appreciation are proof of beauty, the physical appeal of the women in my family is well established. My mother was born during the Great Depression in 1934, the only child of a buxom and statuesque knock-out named Gladys.

Glady was a well-put-together working-class woman blessed with a gorgeous face and an hourglass figure. Family members who recall her younger years tell tales of the desperate measures to which men were driven to win her favour before she finally chose a husband from among them. She never did say why she accepted

George, a short, unremarkable Dunlop factory worker, over the
advances of a suave and wealthy Italian named Sammy (whom she
spoke of for the rest of her life), but I imagine Sammy may have
had a wife stashed away somewhere and that my grandmother did
not see herself as mistress material. In addition to her lucky genes,
Glady was a talented dressmaker with a flair for fashion. I fancy
that had she been born in my generation, and been given the
opportunities I had, she might have become a fashion designer.
As a young woman Glady went from brunette to redhead before
morphing into a blonde, her trademark incarnation in which
she became positively Monroesque. Photographs and family lore
testify to the fact that Glady – even during the Second World War,
when she worked factory jobs, and items like stockings were a rare
luxury – always dressed up and looked a million dollars. Despite
her famous flirtatiousness Glady was 'frigid', at least according to
my mother, and I do recall her freely admitting to not enjoying
sex. The union of Glady and George was not the happiest of
marriages, though he was not a violent man nor a drinker, and
it ended in divorce well before I was born. Glady took comfort
in her cherished, sickly daughter, Dawn, with whom she was, let
us say, overly concerned. She would doll her young child up like
little Shirley Temple and the two of them made a darling pair.

101 Lazy Girl Makeover Tips (Marie Claire)

When my mother spoke of her youth, she described a childhood
and adolescence outshone by Glady's awe-inspiring voltage. She
had spent her childhood in bed reading books and watching
films from Hollywood's Golden Age, star struck by the glamour
of her favourite actors. It can't have escaped her notice that her
mother was both beautiful and alluring enough to have been
one of them. My mother described herself as a plain child and

an 'almost pretty' teenager. This statement is supported by her wedding photos, taken when my mother was twenty; it is a middle-aged yet luminous Glady who seduces the camera. But in an incredible evolution that my father, long divorced from my mother, still recalls with wonder, a new Dawn emerged, quite organically, in her late twenties. Around the time I was born, the pudgy 'almost pretty' face of the woman he married metamorphosed into a visage of delicate loveliness. My father, who was working as a photographer at the time, took a series of photos of my mother and me in the garden in the period immediately following her transformation.

I am a chubby toddler and her slender arms hold me firmly. I am touching her, kissing her, and gazing at her with what looks like overwhelming fascination and admiration, as if I understood, even then, the power of feminine beauty. My mother's eyes are downcast. She is hard to read. There is something in the expression on her face I have returned to again and again.

I've long considered that my mother approached the classic narcissist, and that much I could identify in these shots. Freud said that the combination of feminine beauty and narcissism was irresistible to men who, though drawn to such women, would find themselves shut out by a cone of self-obsession and therefore doomed to neglect or rejection. I saw in these images that my mother was consumed with herself and could not, in some critical way, register me. Beyond this painful realisation I sensed something else, some elusive quality I could never quite name. One day, when I was in my thirties, I had an epiphany. It was not merely my mother's narcissism my father had captured in his lens; the photos depict an insecure narcissism, the state of one who sees and is absorbed by a pleasing reflection and yet still doubts it.

Dawn spent much of her early life playing second fiddle to my grandmother's charms, so it makes sense that in these photos, taken shortly after her flowering, she is wrestling with a newfound self-image. Her emergent beauty must have been at odds with

a deep sense of physical inadequacy. As a young child I was not consciously aware of that sense of inadequacy. I couldn't perceive that it gnawed at her and drove her. I was aware only that I had a pretty mother, a mother of whom others approved, a mother whose veneer of confidence and sophistication was effective and convincing, a mother whose rituals of beauty mesmerised me as I watched her on so many mornings dressing and applying her make-up at her big brown dressing table, her sense of self and mood altering, intangibly, as she did so.

80 Beauty Tips & Tricks Every Woman Needs to Know
(Stylecaster)

I stand before the mirror of my bathroom, the unforgiving morning light revealing a face alive for fifty-plus years, no longer young. I see the eyes sinking deeper, looking more like the eyes of my mother's mother as she aged. I see the dark circles and the gravity-laced sagging of the jowl. A spike of fear pierces my mood as I remember the St Bernard–like jawline of my once-handsome paternal grandmother in her last decades, glimpsed, with a stab of portending apprehension, in my father a few years back when he impulsively shaved off his beard (he instantly regretted it and promptly grew the beard back). I think back to my vicious self-assessments of the past and to the relentless comparisons to other women and I try to breathe through the fear, to relax it, to bring gentleness to this moment in which I encounter myself falling short of the myriad youthful ideals of beauty feverishly produced and promoted by a constellation of industries and media, surrounding us like an expanding universe fuelled by the dark energy of our own self-loathing.

There's a freedom in growing older and caring less about beauty. As a young woman you hear a lot about how hard it is to 'lose your looks'. No one tells you how liberating it can be to age. And no one tells you how women are, in the words of Michelle Smith, 'set up to fail', because very few of us relinquish caring altogether. Smith, a research fellow at Deakin University, published an article in *The Conversation* in July 2017 titled 'Double standards and derision – tracing our attitudes to older women and beauty', in which she discussed older women as damned if they do and damned if they don't, caught between a trying-too-hard rock and a not-trying-hard-enough place, walking a fine line between 'looking acceptably young and unsettlingly unnatural'. Mature women face increased 'policing of their clothing and cosmetic choices': we are harshly judged – and often disadvantaged socially and professionally – for not ageing well, yet we are also 'imagined foolish and vain' if we seek to improve our appearance. I don't claim to have risen above the attachments and investments that drove my mother and grandmother, and if I enjoy a greater sense of release from them as a result of several decades attending to my traumatic symptomology, I still tread that fine line of which Smith speaks as I make my way through my days. I notice it most when the stakes are high or in times of stress, when my defences are down and the old spooks come out to play. The hard-won sense of self that now cores me weakens and distorts, slides back into a preoccupation with how others see me and what others think of me, shakes with jelly-like fear at my centre, giving way to critical superego-speak and paranoid thoughts.

Russell Meares offers an insight into the way trauma affects self-image, describing distorted perceptions of appearance as informed by affect bound to trauma: 'Trauma, whatever its kind, has the effect of impacting upon the psychic system like a loud noise.' Elaborating, he goes on to say that when a trauma occurs the 'sense of inner life is knocked out', by which he means trauma involves a temporary obliteration of the inner life, the identification of 'me-ness' at the centre of the sense of self. 'The feeling of "me" shrinks as a function of the intensity of trauma,' and since it is impossible to separate selfhood from the body the shrinkage of me-ness manifests as altered perceptions of the body. Generally speaking, these deformed perceptions will have a negative cast; the self will be experienced as insubstantial or flawed.

I've thought about beauty a great deal, and I've thought about trauma a great deal, and it seems obvious that the business of beauty – our observations, convictions, vulnerabilities to manipulations, and emotional contagions – can manifest as an expression of trauma. There are, in other words, profound connections to be made between the more troubled aspects of our preoccupation with beauty and the web of patriarchal traumata.

I hope you don't think me a wowser, a body-negative prude bent on neutralising beauty and its syndicate with power and sex. It's not that being beautiful, enjoying beauty or participating in beautifying activities is inherently wrong or problematic. It's a law of nature that youth is, generally speaking, more pleasing to behold than age in terms of physical appearance, and that beauty, at any age, is compelling: it makes you want to look. It's human nature to respond with delight and admiration. But modern-day beauty involves sufferings upon sufferings, lethal methodologies and outright tragedy. And these warrant deeper considerations than the stock-standard knee-jerk criticisms of the media and cosmetic surgery, which are routinely tagged as the 'cause' of women's obsession with beauty and associated complications, such as epidemic eating disorders.

Western beauty customs and procedures are often criticised as a sign of societal ill-health, but of course many non-western and pre-modern cultures have practised no less invasive or extreme beautification rituals. Numerous cultures, from China, where women bound their feet over many generations, to the Maasai tribes of Kenya to the ancient tribes of the Amazon have subscribed to radical bodily modifications. Though some have ritual and ceremonial significance, many are motivated purely by a desire to conform to that society's notions of beauty. In Sudan, Dinka children are facially scarred by the local sorcerer and the marks are considered signs of identity and beauty. Kayan women in the north of Thailand stretch their necks with brass coils. In Mayan cultures, teeth that were sharpened to a point, sometimes with designs etched into them, signified a citizen of high class, and historically lip plates (worn to stretch out the lips) have been used in various locations, including Sudan, Ethiopia and Ecuador. It is thought a handful of social groups in Africa and Amazonia still use them. What, then, do we make of the Kayan women? Do we judge them for their 'vanity' in desiring a long neck? Do we assume Africans wearing lip plates suffer from crippling 'low self-esteem'?

How do cultured assumptions stack up here in the west among those who spend considerable time pondering and researching body modification and cosmetic surgery? 'I generally try to steer clear of connecting cosmetic surgery to psychological trauma,' says Dr Meredith Jones, a reader in gender and media studies at Brunel University and author of *Skintight: An Anatomy of Cosmetic Surgery*. Jones sees this trauma-as-motivation link to cosmetic surgery as a party line among psychologists, but tells me it 'doesn't bear up in the interviews with real people'.

Even where associations are made between body modification and trauma, it's not always negative. Sociology scholar Dave Paul Strohecker notes that '[m]uch has been written about body modification as a form of self-empowerment for women' before citing reports that the three waves of modernist feminism have been associated with an increase in women engaging in tattooing. Such research suggests that 'body modification serves as a means of stress management for the disenfranchised, the marginalized, and the subordinated'. Strohecker draws striking correlations between body modification and trauma in discussing the work of Victoria Pitt, who reported tattooing as a coping mechanism related to 'various forms of oppression (gender, sexuality, race, class, etc.)', and whose research with women with histories of sexual abuse concluded the 'tattooing ritual helped them to overcome these traumatic experiences and locate their bodies once again'. Modification is not all or nothing; rather, we all modify to some degree. It's just a question of how far we go, to what ends and with what motivations. And after all, questions of ethical production aside, is there really a substantive difference between having one's brows shaped or one's hair cut and coloured at a salon, which many women do without thinking twice, and having a facial peel, a laser treatment or collagen injections?

But let's be clear: when we consider western women's relationship to beauty we're not only talking about specific practices that have cultural significance, the possible benefits of self-determined bodily practices among those who have experienced bodily violation, or the productive subcultural tribalism of certain body-modifying communities (I take it as a given that women have the right to do what they choose with their bodies). We're talking big business based on patriarchal power structures. These manipulative, profit-making mega-industries, which are brainwashing and exploiting a largely traumatised populace, are what I want to attend to in my exploration. We're talking beauty in the context of a turbo-capitalist, technologically advanced patriarchy, and simplistic cross-cultural comparisons, any way you swing them, don't further an examination of possible links between trauma and beauty in that context.

In my family there were glaring links between trauma and beauty that took lifetimes to play out, and decades for me to understand. I can't remember my mother's first foray into plastic surgery, but it took place in the short years between the photos of us in the garden and my parents' divorce. My father says he disapproved of my mother's 'nose job'. He liked her original nose and says he would have refused to pay if she had asked him. This admission made me wince, evoking, as it does, a patriarchal order not so long in the past, and indeed not past in some cases, where men exercise power over women's choices and control the marital purse strings. In any event, my mother didn't need to ask him to fund it: Glady willingly covered costs. My mother and grandmother were bound to each other in their pursuit of perfection, as I, too, became bound.

It wasn't commonplace for a 1960s housewife who passed her days in Sydney's sleepy suburbia to surrender a body part to a cosmetic surgeon. Looking at before and after photos (the pictures from the garden fall into the first category) and comparing her pre– and post–cosmetically reconstructed nose, I, like my father, much prefer the original. The latter, though more 'perfect' and conventional, was much less interesting. The original had a beguiling bump in the middle. It had character. It suited her. It was her. And she was all the more beautiful for it. Herein lies the paradoxical truth that is unfathomable to trauma-driven body perfectionists: imperfection can be beautiful, special, admirable, loveable – and even preferable.

My father recalls his alarm at the sight of his wife propped up in her hospital bed, eyes swollen and bruised, nose smashed and bandaged. It may appear curious that it is he, not she, who seemed most affected at the time but, on reflection, it's hardly surprising that a woman who decided to undergo such a procedure would need to minimise the violence involved.

The timing and nature of my mother's second procedure strikes me as significant. I was twelve and she was forty-one when she had breast augmentation surgery. My mother was one hundred and fifty-five centimetres tall, a petite woman whose smallish breasts suited her shape and size. She decided, however, to have them enlarged with silicone. My own breasts were developing and I was experiencing the flux of a changing body. At the time my mother was having her 'breast job', I was learning about the critical relationship between beauty and sexuality. Around this age I began to notice a seismic shift. Men and boys stared, middle-aged women looked at me misty-eyed, friends' mothers said things like, 'Aren't you going to have a nice little body.' I was peaking while my mother was tormented by the visible signs of ageing and the bearing of two children. I found her breast job baffling, intriguing and affecting.

Secrecy surrounded the whole affair. I was instructed to inform anyone inquiring about my mother's stay in hospital that she was suffering from 'women's troubles', a telling phrase that implies a double bind: *I am ashamed that this body is not perfect and I am ashamed of being ashamed, of wanting myself altered.* I demanded to see the new breasts as soon as she was able to remove the bandaging. The impact of the row of big blood-raw stitches under each big, bold breast was repellent and visceral (the procedure has since been modified and scarring is minimal). I think I must have experienced that moment with the same incomprehension my father had felt ten years before upon sighting my mother propped up in bed, post–nose job. I was curious but I recoiled from the bloody evidence of interference, and I didn't like the new breasts. I never did get used to them. There was something about their shape, about the way they threw her body out of proportion. I disliked their hardness when I held her close. I couldn't quite bring myself to accept them as part of my mother's body.

Some take a social constructionist view of beauty, maintaining that society teaches us to measure, and respond to, human beauty in keeping with the conventions of culture and the times. Others view the determination of, and attraction to, beauty as strictly biological, insisting that it boils down to hardwired genetic selection, with basic biology explaining the relationship between beauty and sexuality: a young, healthy, good-looking mate promises a healthy baby and survival of the species. This is a dispute for social theorists and scientists but, whatever the fundamentals of beauty, few would argue with the observation that girls and women have increasingly been conditioned to be beauty-product consumers, and to value and produce beauty as a kind of currency. Men are also increasingly concerned with their physical appearance and targeted by the multifaceted beauty industry. Barely a day passes when the average computer-literate or city-dwelling individual is not bombarded by pornified advertising, journalism, film and television, reiterations of the ideal, and relentless handy hints and hard sells on how to achieve it. It is this order of beauty obsession that is most often critiqued, but those criticisms usually fail to illuminate why we are so susceptible to brainwashing and manipulation and how 'normal traumatisation' sets us up to be shame-based, compulsive consumers.

Weight Loss Tips and Diet Advice for a Bikini Body
(Shape Magazine)

Behind closed doors, another layer of learning is in process in the unique microcosm of each family. My mother and grandmother championed beauty the way others barrack for a sports team. Natural-born beauty was highly prized but they also valued glamour. They wore make-up religiously, were partial to wigs, and even bought, to my dismay, a fur coat each with the proceeds of Glady's miraculous mid-'70s trifecta win. This layer of artifice offered them protection, provided a shell for their vulnerable beings. My mother had beautiful girlfriends. My uncles' wives were both gorgeous. My mother, dazzled by the beauty of her friends and my aunts, considered herself inferior to them in looks and style. The flipside of this veneration for beauty was a sharp critical eye. Nobody was sacred. Contented evenings of watching TV beside my mother on the sofa (sometimes wearing matching mud-packs) were marked by a running commentary on people's appearances. Our favourite targets were famous people and contestants in beauty pageants. While Miss Brazil or Miss Sweden posed in their bikinis and confirmed their wish for world peace, my mother and I would nit-pick. Thick ankles, she might say. Big teeth, I might add. This attention to flaws and detail was, in the end, turned most mercilessly on ourselves.

Not long before I turned fifteen my mother and I decided that I had the foreshadowing of a double chin. I was still girlishly lithe, but the slight lack of definition around the jaw sent us into a panic, which spiralled into farce. My mother thought it through and figured that the best way of reshaping the inadequate region might be to apply a vibrating device. We researched back massagers but they were not shaped for our purpose. It was my idea, I think, for I was neither a sheltered nor an unresourceful child, that your average sex-toy vibrator might fit quite nicely under my chin. And so, while I waited in the car, my mother snuck into a city sex shop and bought her teenaged daughter a shiny gold dildo. Needless to say the chin routine was ineffective and short-lived, and a more traditional application soon followed.

If I were in my early teens today and disappeared my temporary and ever-so-slight double chin through cosmetic-surgery magic, it would not be especially noteworthy. It is no longer only women who fill the coffers of this industry. Children and men are a rapidly growing client base. Would my mother and grandmother have paid for surgery? Almost certainly, if my distress, or the offending shortcoming, was deemed significant enough. The American Society of Plastic Surgeons reported that more than 64,000 cosmetic surgery patients in 2015 were aged between thirteen and nineteen, adding: 'Teens frequently gain self-esteem and confidence when their physical problems are corrected.' That sounds, cheerily, like the end of the story, a plainly desirable outcome, but if trauma is a motivating factor, might the focus shift to dissatisfaction with another aspect of physical appearance? Meares teases out an operation that might offer answers.

Evoking trauma researcher Lenore Terr's finding that an isolated trauma is typically remembered, while recurring traumas are associated with poor recall (Terr differentiates these as Type I and Type II trauma), Meares states that multiple traumas of sufficient impact to disrupt effective psychic processing and reflection are processed by a different memory system from that of the indexical memory of ordinary consciousness. Such traumata are 'not recorded as incidents, but as a form of "knowledge"'. This knowledge involves the 'creation of quasi-narratives', which give the unprocessed traumatic experiences meaning. These quasi-narratives are expressed as negative self-characteristics and experienced as feelings of inadequacy. Thus, a person can come to the conclusion they are 'bad, stupid, ugly, incompetent, or a failure', based on both 'normalised' gendered trauma – those disapproving looks or admonishments that boys might experience for wanting to play with a doll or that girls might encounter for expressing anger – and more extreme forms of trauma, such as childhood sexual assault by a neighbour.

I'm glad the option to undertake unnecessary surgery wasn't available to me then. I know, from painful personal experience, that resolving one site of imperfection is never the end of the story when this kind of trauma-as-quasi-self-loathing narrative is in play. As a young woman I gained weight and lost weight, and gained and lost again. I was less burdened by relentless self-criticism when I was slim, felt better in my body and, yes, more confident in the world, but I was no happier, no less ashamed at root, no less traumatised. My quasi-self-loathing simply recalibrated, expressing itself in other ways, in other perceived failings. In other words, when trauma embedded in the psyche attaches to a physical attribute, changing the offending attribute does not dissolve the internal trauma: it just reasserts itself via another route.

I endured a vicious bout of chicken pox in my early thirties, which left visible pockmarks on my face. I underwent laser treatment to reduce the scarring. And during my forties,

I developed rosacea, a common and progressive vascular condition that primarily affects facial skin. I have yearly laser treatments to help manage it. It goes without saying there is great value in technologies such as these and in reconstructive surgeries and their ability to improve the lives of those with abnormalities or disfigurement. Some of these people have suffered traumas relating to accident, abuse, bullying and social disadvantage. But there are those who undergo such treatment pathologically imagining themselves flawed, and who are at risk of cosmetic intervention becoming an addiction. Medical literature is rife with studies on the psychological make-up, motivations, adjustments and needs of people who present for cosmetic surgery while suffering from body dysmorphic disorder, which is characterised as an obsessive preoccupation with an imagined, or grossly exaggerated, defect in appearance. It's yet another label that might perhaps be added to the long list of trauma symptomology.

Many women report life-changing inner and outer transformations as a result of the cosmetic industry. A friend of mine who underwent breast augmentation surgery is overjoyed. Having been as flat-chested as a boy, she now feels more confident and contented in her body. Trans men and women now more commonly undergo medical transitioning that involves surgery. Many people sign up for cosmetic surgery for pragmatic reasons, such as extending the life of a career in a youth-obsessed industry (though that road leads back to a proverbial and patriarchal Rome). Results aren't always as hoped for, and when things go wrong, surgery can be traumatic, ruinous or fatal. But does that give us the right to condemn a person for seeking to address a physical attribute they want transformed? Even if there has always been a human urge towards bodily revision, there is a critical point to be made about choice. I baulk at culturally enforced prescriptions and revisions forced on children or indoctrinated in such a way as to rob people of choice in any culture. I don't begrudge people who seek out cosmetic procedures that I'm unwilling to undergo. I can see the value of an extended career or increased confidence, but I question the patriarchal base and ingrained sexism of a society in which a youthful, sexualised appearance is a prerequisite for being able to continue to do one's job, especially when this applies primarily to women.

Kim Kardashian Weird Beauty Treatments (Elle)

I'm digging down here, through layers of thinning skin, into memory, history, into the muscle and bone of the western world, fat and malnourished. I'm going back in time to the girl that I was, to the torments of my early teens when I learned to sacrifice comfort at the altar of beauty. Back to the longed-for blonde hair, to the two-day grape diets, to the over-tweezing, and the zealous shaving, and the agonies of acne – the many micro-traumas absorbed and regurgitated as self-hatred, the body blows that shattered the inner world, shrinking me, distorting me in the dogged chagrin of not-good-enoughness, of body as worth, of *I do not deserve*, of *I am unloveable*.

I was so bonded to the notion of physical beauty equating to worth and value that I would sit on buses in my twenties and wonder, when my eyes fell on someone no longer young or someone I thought of as unattractive, how those people could stand to live. It shocks me now, to recall a self capable of this thought until I remind myself that I was, at the time, young and generally considered attractive, and even so, I could barely tolerate myself enough to go on living. It's hardly surprising, then, that suicide might spring to mind.

Years later, after I learned to be less caustically critical, I began to have entirely different experiences in public spaces. One day, when I was living in New York, I experienced a moment of unexpected and mysterious poignancy. I was sitting on a bus looking around at the faces and the bodies slumped in seats when I was suddenly overcome by some kind of transcendent beauty in people – big, small, young, old, light-skinned, dark-skinned, spent and ravaged. Struck by a beauty to do with presence, with its proximity, its possibility, and by a closeness of bodies and a tenderness of energies beyond the superficial separations. It felt like a flash of insight into beingness as love embodied.

Perhaps I judged people so harshly as a young adult because I felt my best years, looks-wise, were behind me by the time I'd reached my mid-teens. My Nabokov-loving twenty-one-year-old boyfriend had pegged me as a nymphet at fifteen. It is the nature of nymphetness to peak early; my Lolita-like revelling in the powers of youth and sexual appeal only just outlived the loss of my virginity that same year. By the time I turned sixteen and arrived in London, two major changes had drastically altered my body and my relationship to it: I had quit dancing classes and I had left home, embarking on a lifestyle that revolved around smoking, eating take-away food and drinking cheap booze. The hamburgers and cask wine piled it on.

Seemingly overnight, I went from exuberant self-assurance and the 'nice little body' my friends' mothers had clucked over, to being plump and disgraced. One minute I seemed set to be the successful heir to my beautiful mother and grandmother's legacy; the next I was a disappointment. The extra weight I was carrying hardly constituted obesity but it was enough to result in a passionate dislike of certain body parts. I was travelling the highways in an effort to outrun my history. The more depressed I felt, the more I ate and drank; the more I ate and drank, the more depressed I felt.

When I was living in London I struggled to get by, scrimping Tube fares and money for doner kebabs. When my grandparents wired their hard-earned money every fortnight to boost my meagre income from the gallery cafe, what did I do? Pay up the rent? Stock up on groceries? Take up a course of study? Buy the decent winter coat I desperately needed? No. I spent it at the local beauty salon on a series of snake-oil cellulite treatments that involved the application of some unknown substance followed by the rotating pressure of a loud, useless machine, all of which had no impact whatsoever on the size of my despised thighs. I distinctly recall the contempt in which the staff of this salon held me. They saw me coming as I rushed, crippled by self-loathing and craving affirmation and sexualised attention, to be scammed. I still recall the anguish I felt in their presence: shame, of course, for being imperfect to begin with and for having to expose those imperfections in an effort to correct them; fear that I was unloveable, unacceptable, short of those taunting imperfections being corrected; and bewilderment – I was little more than a child, thousands of miles away from family and familiarity. There was also a faint hope and a trace of excitement that the ridiculous treatment might, as my deluded fantasy insisted, actually work and transform me into one in possession of the only form of power I thought accessible, or at any rate the only form I desired: sexual power based on beauty.

I wonder now how those women would respond if I asked how they justified the callous treatment and financial exploitation of a girl in the grips of a daily body-image nightmare? It might seem hard to imagine anyone treating such a girl with anything but tenderness and compassion, but the patriarchy pits women against each other in myriad ways, and they, too, have their story. They were but worker bees in the buzzing beauty industry, the sprawling, many-armed multinational marketing machine that peddles the illusion of bodily perfection – spruiking its association with sexual desirability. It was not their job to question or concern themselves with my inner sufferings and misconceptions. It was their job to deliver the treatment the customer wanted, to diagnose 'problem areas', to make money for the business and, where possible, to bring about some improvement. I offered little opportunity for job satisfaction.

During the year before, the year I left home to tear around Australia with compulsive fervour, I had tried to turn my back on my Be Beautiful familial and cultural training. This rejection of the mainstream beauty project was not born of feminist commitment – though the second wave had surged around me throughout my childhood, I was some way yet from understanding or commitment on that front – but more in service to my new drop-out lifestyle and vaguely post-hippy anti-establishment worldview. My clothing style went from high street fashion to nomad shabby chic. I stopped wearing make-up and often went barefoot.

My apparent withdrawal from the beauty game, along with my weight gain, proved difficult for the women in my family, particularly my grandmother. Upon our meeting, Glady would look me up and down quickly and, seeing I was still overweight and unadorned, she would turn her head ever so slightly in disappointed disdain, refraining from comment in the spirit of if-you-can't-say-something-nice-don't-say-anything-at-all. But I clocked her silent disapproval just the same and at other times it leaked out in subtle ways that left me wondering whether I was imagining an indirect covert criticism or being 'over-sensitive', as my father once announced me. As we watched television, or walked around a shopping mall, she would note the pleasing features of other young women in a satisfied tone. 'She looks after herself,' she might say, or, 'She's a good weight.' I use the phrase 'apparent withdrawal' from the beauty game because despite my attempts to break free from the spell my mother and grandmother were bound by, and despite my appearance no longer seeming in step with it, inwardly I remained every bit as entranced as they were. Because of that I experienced these barbs, real or imagined, as excruciating.

This Is What Elle Macpherson Eats in a Day
(Harper's Bazaar)

I was tormented throughout the first four decades of my life by an ideal that shimmered just off the field of my vision. It was a constant presence, as was my awareness of falling short of it. The ideal changed from time to time, from scene to scene, and there were moments when, seeing myself positively reflected in a lover's eyes, the gap of that falling lessened so much that for a while it might be imperceptible, but sooner or later I became aware once again of my unfortunate defectiveness.

As I write, I ask myself how I know this has changed, and whether it really has. I'm not sure if I can articulate it. Somehow I gradually came to inhabit myself more willingly, more happily, imperfectly. Ideals still inform my self-assessments, but they don't loom super-ego large at the front of my mind these days, and I care less about my physical shortcomings even though I have more of them, thanks to the process of ageing. There are other things to focus on, other kinds of power to enjoy. Most gratifyingly, I no longer measure myself against other women in the brutal way I did as a young woman (imagining myself better looking than another woman was no less painful than imagining myself worse looking, since in essence it all fed the same bête noire).

Countless hours and endless energy went wasted in my youth. Driven by desire for beauty, I spent an uncalculated fortune on skin and hair products, endured more than my fair share of disastrous perms (attempts to silence my mother's internalised 'we don't have good hair' mantra), submitted to the requisite fad diets and exhausted myself with compulsive exercise jags. My teens and early adulthood were by far the most unforgiving period for Be Beautiful self-berating. During a particularly anxiety-ridden patch in my mid-twenties, I noticed I had chewed my nails down to ugly stumps and decided something should be done.

Once again, I was awash with that horrible doubling of affect, anxiety upon anxiety and shame upon shame: the badly bitten nails a sign of my anxiety and shame compounded by anxiety and shame that my anxiety and shame had been manifested bodily, now visible to all. I hightailed it to a beauty salon where I underwent a treatment in which acrylic nails are built onto the original – a worthwhile improvement, I assumed, on the tacky business of sticking falsies over the top with glue, which I saw as garish and unseemly. I paid my money, sat patiently while the time-consuming nails were applied, and walked home feeling sophisticated, admiring my new talons. An hour later, I sat on the sofa staring in despair at my hands. I hated the nails even though they looked convincing. I found them grotesque and impractical. I couldn't do a thing around the house, couldn't pick up even the most commonplace object, and worst of all, though I'd been seduced by the suggestion of semi-authenticity, I couldn't shake the thought that I was a phoney. I spent ages painstakingly removing them, feeling embarrassed and foolish.

I've tried several body modifications and some have stuck: the piercing of my earlobes, for instance, which I begged my mother to let me get when I was thirteen; and the now-faded tattoo on my back. For me, motive matters, the spirit in which I get the thing done, the integrity of both my approach and the product. The desire to be more attractive, to modify the body, may or may not be driven by traumatic shame. It's not only the choices I make, but also the way I make them that matters. Even so, there's no denying the fact that the Be Beautiful business is paradoxical in its capacity for ugliness. Much of the beauty industry involves the exploitation of women, children and animals – the traditionally 'feminine beings' deemed possessions of men in patriarchal societies. Sweatshops staffed by Third World labourers (often women and children) produce a huge percentage of the clothing and items western women buy and wear. A gruesome reality hides behind the glossy promise of 'scientific' anti-wrinkle creams. Despite growing numbers of women choosing cruelty-free cosmetics (which are now widely available), the majority of consumers still patronise companies that either test on animals or use ingredients that others have tested on animals, and millions of animals continue to suffer and die unnecessarily. Each batch of the enormously popular Botox has to be tested, often by way of the barbaric LD_{50} method, which involves poisoning animals with a substance until half of them have died, thereby establishing the lethal dosage. Though Allergan, the manufacturer of Botox, has developed a cell-based test to replace LD_{50} and the use of animals, the company has not made an airtight commitment to alternative methods. According to Animal Aid, LD_{50} is still used in the UK despite the government's claims it has banned the test. We turn a blind eye to please ourselves, to please others, protesting or condoning unethical practices with every dollar we spend. In these ways, we western women, who fought, and continue to fight for our own gains, collude in the oppression and traumatisation of other sentient beings, those trapped on the lowest rung of the hierarchical ladder established by patriarchy.

A couple of years after the acrylic nails experiment, at the age of twenty-seven, I gained entry into a prestigious degree and resumed the formal education I'd turned my back on at thirteen. During my first year of university, Naomi Wolf's *The Beauty Myth* hit the scene. Wolf's instant bestseller proposed that the progress made by earlier feminist waves and wins – women's greater access to social options and power, and their unprecedented engagement and representation in public discourse and institutions – masked another, retrograde development: increased pressure to meet unrealistic standards of beauty constructed and circulated by those with commercial interests. Citing a rise in pornography, eating disorders and cosmetic surgery, Wolf claimed that the myth of an impossible, flawless beauty generated a self-hatred that kept women consuming, striving for an unachievable ideal: 'in terms of how we feel about ourselves physically, we may actually be worse off than our unliberated grandmothers.' This makes broad sense, since advertising as we know it and advanced capitalist consumerism came together in the post-war boom of the twentieth century, right before second-wave feminism emerged.

From the start, advertising used women to con other women, initially (and ironically) under the guise of first-wave feminism. The documentary *The Century of the Self* tells the story of how Edward Bernays, the American-based nephew of Sigmund Freud, got women to smoke by slyly manipulating gender politics. Bernays was a propaganda specialist who set up business in New York City, having invented the term 'public relations' to replace 'propaganda' on account of the Nazis having given the word a bad rap. Drawing on his uncle's theory of the unconscious, with its hidden desires, sublimated instincts and irrational emotions, Bernays set out to work out a way to profit from what he saw as a positive form of group mind control. When the president of the American Tobacco Company (ATC) approached Bernays, there was a firmly entrenched taboo against women smoking, and the ATC wanted Bernays to crack it so as to double their market. With his uncle in Vienna, Bernays consulted New York's top psychoanalyst and asked him what cigarettes meant to women. Unsurprisingly, the good doctor advised that cigarettes symbolised the penis, male sexual power.

Bernays then recruited a group of attractive and wealthy debutantes to hide cigarettes while marching in a popular public parade. They were to light the cigarettes when given the signal. He ensured the press gallery was in place, and informed them that a group of suffragettes was staging a protest by lighting up 'torches of freedom'. It was a sensation, and thereafter women who wanted more than the oppression that was their lot were obliged to demonstrate allegiance by taking up smoking. Women started smoking in droves and cigarette sales went through the roof. We've been falling for the smoke and mirrors ever since. This is just one example of how women's desire to Be Beautiful, and men's desire for women to Be Beautiful, is inextricably bound up with the imperialist, capitalist, patriarchal project of post-'Enlightenment' modernity and its sprawling traumata.

In the introduction to the most recent edition of *The Beauty Myth*, Wolf suggests women have more 'breathing space' from this myth than they had at the time of the first edition, but warns: 'The beauty myth, like many ideologies of femininity, mutates to meet new circumstances and checkmates women's attempts to increase their power.' One of those very mutations is evident in the response to a more recent public outing by Wolf, where she discusses her understanding of third-wave feminism on the Big Think YouTube channel. What Wolf has to say in the clip is, as feminisms go, relatively benign, easy listening and notably man friendly. She coined the term 'third wave', she explains warmly, to entice a revival of a flagging feminism for a new generation of young women. She goes on to say that some of its characteristics include a more pluralistic and less dogmatic approach to sexuality, fashion and make-up, more attentiveness to issues of class and race, and a canniness regarding the use of media or consumer practices 'for a good outcome'. Despite the mildness of Wolf's words the comments range from raging ignorance to sickening misogyny:

- Fuck feminism.
- 3rd and 4th wave feminists use sex as a weapon. They dress provocatively, tease, and reject men in an effort to dominate men through sexual frustration. They manipulate unknowing, brainwashed men to get what they want then leave them high and dry. The only way to reverse 3rd, and 4th wave feminism is for the majority of productive, and professional men to become MGTOW [I had to look this up – it's an acronym for 'Men Going Their Own Way', a movement of men who subscribe to this term as 'a statement

of self-ownership, where the modern man preserves and protects his own sovereignty above all else' – in other words, it's a separatist, pseudonymous, online community that inhabits the 'manosphere' associated with the 'alt-right'].

- what is she doing outta the kitchen?
- The feminist UGLY FUCKS tried to change our video games, now they're ruining our films!
- feminazi bitches
- Third Wave Feminists are so sheltered they get triggered over anything and thing [sic] men are so inferior that they made a law against "manspreading." It's not the guys fault that they can't sit a certain way because they have a dick.
- Third wave feminism is full of sexist cunts who think the world owes em something
- Here you have Naomi Wolf, a feminist, boldly and happily admitting that she completely made something up and then invented a lot of nonsense to describe this thing she made up to along with it as well ... So, why should we believe anything Naomi Wolf says? Oh but wait, facts and credibility mean nothing to feminists, so, it's all good then ...
- so.. shes the one we shoot. got it.
  how?
  with a bullet?
  with ejaculate you ninny
  she would talk and i'd go limp [sic]

Toxic masculinist trolls like these stalk and abuse women online routinely, and Wolf's 'beauty' is used against her as she dares to take up public space and express a point of view ('she would talk and i'd go limp'). While I don't agree with Wolf on all points, I vehemently defend her right to give voice to her ideas in the public realm without being subjected to abuse. Is this hatred, unleashed with abandon on countless public threads, a fair measure of the state of masculinity in the twenty-first century? While some of the researchers furiously studying this behaviour link self-identified trolls with narcissism, psychopathy, Machiavellianism and sadism, others, such as Whitney Phillips, maintain trolls are 'mostly normal people'. If this statement appears to be pointedly neutralised in terms of gender, Joel Stein, the *Time* journalist who noted the above findings, lets slip when he writes: 'Trolls are turning social media and comment boards into a giant locker room in a teen movie, with towel-snapping racial epithets and misogyny.' Unsurprisingly, then, women are among their favourite targets and attacking women's appearance is a primary strategy.

I suspect the men most likely to exhibit this kind of toxic masculinity are those raised with a particularly virulent version, or a high proportion, of old-school masculinist traditions – the kind that puts stock in the superiority of men over other beings and believing their dominance therefore justified. It also stands to reason they are likely the least resourced to develop the skills and capacities in a post-patriarchal society. Women who adopt a strident politics of feminism in combination with a legacy of unaddressed personal patriarchy-related trauma also prove problematic in interpersonal and political realms, but militant male-separatist feminists and bona fide misandrists are relatively few in number compared with the swelling armies of hate-speaking trolls and ruthless male terrorists.

Patriarchal conditioning entwined with transgenerational trauma is the root of the problem, but the secondary problem is the entrenched resistance to addressing it. At its least damaging the resistance to taking responsibility results in turning the other cheek when witnessing sexism or shoring up the last bastions of patriarchal male autonomy via poison-penned chest-beating cheap shots, and at its most damaging it explodes in crimes against humanity like the rampaging murder of blonde women in 'retribution' for sexual rejection, or blasting apart a venue full of dancing young people in the name of a fantasy patriarchal-religious God-head. Defending against the loss of certain privileges and beliefs causes some to cling to the remains in a mess of confusion and submerged distress. Those who show up to work with us, side by side, through this mess, deserve a sympathetic ear and support. Those willing to question their conditioning, to give up its payoffs, and to be held accountable and attend to their trauma, so that they may contribute to transforming society for the better, deserve ardent respect.

This Flawless 45-Year-Old Model Will Make You Question Your Anti-Ageing Routine (Popsugar)

Am I invisible? I hear other women my age talking about no longer feeling seen in public spaces, about no longer being socially validated. I like moving around, day to day, sans make-up, dressed down, flying under the radar, going about my business. I like this cloak of invisibility – if visibility means being primed for objectification and being eye-candy for men. I like getting dressed up when I'm in the mood. I still enjoy being noticed by certain people. I realise how differently I am seen in the world when I wear make-up, and I remember when I first cut my shoulder-length hair very short in my late twenties: I was instantly less visible to 90 per cent of men. Happily, they were the 90 per cent of men I most welcomed being invisible to, but it was difficult, back then, to get used to it, since I had been raised from birth to crave the approval of men I had no desire for.

I was a third-year mature-age undergrad student in the early 1990s, at the time of that first short-short haircut, and during the course of my studies I launched into a lengthy survey of feminist discourses about objectification, the relegation of women to the realm of the body and the sphere of the private, and the cinematic 'male gaze'. My attempts to understand inculcations around beauty, and my struggle to free myself from their hold, surfaced in my university work. I was particularly interested in post-Freudian psychoanalytic theory. Julia Kristeva's take on beauty and artifice as the sublimation of loss, to mask a state of mourning, made thrilling semi-sense to me. In 'Beauty: The Depressive's Other Realm', a chapter from her book on depression and melancholia, *Black Sun*, Kristeva takes an essay by Freud as her starting point.

'On Transience', Freud's meditation on beauty and its passing, implies beauty is bound to loss. Walking in a fecund garden one summer's day with a 'taciturn friend' and a famous young poet, Freud was astonished to learn that his companions took a dark view of the natural beauty all around them, declaring an inability to enjoy it since it was 'fated to extinction' – the witnessing of beauty instantly reminded them of its inevitable fading, of death. Freud argued against this pessimism: 'A flower that blossoms only for a single night does not seem to us on that account less lovely.' Nor, he continued in protest, could he understand 'why the beauty and perfection of a work of art or of an intellectual achievement should lose its worth because of its temporal limitation'.

Upon further reflection, Freud concluded that what he had encountered in his friends that day was a kind of revolt against mourning. Upon seeing the beautiful and valued object, these two sensitive men, he reasoned, had perceived the mourning inherent in loss and struggled against it. Foreshadowing his major work on mourning and melancholia, which would not be published for another two years, this essay was written during the First World War. War had been looming over Europe the day the men had taken their walk together. 'One year later,' Freud writes in the essay, 'the war broke out and robbed the world of its beauties. It destroyed not only the countryside through which it passed and the works of art which it met with on its path but it also shattered our pride in the achievements of our civilisation, our admiration for many philosophers and artists and our hope of a final triumph over the differences between nations and races.' Yet even in the face of war's mass devastation, Freud held firm that those who refused beauty because of its transience were 'simply in a state of mourning for what is lost'. He stated that beauty's transience gives rise to two different impulses: one is the refusal, the 'aching despondency' of his companions; the other is 'rebellion against the fact asserted', the rejection of transience and an unreasonable and impossible 'demand for immortality'.

Kristeva's move, following on from Freud, was to pose, and somewhat address (the chapter is very short), the following question: 'by means of what psychic process, through what alteration in signs and materials, does beauty succeed in making its way through the drama that is being played out between the *loss* and the *mastery* over the self's loss/devalorization/execution?' Death and trauma hover over Freud's thinking on beauty and transience, and death asserts itself even more overtly in Kristeva's treatment. 'In the place of death and so as not to die of the other's death, I bring forth – or at least I rate highly – an artifice, an ideal ...' She goes on to explain the way in which the psychic process of idealisation functions as allegory through a dynamic construct of sublimation. 'Like feminine finery concealing stubborn depressions,' suggests Kristeva, 'beauty emerges as the admirable face of loss, transforming it in order to make it live.'

My move, humble undergrad style, was to submit a philosophy essay drawing on these brief moments in Kristeva's and Freud's oeuvres to make connections between patriarchy-related depression in women and the endemic preoccupation with youthful beauty. I argued that women in advertising-swamped contemporary culture are positioned and conditioned en masse to use 'feminine finery' to conceal 'stubborn depressions' born of aeons of patriarchy. As a result, women and girls tend to be obsessed with achieving and maintaining an ideal of physical beauty to mask centuries of structural losses, resulting in a collective preoccupation with beauty that serves as a bandaid on a gaping socio-political wound – beauty, socialised and industrialised as a form of currency, provides a way to exist in the face of those losses and lack of access. I did not quite understand at the time that I was getting at collective trauma as a multi-generational, gendered operation, but I felt sure I was tapping a vein.

For another student assignment, I mined the work of philosopher Georges Bataille, for whom beauty sets the stage for physical eroticism, itself understood as a death-denying and death-defying transgression (the good old sex/death equation). According to Bataille, we human beings experience ourselves as inescapably discontinuous (we die) and long to experience ourselves as continuous – a contradictory state of flux. We seek to transcend the limits of life without going so far as to cross the critical life/death boundary. Profanation serves as an achievable transgression and beauty is something of a gateway. Bataille maintained that beauty is valued for the way it conceals our animal aspect (the hairy parts, base characteristics) – until sex comes along to reveal it. The further removed from the animal we are – the more polished and preened – the more erotic and exciting that animalistic revelation ultimately is. In his view, eroticism marks the fusion (or promise of fusion) of separate entities involving the play of discontinuity and continuity. In the Introduction to *Eroticism*, Bataille speaks of the Marquis de Sade's assertion that we come closest to death (continuity) through the 'licentious image'.

Combining this strand of Bataille's work with Angela Carter's reading of de Sade's novels *Justine* and *Juliette*, about two sisters with very different temperaments and trajectories, I wrote a philosophical pop culture essay postulating that Marilyn Monroe and Madonna (at least in her then early-'90s incarnation – the era of the Gaultier cone bra and her *Sex* book) respectively mastered the art of beautification as the 'Blonde Goddess' ideal of their times. (Blondeness is crucial here as an erotic signifier in pop culture conferring as it does a halo, an ethereal 'lightness' suggestive of sacredness and continuity.)

Though they shared many characteristics – both American, both young women when they rose to fame, both having lost their mothers at an early age – they evoked eroticisms of different kinds: Justine/Monroe was ruled by the heart; beauty used, abused and defiled, while Juliette/Madonna was in control; a survivor and a libertine who subverted her symbolic blonde invitation to be profaned by actively taking part in profanation. MM and Madonna, I proposed, were twentieth-century Justines and Juliettes in terms of embodying distinct types of feminine positions and behaviours in the patriarchal social order. But, I argued, their films *The Misfits* and *Madonna: Truth or Dare* revealed a kinship between the two women in these works. 'Something haunts the screen and it is this,' I wrote: 'the sisters' unavoidable cultural roots as women. Even as Madonna sucks on a bottle in faux fellatio, even as she simulates masturbation on stage or scolds her messy young dancers there is something melancholic about her, a vague relationship to Monroe.' In other words, even though Juliette appears to be more feminist, more liberated, wielding power and enjoying freedoms traditionally only available to men, both figures perform a masquerade of glamorous blonde beauty over the top of cultural wounding. As Carter points out, Juliette's triumph is 'just as ambivalent as is Justine's disaster. Justine is the thesis, Juliette the antithesis.' 'For Carter,' I wrote in conclusion, 'neither Justine nor Juliette is a worthy role model for the women of today and it would seem to follow that neither is Monroe nor Madonna. Carter did speak of "a future in which might lie the possibility of a synthesis of their modes of being, neither submissive nor aggressive, capable of both thought and feeling".' I ended the essay with the claim that the challenge of realising this vision is to be met not in the spotlight, but in the privacy of our own beings and the forum of our own lives as we struggle – whatever gender identification or hair colour – towards a meeting of heart and head. Are we there yet?

My theoretical explorations re beauty were instrumental to my education but they failed to purge me of my painful personal obsession and my incessant sense of falling short of beauty's demands. The therapist I found myself hashing it out with took the view that my perfectionistic obsessiveness and boundless insecurity stemmed from a vortex of shame, fear and heartache, born of childhood abandonment. There was a void, she said, where a solid sense of self ought to be, and I filled it with a need for perfection and attention, and medicated it with approval from others. Unmedicated, I went into withdrawal and felt the presence of the underlying 'dis-ease'. The solution was straightforward but far from easy: stop the bandaid behaviours and, with help, allow buried fears and feelings to surface. The process took its clumsy, incomplete course and, with the passage of time and maturation, it brought some relief.

Over the years I've softened towards the body parts I railed against in my youth. I no longer spend unhappy hours meditating on every flaw, though I occasionally catch sight of myself in unflattering lighting, or see a bad photograph, and slip back into disparaging thoughts of old. People speak of self-acceptance as if it's an absolute that one either possesses or doesn't, but I view it as a continuum, a sliding scale. Hokey self-acceptance memes circulate in the scrolling social-media simulacrum like hyperreal pep talks, yet platitudes don't help us where we hurt. When I think about the countless hours of my life lost to perfectionist gloom, I regard that self-obsession as a brutal taskmaster that held me hostage. As a young woman it kept me from making love with abandon. It kept me from wearing what I liked. It kept me from going swimming in summer. I wonder what I might have done with that time, what I might have achieved, had I not been so oppressed by the weight of perfectionism.

I've learned a little, too, about the warm comfort of allowing oneself to be loved and appreciated, imperfections and all. I remember sitting on my bed covered in unsightly chicken pox,

horror-struck by my scab-ridden face, while my then-partner
gently applied calamine lotion to each and every scab to help the
itch. It seemed to me one of the most intimate moments I had
ever shared with a lover, and I was so overwhelmed by it that I
cried – not in distress, but out of sorrow for having not allowed
myself to be loved like that in my self-conscious perfectionism.
I don't want to be enslaved to an ideal of beauty, or to be invested
in it for a sense of worth, but I want to look my best. There are
good reasons to care about how we present. Just as there is a
continuum of self-acceptance, there's a continuum of artifice, and
we each have our own choices to make in terms of defining our
position on that continuum.

I watched my mother and grandmother pass through their
fifties, where I now find myself, a time of life when visible
ageing begins to assert itself more forcefully. There's a photo
of my grandmother in one of my mother's albums that's been
there as long as I remember. This photo and the story that
accompanies it entered family lore as a testimony to Glady's
character, capturing her quintessential tendency to deny the
blatantly obvious. It's a black and white Polaroid taken in the
Maroubra council flat my grandparents occupied all through
my childhood. She would have been in her late fifties or early
sixties. Though she stands posed in stilettos and lacy underwear
wearing a coy, expectant expression, she steadfastly claimed
Johnny had snuck up on her and snapped the picture. My mother
and I found it funny and ribbed her about it over the years
because her story seemed to us the height of improbable false
modesty. But looking at this remarkable image now, I don't find
it quite so funny. I'm searching for the right words, typing and
then erasing words, unsatisfied with words. I look at this photo
and I think of selfies and the way those who routinely take and
post them are so often disparagingly cast as narcissistic. I see the
kitsch of that apartment and the white vase in the background,
one of the few items my grandfather's family brought with them

when they emigrated from Myanmar. It's in my living room now, one of my most cherished belongings, the only thing of his I possess. I look at my grandmother frozen in this moment and I realise my mother and I missed something crucial: this photo not only reveals the central paradox of Glady's obsession with beauty; it also testifies to the way society sets women up both to be highly invested in their sexualised image and to feel shame around – and try to hide or minimise – that investment.

Even now, with my mother and grandmother long dead, it's hard to speak these family secrets. There's viscidness to this business of beauty, to the way it veneered across the three of us.

Having outlived breast cancer, the sudden death of her only child, and the passing of Johnny, her husband of forty-eight years, Glady endured her last year on SSRIs with her two cats, and what remained of her formidable resilience and good humour, in a pokey housing commission flat in Sydney's north-west, from which she steadfastly refused to relocate. She was a good-looking woman, even as she aged, not above flirting with my unsuspecting boyfriends, nor outdoing me in heel height or neckline. She never surrendered to comfort over glamour, refusing to cut her hair short even as it thinned to wisp-like strands, and rejecting the casual sportswear now favoured by many older women. Even towards the end, she fretted about her appearance, complaining if visitors caught her unprepared. She took time each day to prepare her face and hair, and she kept her floral make-up bag within easy reach beside the beige velvet armchair in which she could almost always be found in those last months of her life.

Breast Implants Sydney – Creating Beautiful Breasts:
Affordable Perfection, $9,900 (Ads by Google)

As my mother grew older and more reflective she regretted the surgeries, particularly the breast job. She became convinced that the implants contributed to her ill health and she joined the class-action suit against Dow Corning. It was impossible for her to prepare a comprehensive claim as she had undergone the surgery in the 1970s and there were limited hospital records, but she lodged what documentation she could gather, and when she died in 1997 I took over her claim as executor of her estate. In the end, after it had dragged on for many years, the women won the case and I received a measly payout of a few hundred dollars from the multi-million-dollar settlement. But there was more than dodgy implants to my mother's regret. She expressed remorse about the shaky sense of self that drove her to surgery. She felt ashamed at what she felt was vanity and her gullibility to being swayed by Al's encouragement at the time. In an understated way her change of heart acted as a final release from the burden of my long Be Beautiful apprenticeship. During the time in which we both wrestled with our demons, I felt sad every time we embraced and the two hard, alien implants pressed against me, but mostly I felt sad that my mother never knew how beautiful she was. I only hope that in those years of soul searching she came to understand how much more she was worth than appearance alone.

We tend to think of beauty and vanity as flippant, trivial pursuits, as if this concern with surfaces is itself inherently superficial. It is anything but. The body and appearance are bound up with more complex and weighty matters, with histories private and social, personal and political. Biology and nature. Reproduction and the survival of the species. Matters of the heart. Perhaps it is here that beauty's deeply rooted connections to trauma can be most productively traced.

My mother and I had both been, in some crucial sense, fatherless girls. We grew up in the shadow of absent and withholding men, yearning for their presence and affirmation. We learned soon enough that sex was the way to get attention from men and that the primary way for a woman to be sexually desirable was to Be Beautiful. As I emerged from a childhood marked by a frightening dependence on addicted and violent adults, the biological bloom of adolescence brought the heady discovery of a newfound power, a power I did not hesitate to use and abuse in my quest for freedom from those formative wounds and terrors.

It seemed a logical progression, then, that as I lathered thick gooey collagen creams into the wrinkled faces of Potts Point dames I had a head full of men and dreams of escape.

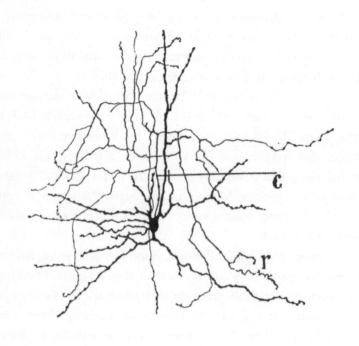

It's 1979 and I'm fifteen, fucked up and restless. My mother and I are living alone after years of mayhem with her deranged or drunk boyfriends. Finally, everything is quiet. Too quiet.

School is a year or so behind me, and I've killed time learning to be a secretary and a beautician, but I'm hopeless at both and will not work a day in my life as either. I'm not going to fit into a job or mainstream society anytime soon. I pass aimless hours roaming the streets of Glebe, daydreaming and staring off into the distance, conjuring up the ideal man with whom to lose my virginity. I see this event as some kind of magic portal into the hallowed realm of adulthood, and I'm itching to be an adult. It seems to me far better to be one than to be at the mercy of one. I imagine sex will transform me, making me instantly wise and womanly. I expect, from having read articles in *Cleo*, from years of films and songs and advertising, and from observing the lengths to which people seem to go for sex and romance, that the heavens will open up and all that is glorious and worth living for will reveal itself in a blinding flash. Meanwhile, during the days, I size up guys I come across as potential candidates. I imagine my hero as several years older, a surfer, with long honey-brown hair and tanned lean-muscled arms. In my mind's eye, he glides on his board through sparkling pipes of aqua waves with the grace and strength of a dancer while I sit on the beach watching in awe, heart swelling with pride.

To break up the boredom while I wait for him to show, I visit grown-up friends, like Ernest, the elderly English gentleman around the corner who helped me break out of school and lets me bludge his Peter Stuyvesants, or the household of sex-worker lesbians where I eat Vegemite toast and grill the girls about blow-job technique. I have few friends my own age.

Michelle Rutherford is one of the few and I spend more time with her than anyone else. The youngest of a large Irish-Australian Catholic brood of eight, she goes to St Scholastica's, the boarding school around the corner. I've also befriended her brother Pete, who occasionally rolls into the city, taking leave from the country town out west where he works as a farmhand. I figure it was their dad's multiple sclerosis that forced the family to move to the city. He's in a wheelchair and he's hard to understand on account of the MS, which has ravaged his speech, but he's nice to me. Michelle's mother, on the other hand, doesn't like me much, and over time she'll come to loathe me, not altogether unfairly, but the Rutherfords run an open house, so there's no keeping me out.

The oldest brothers, James and Jeremy, are absent. James is a law graduate who was an anti-conscription activist during the Vietnam War. Now he's a respected journalist, having cut his teeth covering the Whitlam government. His career keeps him busy so we don't see him much, but he does get me my first-ever job when he secures filing work for Michelle and me at the National Trachoma and Eye Health Program, established by Fred Hollows, who has been studying and treating eye defects in Aboriginal communities. Jeremy is off travelling somewhere. There are older sisters who come and go, the kind of women who might not shave their legs. One of them helped establish Elsie's up on Westmoreland Street, the first refuge for women and children in Australia. I find her and her friends scary (they seem very serious and vaguely disapproving) but I'm curious.

One day I go down to the Federation homestead looking for Michelle. The Rutherfords' door is always open and the rooms are bright and airy. I walk through the empty house, searching for signs of life but finding none. I reach Michelle's bedroom, where I'm startled to see a tall, sandy-haired young man lying on her bed reading. It's Jeremy, back from his latest adventure: Spain. We talk. We start spending time together. It feels like destiny. He's not the handsome surfer I've imagined as The One, but I'm losing patience, and to my fifteen-year-old self he seems exotic and sophisticated. Most importantly he's available, and for a girl in a hurry that's everything.

Jeremy's not like anyone I've ever known. He's only twenty-one, but he has the air of an old man, jaded and knowing. He is bookish and smart and he aspires to write, a combination that leads him to cast himself as Humbert Humbert to my Lolita. He smokes roll-your-owns, mumbles and shuffles around barefoot in second-hand suits. His hair is a wiry mess and he drinks vast amounts of cheap wine. He has round-the-clock stubble. I don't know if I'm impressed by him or embarrassed by him. I already understand the currency of sex appeal, as I've spent years learning the sly art of manipulation, testing the ways being cute or sexy or childlike or flirtatious or suggestive or playful can get me what I want. But in my mind, I won't be a woman till I've Done It.

The topic of losing my virginity became a running theme in conversations with my mother and friends, until the day came when I confided to my mother that I'd decided to go all the way with Jeremy. She took me to a doctor who fitted me with a diaphragm. One night soon after, when my mother was out for the evening, Jeremy and I had sex on my single bed. I was expecting blood, but I don't remember there being any. It hurt – I do remember that – and it was over quickly and the heavens did not open and nothing was revealed and afterwards I did not feel transformed. I felt a sense of satisfaction, though, swanning around in my short satiny dressing-gown the next morning. I suspect I imagined it meant that childhood, with its attendant dependence and sufferings, was over.

If I had been honest with myself I would have admitted to disappointment, but to be fair to Jeremy I don't know if any lover could have led me to revelations then. I was so entirely oriented to the notion that I existed to please men, and that my body was for their pleasure rather than mine, that I was not yet ready to explore its depths and delights in the presence of a man. Over time I learned to perform sex and fake it, which seemed to suit most men just fine. I was not willing, or able, to desire, to surrender control. I had only just discovered the power-by-proxy that came from being desired, and I was milking it for all it was worth. After years of gendered 'normalised trauma' and heteronormative Be Beautiful training, my focus was all wrong. There was no room for anyone else. It was all about me, and yet there was no room for me either. Sex was a facade, a function, an end of a means.

Jeremy has already been north, and he tells me about the Top End. He speaks of Darwin as a Mecca. It's not so much the place itself he waxes lyrical about; it's the mindset, its experiential essence. He describes a roughed-up wonder-world populated by a loose-knit network of nomads who crisscross each other's lives and days in a cosmic ballet of anti-establishment bonhomie. It's less than five years since Cyclone Tracy flattened the community, but Jeremy makes it sound like the place to be, and I become enthralled. Jeremy is charmed by my precociousness and promises to take me away. London's not yet on my radar – that's a year off. I'm still only fifteen, freshly deflowered, and what I'm most in the mood for is an epic road trip.

I'm not sure why I latched on to Jeremy's Darwin, why going there became an all-consuming mission. Probably it was because it gave me a vision, and I needed a vision. It was the furthest, most unimaginable site within reach – an irresistible destination. I was floundering around, not sure who I was, what I wanted to do with my life, or what kind of people I liked. Jeremy, for his part, had strong preferences about who was, and who was not, good company. He scoffed at the earnest idealism of flower-power hippies, and was nonplussed by 'punk', which in any event seemed a tad redundant in post-near socialist, sunny Australia, where the living was relatively easy (so long as you were white). Jeremy and his friends were sardonic, relaxed, generous and anti-fashion. They tended to be literary-minded, to be hard drinkers, and to share contempt for wealth, the workaday world and materialism. The cardinal sin in Jeremy's eyes was pretension. For his ilk, raised on *The Catcher in the Rye*, phoney was the worst thing you could be. Darwin became the symbol of their doctrine, the spiritual home of a tribe of outcasts. It was not a tropical paradise in which to find yourself. It was simply a place to be.

In the Sydney autumn of '79, it shimmered like a Shangri-La and I couldn't wait to get there. Our departure was presented to my family as a fait accompli. I told my mother she had two choices: she could let me go, in which case I would stay in contact and let her know where I was, or else I would run away. My grandfather drove us up Parramatta Road to look at bombs in second-hand car yards. We bought a puce-pink EK Holden station wagon with orange nylon curtains for a few hundred dollars and threw a mattress in the back. Jeremy packed the car with boxes of books and I chucked in a bag of clothes. We hit the highway on a crisp autumn day.

I look back now in disbelief. How the hell did we pull it off? My terms left my mother few options, and she was, predictably, hesitant and worried. My grandparents frowned upon my leaving home so young and objected in their muted way, though Glady seemed more distressed that I was abandoning my mother – or at least that's the perception I'm left with. Jeremy's mother also disapproved, but no one put up much of a fight and members of both his family and mine showed up cheerily to our goodbye party as if I were not a minor, about to leave town with a man six years my senior who was technically a criminal for having bedded me.

As I write this, I feel conflicted. I want to climb into a time machine, walk back into the Rutherford homestead where that party is taking place, and take each one of those adults – who knew so much better than I did how vulnerable I was – to task. I want to thank them for letting me be the wild and wilful young thing I was, for letting me go. I want to ask, what were you thinking? I want to say, hey, it was the '70s. It was a different world.

The road trip begins sedately enough. Our relationship is new. Jeremy and I are still getting to know one another, or what little of ourselves we'll allow the other, allow ourselves, to know. I sit in the passenger seat with my feet on the dashboard, watching the world go by, probing Jeremy for his fascinating thoughts and feelings about me, helping make the practical decisions – where we'll stop, for how long and for what purpose. We amble through hippie country. Bellingen, Nimbin, Mullumbimby, sleeping in the wagon parked in secluded spots where I practise my fledgling sexual skills and sleep with my underpants drying over the elastic curtain cords.

The car breaks down on a winding road deep in the hinterland of far northern New South Wales. The local mechanic takes pity on us and tows us to his garage, where we live in the wagon for days on end while waiting for a new engine. His wife delivers food on a tray every now and then, and we sit in the front seat with a view of her Hills hoist. We run out of things to say to each other. There are only so many times in one day I can get him to tell me I'm beautiful. I'm restless. I turn to the boxes of books and for the first time in my life I begin to read in earnest. Jeremy has varied taste but he tends towards braggart writers like J.P. Donleavy, Henry Miller and Charles Bukowski. I discover the modernist classics. Dorothy Parker and T.S. Eliot are my favourites. I learn Eliot's ode to ageing – 'The Love Song of J. Alfred Prufrock' – off by heart; the irony is lost on me. I don't know it, but this move, this digging down into the boxes, is the beginning of who I will become, the beginning of the vocation and education that will shape my adult life. I'm discovering the salve that will see me through everything to come. The books and songs that will make this life bearable. More, that will make it profound.

'Memory fades, memory adjusts, memory conforms to what we think we remember,' says Joan Didion. I struggle to remember what that girl thought, what she felt sitting there in the front seat, feet up on the dashboard, Hills hoist ahead, reading. They're gone, those memories, vanished now in the tincture of time. Memory conforming to what I think I remember: the slow awakening to the other worlds in the pages of a book, in the minutes of a song, other worlds one can travel to, worlds that not only provide an escape from this one but also help make sense of it, or revel in its impossible quandaries, or lay bare its tender absurdities. I read Eliot's 'Portrait of a Lady' and I am captivated by the rhythm of a passage. I recite it to myself over and over, transported by its musicality, tapping out the beat. I'm especially fond of the line about youth being cruel and having no remorse and smiling at situations it cannot see, followed by the narrator's confession of his smiling, youthful sipping of tea. That irony is not lost on me.

When I'm not reading or listening to music I'm crippled by self-consciousness. Not shyness exactly, for I can be a gregarious creature in my ambivert way. It's more a relentless awareness of my own presence, of the effect I have. I harbour an excessive concern about what others think of me, how they view me, how they judge me. I know I'm pretty and I have a nice body, but that's not good enough. I want to be excruciatingly beautiful, impossibly smart, exceptionally talented, worldly, charismatic, famous and dazzlingly special. I soak everything up, re-imagining my identity with the books my hand is drawn to, with each person I encounter, with every mile we clock up. I gaze out the window, fantasising about my future. I know this journey is only the start, and that Jeremy is only the first. I like Jeremy, but what I like even more is the way I see myself reflected in his eyes.

At first, Jeremy's lust for me was fun, but now I tire of its demands. I try to work out how much I can withhold and how much I must concede to keep the balance of power exactly how I want it. What I do like about sex, what I'm drunk on, is the fact that once you hook someone with it, or with the suggestion of it, you can make them do just about anything.

I focused on pleasing Jeremy because there was some satisfaction in that. Besides, it was strategic: I needed him. The further north we headed, the more I felt myself in uncharted territory. Each mile pushed the familiarity of my childhood further behind. The fact that I had no ground beneath me didn't bother me. My only fear was going back, back to childhood, to entrapment, to powerlessness. Anything else – any hardship, deprivation, misgiving or humiliation – was tolerable, even preferable, so long as it did not send me back.

I didn't realise how unusual it was for a girl my age to be on the road. If I missed home and my family I did not allow myself to acknowledge it. I was perplexed most of the time but I willed myself to appear at ease. Always on the move, I couldn't anchor myself or weigh myself down to steadiness, and this was the paradoxical attraction of the transient life. It was as if I believed I could outrun myself if I moved fast enough, could outwit the terror and grief if I kept one step ahead of it. Years later, in rehab, I would learn that this is deemed a 'geographical': a misguided attempt, commonplace among addicts, to escape an unhealthy inner world by changing one's external location and circumstances. I passed the time and amused myself by playing mind games with Jeremy, who flattered me and stroked my endlessly needy ego while providing a baseline of security in our ever-changing landscape.

We enter Queensland and pick up two hitchhikers, Frank and Danny, and their two small dogs. I'm already weary of play-acting at a proper relationship and I'm grateful for new blood. Frank's Aboriginal, from the Riverland, on the rebound from a bitter break-up, and Danny's a light-hearted larrikin.

The four of us have longwinded singalongs as we barrel down the highway. Jeremy likes to sing sacred songs (his favourite is 'Nearer, My God, to Thee') and he's fond of Bob Dylan. I follow the rise and fall of his voice as he belts out the hymns, and watch his carolling profile, his permanent bed-hair blowing in the breeze of the open window. We listen to a lot of Leonard Cohen. We smoke rollies and survive on a diet of flagon wine, middies of beer, fast food and soup-kitchen slops. It's the late '70s, the halcyon days of social security. We have no fixed address and simply transfer from town to town, picking up counter cheques as we go. I have no problem collecting welfare despite my age. On cheque days we spend our money readily and enjoy our most substantial meal: a pub counter lunch. Most of the time, we beg on the street, pick through the car ashtray for decent butts, and siphon petrol out of parked cars in the dead of night, which has the added bonus of a (headachy) high. Personal hygiene is maintained in service-station bathrooms in between occasional showers. (Have you registered the thought 'where was her mother?' yet? If so, have you then reflexively wondered why you didn't ask 'where was her father?'?)

I feel a niggling sensation when asking strangers for money or plucking butts from the EK's ashtray, but I'm not aware this feeling is called shame. I'm not aware that shame is so woven into me that I no longer feel it as notable. It is a way of being that is normal. I am oblivious to it. I've reversed it into a point of pride. I romanticise poverty and scavenging. So do my companions. Perversely, we feel it makes us better than everyone else. We watch the plebs shuffling to work and back in their waking sleep, living their dull, conformist lives, and we pity them.

I had little knowledge of Australian history and even less about Australian politics, though I was aware my family were Labor voters. But you didn't have to be a political brainiac to sense the conservative chill across the state border. Queensland was Joh Bjelke-Petersen's turf back then. I was appalled by the lines up the middle of Brisbane's footpaths: those walking one way filed down one side, those going the other way up the other. It felt trapped in the 1950s. Women in house dresses baking pumpkin scones and men in Akubra hats working outdoors. The further north we went in the Sunshine State, the surer the menace in the air. There were places we were unwelcome. Between Brisbane and Townsville we'd often sleep out on beaches, and evenings were passed in parks drinking with local Aboriginal people. Once the police descended on such a gathering. Jeremy, Frank, Danny and I were ordered to move on. We did as we were told. The next day we were told that two of the women we'd been drinking with were taken off to the cells and raped.

We reach Townsville and ferry over to Magnetic Island. We park the wagon in the car park of the pub down by the wharf and spend the night drinking with a local man in shorts. I pass the evening in a blacked-out blur. The next morning I find myself lying on the ground of the car park. The man in shorts is poised above me with a pair of scissors: he has sliced my dress open with a clean cut up the middle. He runs off when I wake, and the others sit up, stunned and hung over.

I am shaken to the core. For the first time I acknowledge the danger in what I'm doing. I allow myself to feel – for a split second at least – how young I am, how alien the people I'm meeting. I have the bone-chilling realisation that men can be as threatening in my shining new adult life as they were in my childhood, that the power I think I have over them can, in an instant, be turned on its head. As the heat of the day gathers, I stand in a phone booth by the beach, crying down the line to my mother as the waves lap the shore. I don't say what has happened, or how scared and lonely

I am. I tell her only that I miss her and love her. She begs me to come home, her voice pitched between pain and panic. I refuse. I long to go home – to my mother, to comfort, to familiarity – but I tell myself I cannot. I have not yet reached my goal, have not yet made it to Darwin. Going home would mean accepting defeat, admitting that I'm a child and can't cut it in the world of adults. I won't give up, whatever the risks on the road.

Despite this disturbing introduction to the island, we stay on, exploring its sparkling nooks and sublime crannies, lolling around on idyllic beaches with crystalline water in the perfect heat of a tropical winter.

I was not particularly attracted to Frank but he fitted the critical criteria: he was there, so we began an affair. Danny turned a blind eye, but when Jeremy made the inevitable discovery our little foursome turned suddenly sour. When I think back to this time I can't help but wonder why Jeremy took me seriously enough to be as affected as he was, given my obvious incapacity for emotional connection or loyalty. But of course, despite his grand persona and erudite ramblings, he wasn't far from boyhood himself. Though the tension was thick, we continued as a quartet, careening out of Townsville for the trek north-west to Darwin with a furious, suicidally speeding Jeremy at the wheel, with only semis for company on the numbing highway, and passing the odd tin shed in the dirt with a cattle dog out front.

We cut across the border between Queensland and the Northern Territory on an incessantly nondescript road, and nothing seemed to change, except it did. If Queensland felt oppressive and stuck in time, the Northern Territory felt exposed and forgotten by time. If in Queensland the heat of the law was your biggest threat, in the Territory it was being left to your own devices, cast into a state of lawlessness, that could do you the greatest harm.

By the time we reached Darwin I was exhausted. I was tired of being dirty, tired of being hungry, tired of the wagon, and tired of Jeremy, Frank and Danny. I needed to recuperate.

I checked into the local women's refuge the way most people check into a hotel. I spun some 'he done me wrong' line to the well-meaning women workers to justify my abuse of their favours. With no awareness that my own story was justification enough – I was, after all, a fifteen-year-old girl, 4,000 kilometres from home, fleeing trauma in the company of adult men – I lied. By then, scamming had become habitual; I no longer knew which of my stories or needs were real, and which of them were manufactured.

I recover at the refuge for a couple of days, listening to a constant stream of Joan Armatrading, eating regular, healthy meals and enjoying such strange normalities as watching television, taking daily showers and sleeping in a properly made bed. I hide from the men and the confusing emotional complexities between us. But once rejuvenated, I grow edgy. I remember why I've come to Darwin and I'm seized by the urge to join the boys and meet the mysterious drifters Jeremy's told me so much about. So I leave the refuge with a wave and a thank-you and go off in search of the men. They aren't hard to find. The Vic Hotel, with its big overhead fans and balcony overlooking the mall, is a favourite of the itinerants, as are the Animal Bar on the Esplanade and the Workers' Club.

We live for the day, for the minute. I rarely know where my next meal is coming from or where I'll sleep. I tell myself this is freedom and that I like it.

We spend time at Lameroo Beach, which has long been an established camp because of the hippie trail to Asia. It fills up year after year in the dry with cliques of ganja-smoking, guitar-strumming youth, and tree houses remain as evidence of their initiative. There are mutterings about the nomads who were blown away from the beach on the night Tracy hit and were never counted as missing – to be counted as missing, one has to belong in the first place. But this is likely an urban myth: as Jeremy points out, the fierce mosquitoes alone would prohibit camping there in the wet. Even in 1979, Lameroo is a permanent party, and there is something notable about the drifter parties: there are hardly any women, and those who are part of the pack tend to be tough and working class.

The women view me with disdain and treat me like the middle-class princess I'm desperately trying not to be. I am dismissed because of my age, disliked because of my sexual game-playing, and told more than once to 'go home'. It's delivered with condescending scorn and it only makes me more determined to prove myself by staying. The rejection, and not being taken seriously because of my age and girlish prettiness, is a source of disgrace. I want friendship and approval but have no clue how to win it. I focus on gathering allies where and how I can by flirting shamelessly with the men. I can't match my adult comrades in terms of wit and knowledge, so I learn to observe. I pass long hours at their feet, watching, listening and drinking. Taking it all in. Like Jeremy's books, learning to observe, to listen, will prove to be invaluable training for a writer. But at this point, I have no ambition save to experience life, to forge my own path through it.

Nobody ends up in New York by accident and no one really cares where you come from or why you've arrived. Being there says it all. Similarly, nobody ends up in the far north by accident, and in the 1970s no one was interested in personal history. Being there marked you. Though my underage status stamped me as different, I was not alone in trying to outrun the past. We were united in our commitment to denial and bravado, and we supported each other in a lifestyle fuelled by alcohol and financed by the dole, charity handouts and petty crime. This fuzzily defined kinship had a generous and egalitarian spirit, marked by a sharing of resources that evoked a socialist sensibility. When one person's dole cheque arrived it was for all. When cash ran dry, a meal, cigarette or middy would appear. The EK became communal property. Jeremy never hesitated to lend the Holden out whether he'd known the person for years or minutes. It might come back in two hours or two days. Amazingly, it always came back.

Darwin itself was not a pretty place. It was little more than a township, and still being rebuilt. The sprawling landscape was relentlessly flat, and the community was recovering from a disaster that would shape its future identity. I wasn't disillusioned, though, because I didn't go there for pretty. I went for new horizons and a sense of belonging among others who didn't belong, and I found what I was looking for: passing afternoons fumbling with men on sagging single beds in rundown rooms; the joie de vivre of gatecrashing the locked-up YMCA in the small hours and splashing around the candescent pool; a glimpse of transcendence listening to the Patti Smith Group's *Horses* for the first time, in the dark windowless office of the boarding house on Knuckey Street while sharing a joint with the manager and his girlfriend. It was, just as Jeremy promised, the outsider capital of Australia.

Back then, Darwin attracted lost souls and seekers, addicts, drifters, losers, chancers. In *Slouching Towards Bethlehem*, a collection of essays about California in the '60s, Didion wrote about the stark reality of San Francisco's Haight-Ashbury in the comedown from 1967's 'summer of love'. She portrayed a counterculture less turned on and more traumatised. Often the young casualties she described were the children and grandchildren of generations who had lived through world wars. The carnage Didion chronicled depicted youth born of a cesspool of trauma and into a sped-up, ultra-modernised, hyper-capitalised, economically booming climate. They walked headlong into idealism only to be spat out in Hades. Unlike those hippies, the young people who travelled the long and dusty highways of Australia during the 1970s were under no illusions as to the promise of revolution or the likelihood of being greeted by a love-in. Mostly descended from convicts and working-class Anglo settlers, we were made of grittier stuff, but we were still, for the most part, casualties of war-torn industrialised patriarchy, even if we had suffered it less than many thanks to our geographical location.

The people Jeremy and I knew were the types who would be reported as missing, who would meet foul play, die young, rot in prisons or disappear into the hills to live as hermits. Some of us ended up reinventing ourselves, reintegrating in part compromise, part holdout, to become 'productive members of society'. I don't know how they survive, the casualties of the generation now coming of age, and how they live, now that the welfare net has been so substantially sewn up. Where does a young person in an abusive home go today? How do they escape? Are they among the booming homeless in makeshift villages of tents under bridges? (No travelling north on counter cheques these days.) Do they simply stay at home, however hellish, joining the bursting ranks of young people force-fed degrees they aren't sure they want, the ones who stare out at me blankly as I lecture, the ones who self-sabotage?

Traumata becomes stigmata: the girl who begged and stole and scammed bore scars and stigma. In her book *Writing Wounds*, which examines trauma and memory in relation to the work of French women writers, Kathryn Robson cites the *Oxford Dictionary* definition of trauma as 'a wound or external bodily injury' and a 'psychic injury, esp. one caused by emotional shock the memory of which is repressed and remains unhealed'. Chronically traumatised people bleed spontaneously in response to both fresh trauma and seemingly benign events. 'The interface between body and mind in psychological trauma may be seen to begin with the wound – or, more accurately, with wounding,' writes Robson, reasoning that it stands to follow that to 'remember and narrate trauma' means to 'attempt to write in and through wounds, through the holes within memory that represent the incursion of the past into the present', which suggests a reckoning with traumatic shame.

Robson turns, once again, to the dictionary. The word 'stigma' comes from the Greek, meaning 'a mark made by a pointed instrument'. It originally denoted the branding of slaves' bodies, leading to the contemporary figurative meaning: to be marked by disgrace, to be shamed. 'The marks of "stigma", impressed upon the skin, imprint the individual's past on the body, so that the stigmatized body becomes a site where history and identity are inscribed.' In the wake of chronic, naturalised trauma, its soul-shattering history is inscribed upon the psyche and the body, a process metaphorically signified by stigmata.

In her discussion on the influential philosopher and feminist literary theorist Hélène Cixous, Robson notes: 'In Cixous's formulation, the wound precipitates either death or healing; its story, she seems to imply, emerges through the scar that marks its healing. If we accept her logic, the scar – the point of suture, when, figuratively speaking, the skin re-mends and the wound is sewn up – is the site of the story, "ce récit".' Cixous' own writings, however, defy such closure and neatness. Robson concludes that the writing of trauma emerges from the open wound rather than the 'closed scar', but later qualifies this, stating that writing is 'bound up not only in the story of loss in the past, the scar, but also in the wounds that open up in the act of telling'. I'm writing through stigmata, but I don't mean to suggest I'm a martyr.

I heal. I bleed. I heal again. One scar seals (thin-skinned) while another weeps. I've made peace with my stigmata. I have my analgesic ways and the body's own miraculous capacity for regeneration. We survivors are resilient. We keep coming with the life force. The fire in the belly dims and then rises again to burn bright. We find each other in subcultural solace. We find each other. I don't imagine these words will fix my wound-scars and I'm certain they won't fix yours, but maybe they can be a portal through which we can meet ourselves, the selves we've forgotten or disowned, the selves that split off in the moment of trauma whom we are yet to meet. 'I think we are well advised to keep on nodding terms with the people we used to be, whether we find them attractive company or not,' advises Didion. 'Otherwise they turn up unannounced and surprise us, come hammering on the mind's door at 4 a.m. of a bad night and demand to know who deserted them, who betrayed them, who is going to make amends.' That girl, the one who settled then set off in search of adventure, she's knocked on my door.

I've long lost contact with those nomadic outsiders. I remember them, and the days and nights I shared with them, as if the film of this entire period is ruined and only select scenes or frames have been saved. Jeremy, now a social worker in the Red Centre, is the only one I've stayed in occasional touch with over the years. I don't remember how I left Darwin that first time, with whom I left or how long it took to get home, but once back in Sydney I couldn't get Darwin out of my mind. I moped around awhile and, incurably restless, I convinced Heidi to fly back up with me.

We move into the Knuckey Street boarding house and get jobs as housemaids at the local Travelodge. I quit after a couple of weeks and take up with a young man with long honey-brown hair and tanned lean-muscled arms.

As the wet approaches, we make plans. The boyfriend and I hitchhike to Brisbane. Passing hours at a time by the side of the highway, listening to Joni Mitchell or Phoebe Snow on a tinny cassette player, we inched closer to Brisbane day by day until we reached its outskirts, where I suddenly found myself living with his family. Not long after I was involved in a car accident. We'd been visiting friends of my boyfriend's on the Gold Coast and I'd gone for a drive with two sisters who were, unknown to me, on Rohypnol, our mission being to get (more, different) drugs. The Kombi van veered off and rolled on the highway, and I lost consciousness for a few minutes. We were lucky to emerge with only minor injuries. I wasn't sure what I was doing in Queensland, with this pleasant guy and his suburban family, but I didn't know what else to do, so I stayed on. After a couple of months, we hit the road again, heading south. When we reached Canberra I decided to go it alone and bought a one-way bus ticket to Perth.

For another half a year I rushed around the country, picking up and discarding companions en route, or travelling solo. The harder it got to outrun myself, the faster I ran. I dashed between Darwin, Cairns, Sydney, Byron Bay, the Gold Coast, Canberra, Adelaide, Perth and Broome. I travelled by bus, train, thumb and plane. I explored a pre-tourist beach in Cairns in a throbbing, tripping grass haze and enjoyed an excursion inland to pick gold tops and swim in a cool watering hole surrounded by the saturated reds and greens of wild tropical growth, but despite tranquil surrounds like these I was not at peace. The denial and bravado slipped, and I began to feel fear, or to acknowledge the fear I'd felt all along. There were interminable stretches rolling down isolated, pitch-black highways in the cabins of speed-freaked truckies. I watched for hints of a psychotic serial killer, as if picking up a sure sign would have helped me out there anyhow. I spent hours waiting for rides on the side of the road, singing to myself, talking when I had a companion, sitting on my bag under the relentless sun. I slept overnight in the houses of locals who grew weirder by the hour. Still not yet sixteen, I relied on the kindness of strangers and was relieved when their kindness was uncomplicated.

I took time out at my mother's house on the Central Coast, where she was holed up with my Uncle Hugh. I wrote in a big A4 notepad for the better part of every day. This caught my uncle's attention. 'Diary of a Little Girl', Hugh titled it – whether with affection or condescension, I wasn't sure. I noticed an expression on his face as he said it, part impressed, part concerned, as if he suspected I might be a budding writer. When I tired of their dramatics and grew bored enough I returned to the city, enamoured with Jake, to fantasise about him in my mother's city studio. I soon followed him to London with a suitcase of summer clothes (heading into London's winter).

Fast-forward eighteen months. Upon my return to Sydney, diminished, I lived in my mother's spare room in a flat in Kirribilli until that fateful day I caught a ferry to the city to watch my brother's band rehearse, got lost, and wound up blacking out and getting fucked by a man who wouldn't let me leave when I regained consciousness. My brother took me under his wing then and we shared a series of flats in Manly while I tried to work out what kind of person I wanted to be, what kind of life I wanted to live. I got a job as a nurse's aide at the Spastic Centre, which I managed to keep for quite a few months despite my problem drinking, and I wrote depressive, Dorothy Parker–inspired poetry.

A good deal has been written about the relationship between trauma and artistic production. There is a plethora of research on the appeal of art for trauma survivors – be it through reading, writing, listening to or making music – and its possible application as an aid to recovery. My academic monograph proposes that a certain kind of creative writing can testify to transgenerational trauma transmissions, and that this testimony is a form of political witnessing.

Quoting world-famous clinical trauma theorists Bessel van der Kolk and Onno van der Hart, Robson notes the traditional importance placed on narrative as a means of communicating trauma: 'Traumatic memories are the unassimilated scraps of overwhelming experiences which need to be integrated with existing mental schemes, and be transformed into narrative language.' Yet she adds that if trauma, by nature, resists narrative representation, 'any narrative of traumatic experience will necessarily modify, distort, even fictionalize, that experience'. This is confirmed by van der Kolk and van der Hart, who view such distortions, whether conscious or unconscious, as the manner by which articulated trauma becomes one's 'life story' (meaning it is always a form of fiction) and that this process of sense-making is closely linked to psychological healing. Robson clarifies, via van der Kolk and van der Hart: 'The modification of traumatic memory works to "soften the intrusive power of the original, unmitigated horror", to dilute the force of the original event.'

When I first started writing I wasn't thinking about the relationship between trauma and writing. I wasn't thinking about trauma at all. I was just writing, transcribing my becoming in words, marking the page as a way of reaffirming my presence to myself and in order to, as Didion would have it, find out what it was I thought and what I felt. The first poem I ever wrote was about a homeless old drunkard. I was thirteen or fourteen years old. Following my literary awakening courtesy of Jeremy's boxes of books, I read up on the classics and scoured second-hand bookstores for poetry collections. I picked up books by poets I'd never heard of before, whom I would later discover to be held in high esteem. I read Eastern European poets, Latin American poets and the Beat poets. I read mostly men because bookstores stocked more books by men, because men were the writers people talked about, and because of internalised sexism (men are geniuses and 'only women bleed').

What was I doing with that writing of words? What am I doing now with this writing of words? I'm writing an autobiography of patriarchy, playing the traumata backwards, chasing it down rabbit holes, twisting it inside out, and if you do that they'll call you a 'confessional poet'. They'll call it 'memoir'. You'll risk being undersold, sidelined, cast as less valuable than Men Who Write About More Important Things Than Their Feelings and Lives.

It was during this Manly period of my late teens that my friend Maggie came back into my life, or rather it was then that she pulled focus. I had known Maggie for about five years, ever since she had taken refuge with Aunt Phoebe and my cousin Rachael, not long after they returned from the Mediterranean. It was known that she had fled her brother's sexual abuse but it was not discussed. I introduced Maggie to Jeremy and they took up together, but that didn't stop her having a crush on me and showing up drunk and adoring unannounced. I was by then quite inclined towards women, and even though Maggie wasn't quite my type I liked drinking with her and the flattery of her barely repressed infatuation. We started taking trips up and down the east coast on the old mail train, mostly staying in pre-tourist-boom Byron Bay and inland Mullumbimby, with Jeremy sending funds from time to time. We played pool, drank all day, chain-smoked cigarettes and lived spontaneously, taking off when we felt like it. Between us there were DUIs and court cases, drunken beer garden spectacles, suicide attempts and psych hospital stays. And there were careless nights in low-rent rooms above public bars, where my bi seductions took no account of her closeted homosexuality and delicate mental health.

By now we were nineteen and running in circles. We careered to a crash one afternoon in the office of a Byron Bay doctor, who promptly admitted us both to detox at the local hospital. We lay side by side in a four-bed ward doped up on Hemineurine, a sedative and hypnotic used for treating alcohol withdrawals. I discharged myself after several days, staggering up Jonson Street under the glaring sun to the old pub opposite the beach, where I began to feel peculiar, not quite right. I went back to the hospital, but the nurses refused to re-admit me: I'd been marked as a troublemaker. They phoned a local rehab for addicts known as The Buttery, on account of its location on the site of an old butter factory. I found myself sitting opposite a friendly twosome who talked about the joys of 'getting clean'. I had no idea what they were saying, but I agreed to go with them. I thought it might be a relaxing holiday, time out from the furious movement, somewhere to gather my thoughts, to see what they might be when they weren't pickled by ethanol. The next afternoon I had a seizure by the banks of a river during an outing.

I spent several months at The Buttery, where I sobered up, ate too much, went back to writing depressive poems, and edited a collection of poetry written by residents, *Polyunsaturated Poems*, which had the significant benefit of getting me out of drains duty when my turn came up on the roster. I'm not sure how much I absorbed, how seriously I took what they tried to teach me about addiction, or whether I understood anything of my own predicament. I do know I left with the best of intentions, and that I tried to practise what they preached upon my return to Sydney, but soon The Buttery and its ways receded into the past. A new chapter began.

It was 1983 and I was closing in on twenty when I started writing poems with fervour, my typewriter set up on a makeshift desk next to my bed. I'd had two poems published while at The Buttery, and I was starting to think of myself as a poet. The turning point came when I met a mouthy redhead named Louise through a stranger with whom I'd hitched a ride back to Sydney after visiting Maggie in the Blue Mountains. (Maggie, by then, had had a flaxen-haired child to Jeremy and had finally come out as a lesbian.) The stranger had stopped off at Louise's pad to buy Buddha sticks before driving me home. Louise and I struck up an instant friendship and I started spending time at her basement flat and accompanying her to gigs. Show by show, she introduced me to her friends, and the night I met The Idol, lionised by local punters as the striking singer of a legendary and defunct band, I wound up sitting on his lap in an over-packed car. I liked his self-effacing manner and piercing blue eyes, his intelligence and sinewy gait. Our paths continued to cross, and a few weeks later I kissed him on tipsy impulse next to the poker machines on the first floor of the Trade Union Club. It was on.

I fell crazy in love. I came alive to myself, to my body, to desire. I learned how to listen through my lover, twelve years my senior. Music became a form of worship. My world opened into ever-unfolding new worlds. References multiplied and exploded into other references. Now, at last, I understood what sex meant, what music was, who I could be. At first I went with it, but soon the ghosts of my trauma came out swinging, shadowboxing me into a corner that would take decades to emerge from.

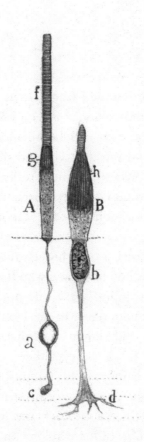

For most of my life I waited (the past in the present) for my father to show up and convince me he loved me. Like Godot, the longed-for father of my childhood fantasies never did come, and like Estragon and Vladimir I passed my days in an absurd tragi-black-comedy where nothing really happened but the marking of timeless time. Countless characters took that stage for a moment, for days, for months or for years, and I looked to each to save the day.

My father slices banana onto his cereal at breakfast. He is far away and frightening. I do not know who this stranger is and why he sometimes appears in my house. I do not feel I belong to him and yet he is of great importance to me. I am confused. He is here before me, my father, and I know he is 'my father' but he does not seem to be *my father*. I don't have a father.

My mother folds laundry in my parents' bedroom. My father bends down and makes a swing of his arms between his legs. I sit on them and he rocks me back and forth. He throws me down on the bed and rubs his whiskers on my cheeks, tickling me. I giggle. He blows raspberries on my bare belly and I laugh, exploding with delight. I have a father. I feel special and loved. I am the happiest girl in the world.

This story, the story of my father and me, of me and my hallucinated fathers, is an enigma, subject to interpretation. My memory is defective, untrustworthy. Time stops.

I was five when he left, when I realised I no longer had a father. I didn't know why he disappeared and I thought about it all the time. I didn't even know how to think about it but I did. Shame: at school the other children had fathers. I didn't know what I'd done to no longer have the father I had never been sure of having, or why my family wasn't the kind of family I saw all around me. Divorce was not unheard of, but in 1960s suburban Australia it wasn't common.

The Idol (three years?) surprised me. A vague supplication. I became a believer. We lived in the night, vampiric. He saw in me a poet and that was his greatest gift to me. I loved him broken-winged, unhinged. How well I knew his flailing flight, his two strong hands, his holy hell and half-blind eyes.

And if he doesn't come? Our troubles didn't arise because (or not only because) I was immature and ill equipped for that order of intimacy. It was as if The Idol keyed his way into the deepest strata of my being, and in doing so inadvertently released the traumatic demons entrapped there. But as is inevitably the case with origin-myth analogies, we're left scratching our heads as to what that really means.

According to Ruth Buczynski, a trauma researcher at the US-based National Institute for the Clinical Application of Behavioral Medicine, it means (ironic spoiler alert) that significantly traumatised people are more triggered by getting up close than less traumatised people. Studies, Buczynski claims, confirm links between 'childhood emotional maltreatment' and PTSD that highlight a tendency towards self-criticism as interfering with the ability to have harmonious and satisfying intimate relationships. Two hundred and eighty-two comments from members of the public follow this short article, one

hundred and sixty-seven heart pourings of pain: 'I had really
low self-esteem, thought I would die if anyone touched me' /
'Relationships With Women Had All Failed' / 'I have a broken
relationship with 2 of my children, and have not seen 5 of my
grandchildren for years' / 'Sometimes I feel she actually wants to
sabotage our relationship' / 'When you are abused as a child, you
learn to trust no one' / 'My step-Dad ... tortured and raped me
almost daily ... and I still can't seem to find a man who doesn't
act exactly like my step-Dad.'

Between the ages of five and eight I have no memory, no
memories at all, of my father. For a long time after the divorce it
feels as if he is dead, or on another planet. At Christmas he does
not come or call. On birthdays there is no word. I do not have
a father. I look at other girls who have fathers and I think they
are prettier, cleverer, better than me in ways I don't see. I look
at other girls who have fathers that love them and I ache with
longing to be loved like that.

I think now about this period, this time in which my father
seems to have disappeared, and wonder if his imagined absence
comes down to the strange patchiness of childhood memories
or if it's a sign of traumatic amnesia, for there is evidence to the
contrary. My brother insists we saw him regularly, but when
my father and I recently tried to piece it together with the
aid of our mutually dodgy memories he confirmed that there
would have been long periods in which we saw little of each
other and times when we didn't see each other at all while he
was travelling overseas or living in Gosford and Queensland.
In any event, I have no recollections of spending time with
him until several years later, when I was around nine, and he
would come on Sundays (I don't recall ever spending whole
weekends with him). Not every Sunday, but some Sundays,
occasional Sundays (again my memory is hazy here – it seems

as if I could count the visits on my fingers, but I suspect there were more than that).

When he did show up on Sundays, every few months (or was it weeks?), I was torn between dread and anticipation. I lived for those torturous visits, counting the days to when I would have a father and hoping that this time he'd be the father I wanted, the father I saw other girls having, the father for whom I would be the Most Important Thing.

He comes to visit. I wear my favourite outfit and wonder where we'll go. He arrives, chats to my mother from the armchair, and then settles down to read. I am bored and bereft.

He comes to visit. He takes me across the bridge to a big house. There are no children. The grown-ups talk and their conversation is white noise. I do not exist. Classical music plays in the background. I sit in a beanbag. I like the beanbag, but there's nothing to do. I listen to my father talk and understand nothing of what he says. People seem to like him, look up to him. I'm not sure why, but I like it. Maybe it means he's special. Maybe it means I'm special.

Sometimes I felt proud of him without knowing why, or as if I would be proud if he were my father, if I had a father. There were moments when I thought he was proud of me too, especially about the dancing, so I danced harder, lulling myself to sleep with visions of dancing on a grand stage, the star, with my family, if I had a family, in the audience, applauding, and the sound of that applause was the sound of being good enough.

He comes to visit, and sometimes he surprises me with fun, or rather I have accidental fun when I'm with him. This happens when he takes me to places where there are other children to play with and adults who fuss over and entertain me.

He takes me to lunch at exotic restaurants. I don't want to go. He never asks where I want to go, what I want to do, what I'd like to eat. He wants me to try food I don't like the look of. I don't want to. He is disappointed I am like this. He insists.

I eat unenthusiastically. I don't like the food. He makes me try something else. I hate it and I want to go home. He goes quiet.

Years later, when I was in my forties, we had a candid conversation, during which my father admitted he didn't like me as a child. There were differences of opinion between him and my mother and grandparents, differences regarding diet, discipline and other aspects of child-rearing. He disliked the effects of my mother's indulgences and my grandparents' spoiling. He felt sidelined, cut out, disrespected. He thought I preferred my mother and grandparents (I did). He gave up. He let them have me. And he disapproved of the person I became under their influence.

It's common sense that the absence of approval and the withholding of affirmation will negatively affect a child and likely cause problems later in life, but can it qualify as traumatic, given trauma's association with shock and extreme events? This lack of admiration was not a blunt-force trauma to the psyche. Most of the time it was a diffusive, amorphous, permeating injury rather than a jarring or violent one, though there were moments I felt it acutely, moments when a critical word or a timely silence or a loveless look would pierce my being to its core and make its pointy, permanent mark.

My father wasn't intentionally mean. He wasn't mean at all. He tried, in his way, to be caring, to reach me, but he never quite met me where I was. His own historical wounds and conditioning gave rise to a subtle form of neglect, part frequent physical absence and part constant emotional disconnect. It's unfair to expect caregivers to meet the emotional needs of their charges day in and day out without faltering. Even the very best unavoidably fail sometimes to meet the needs of those in their care, so where and how do we draw the line as to what constitutes neglect?

In *Running on Empty*, Dr Jonice Webb describes emotional neglect as an 'invisible force' defined by a parent's failure to respond *enough* to a child's emotional needs. Webb views this type of neglect as the opposite of the overt mistreatment commonly associated with child abuse, in that maltreatment is characterised by parental acts, whereas emotional neglect involves an absence of affective connection. This unmemorable failure to 'notice, attend to, and respond appropriately to a child's feelings', this act of omission, becomes 'the white space in the family picture', the 'background rather than the foreground' of loss, a holding pattern of trauma around needs and wants that one may not even be conscious of having had. So while in the foreground I experienced my mother's chaotic relationships with violent and alcoholic men as disconcerting at best and annihilating at worst, in the background my father's emotional neglect erased me.

My father's rejection was compounded when he remarried and his new wife gave birth to a baby daughter. I figured he'd traded us in for superior models. My sister and I have since swapped notes and it seems she shared many of my experiences of his fathering as a child, but at the time it looked to me as if she got the father I had always wanted. I tried to understand why he seemed to love her and not me. I wanted a sister but not like that. I imagined she was better than me in ways I couldn't see. He more or less disappeared out of my life again when they moved interstate.

The English Ex-junkie (two-and-a-half years): sweet and numb and chronically late. Is anybody home? Back and forth and around and about we went until I looked at him and saw the place where my father was not. There's the wound!

I was in my early years of sobriety when I took up with The English Ex-junkie, whom I'd met (it does not get any more clichéd or doomed than this) in detox. It was my first attempt at forming and maintaining a relationship without the aid of substances and though it was, overall, more 'functional' than previous relationships by virtue of not being blacked out or drug-fucked, it hurt. I was slowly coming to the realisation that I was attracted to 'emotionally unavailable men', as the old standard goes. It was the first time in my life I had experienced the pain of this pattern without self-medicating and I found myself spiralling into states of emotional turmoil, sometimes even without an identifiable trigger. I came across a word for this whirlpool: abandonment. One of my best therapists once said that an adult cannot be abandoned, only left, because an adult is not subject to the same dependence-for-survival as a child, and is at a far more sophisticated stage of development with which to deal with a separation or a relational rupture, even a traumatic one. Only children can be abandoned, but people who experience significant enough levels of caregiver abandonment as children are often and more readily triggered into a traumatic re-experiencing of earlier, formative abandonment in the context of a present-day circumstance (the past in the present). I learned that I was highly susceptible to these 'abandonment triggers' and came to realise that once sufficiently bonded to another I lived in perpetual fear of it, and in hyper-vigilant reaction to any hint of it. Yet the knowledge that I didn't need to fear it because it had already happened, way back when I was a kid, was little consolation because I continued to re-create it, or hallucinate it (the past in the present) in visions so real I lost touch with any other reality. I fell for emotionally undependable men and then became excessively dependent in a paradox that wedged me firmly between the proverbial rock and hard place.

I first came across the teachings of John Bradshaw when my coupling with The English Ex-junkie was in its death throes. Bradshaw, who died aged eighty-two in 2016, had been, like me, a teenaged problem drinker. After fleeing the monastery where he spent his young adulthood, he became an author, therapist, public lecturer and self-confessed 'compulsive intellectual'. His 'Where Are You Father?' talk came as a revelation at the time, helping me connect the dots between my childhood experiences with men and my adult experiences with men. Unlike many of the self-help formulations of the day, Bradshaw didn't figure the family as an isolated unit in an otherwise apparently well-functioning society; he called patriarchy to account.

Bradshaw's central thesis is that aeons of traumatising patriarchy has resulted in generationally cyclical conditionings and trauma-bound woundings across the gender spectrum (my inclusive adaptation of his rather more traditional and binary view of gender). Generation after generation of men, pitted against one another in war and business, inherit the patterning of an outdated patriarchal masculinity that 'hides behind prestige, money, and power', prohibits affective encounter, expression and vulnerability, and cripples the very capacities needed for intimate relationship and healthy familial bonding.

There were critics who, cynical of any text and figure associated with the genre of self-help, baulked at his impassioned evangelistic Texan drawl (Bradshaw had spent time in a seminary, which was why preaching had a marked bearing on his masterful oration). Many declared him a charlatan, erroneously assuming he was cut of the same cloth as Tony Robbins on account of his stage presence and ability to draw a crowd. Even *The Simpsons* took the piss out of him in a classic episode called 'Bart's Inner Child'. I understood these reactions, but nevertheless I found solace and sense in Bradshaw, and to this day he stands above the pack in my mind. Unlike Robbins, Bradshaw never promised anyone a trauma-free rose garden. He didn't charge exorbitant prices for his workshops or greet pre-hyped audiences with hyper-masculinist gestures, and he freely admitted that his do-good public works came with regular ego-strokes. He was an intellectually sophisticated and compassionate cultural critic and trauma worker who addressed us as equals in a mutual struggle for harmony and happiness. 'In many ways I failed my son and stepdaughter as a father, even though I was a family therapist and a dedicated father,' Bradshaw said frankly in an interview with Sherry Von Ohlsen. 'I had grown up fatherless. My father was an alcoholic who abandoned the family. I didn't have a father model. I wasn't there emotionally for my son a lot because I didn't know what my emotions were.'

Slowly, over time and in light of myriad influences, I began to identify the effects of my father's absence and rejection on both my childhood and floundering relationships as an adult. I realised my father's abandonment and neglect helped create the conditions for the overtly traumatising experiences of growing up with my mother's alcoholic and violent post-divorce partners – not just, or even, in his initial leaving, but in his failure to engage with me enough to earn my trust and know what was taking place in my home life, and in his failure to intervene on my behalf. I gained some understanding of the way men – and more specifically my father, brother, grandfathers, partners and lovers – had been set up to be socially shamed out of vulnerability and empathy. It dawned on me that trauma isn't always splashy or overt: that it can be inscribed by lack as much as by action, and instilled by what is not done as much as by what is done. Neglect – including emotional neglect – thus becomes an under-the-radar form of trauma that often eludes detection. And I came to see how traumatic formative relational experience establishes destructive patterns – 'scripts', Tomkins called them – for adult relationships, which are further traumatising, or at least re-traumatising in that they trigger CPTSD-bound reactions, feelings and behaviours. Patriarchy and the 'father wound': it all made sense.

The challenge, Bradshaw maintained, was to, individually and as a society, acknowledge traumatic patterning, to grieve traumatic losses (he called this 'grief work'), and create new ways of being and relating, new kinds of masculinity and gender politics through lives and communities committed to healing and to developing the capacity to love. To some degree this *is* taking place, but resistance is strong in some quarters and progress is blighted by agendas of sabotage and nostalgia (chiefly among white men, but also among women suffering internalised sexism and Stockholm syndrome), backlash and ignorance. Bradshaw was out front in saying it would take conscious commitment and effort to undo the conditionings of patriarchy and to address a personal legacy of trauma, work that is hindered by denial, laziness and self-serving attachments to patriarchal payoffs.

Despite his contention that for most of us the gains we make in the face of traumatic legacies require perseverance and labour, he did concede to the possibility of 'spontaneous remissions' from severe or chronic childhood trauma, admitting in an interview to Veronica Hay that 'lots of people work through this stuff just out of their own experience and pain'. Having tried to do so unsuccessfully during his time at the seminary, he cautioned against putting the cart before the horse in terms of turning to religion or spiritual teachings (often rooted in patriarchal worldviews and scriptures) as a salve for the sufferings of chronic trauma. For some, he said, the tendency was to seek spiritual enlightenment as a cure-all to unresolved trauma rather than do 'the pain work' (by which he meant allowing previously repressed emotion to surface) in the human realm. 'I don't deny that someone could go into metaphysics and do the healing of this,' he told Hay, 'but my own experience has been that a lot of people go into various spiritual disciplines and they become what the Germans call "air people" – they're not grounded.' My father was not an air person – though I have seen such people at ashrams and Buddhist monasteries (they have a certain set smile, a saccharine niceness, a floaty benevolence I find hard to trust), but he did take refuge in spiritual teachings in refusal of the messy, oft-ugly business of affect and the struggle of human relationship. There were times when I felt this every bit as much of a barrier to our intimacy as if he'd been an alcoholic like his brother Hugh.

As *The Simpsons* take-down of Bradshaw demonstrates, the concept of the 'inner child', which came to the fore in the 1980s, is an easy target for ridicule (and sometimes justifiably so – like any conceptual/linguistic metaphor, its viability and respectability depend on the way in which it is presented and configured). Unless you've been living under a rock for the past few decades, you'll know that 'inner child work', as it's sometimes referred to, charts a way of attending to childhood trauma from the vantage point of adulthood. In his book *Homecoming*, Bradshaw claimed the benefit of nurturing and learning to, in pop psychology parlance, 're-parent' the 'wounded inner child' was a release of creative energy and the emergence of an essential, most valuable aspect of self, which Carl Jung termed 'the wonder child'. Some people manage to manifest the wonder child despite chronic or extreme traumatic childhood experiences, and Bradshaw gave Veronica Hay the example of Rainer Maria Rilke, whose mother had wanted a girl (hence his middle name). Bradshaw told it this way: Rilke's mother would say, 'Is that the wonderful Maria at the door or the horrible little Rainer?' Rainer would, of course, reply that it was Maria. 'You either grow up to be a great poet, or terribly screwed up. Rilke became a great poet,' he concluded. I became your garden-variety, terribly screwed-up poet.

Much of what Bradshaw said about fathering still rings true for me, but there are flies in the ointment, the most obvious being the apparent heteronormativity of his reading. He never disqualified outright the potential for gay, lesbian, trans and non-binary people to form families, nor did he express any overt bigotry, but his lectures and writings assumed cis and het figurings of caregiver roles. To be fair, though, we need remember that general awareness of the diversity spectrum was far more limited in the 1980s and '90s than it is today. His positioning of the father as crucial might appear to contribute to the problematic belief that any father is better than none. Headline after headline says otherwise: eleven-year-old Luke Batty is beaten to death by his father with a cricket bat at a sporting event. A Father's Day visit ends in suspected murder-suicide. A mother says the accused murderer was a 'loving father' to her children.

Bradshaw is right to identify a woundedness born of absence, physical and/or emotional, that is especially pronounced in a society that promotes a nuclear-family ideal of normal, but he disavows an obligatory duty to parents, acknowledging that, for some, parental presence can be far more wounding. Despite his focus on the damaging 'father wound', he questioned societal sentiment regarding parental reverence, telling Hay that he 'was taught as a child to obey any adult simply because they were an adult'. This is, he stressed, a recipe for enabling child abuse. 'We have been so indoctrinated into honouring Mom and Dad, which can be really dangerous. Obedience without content is very dangerous.'

My father was not dangerous, but neither did he make me feel safe. I knew he meant me no harm. He would never hurt me the way some men hurt children, never do to me (or her) what my mother's boyfriends had done, but I also knew he did not protect me. He was not, as Bradshaw's fellow Texan pop psychologist Dr Phil likes to put it, 'a soft place to fall'.

He comes to visit and announces he's taking me to the movies. I am excited. I love the movies. We have never been before. We drive to the theatre and he buys the tickets and we sit in the dark. I am twelve. It's *Barry Lyndon*. I can't follow and find it dull. It seems to go on for.ev.er.

In the summer he takes me swimming. He knows secret little beaches around the harbour and often we find ourselves alone. I like these outings but, despite my child's affinity with sun and water play, I never quite relax in his presence. Lying side by side on the sand, hot rays burning down, I'm still fretting over what he thinks of me, if he thinks of me, and what he thinks is wrong with me.

Every now and then he makes an effort to take me somewhere

both entertaining and educational, like The Rocks. We visit the Argyle Arts Centre, where we watch a man glassblowing and have a novelty photo taken, pretending to be of the nineteenth century. My father makes a fine gentleman patriarch of the Industrial Revolution. I make a suitably sullen pre-suffragette daughter.

I didn't notice The Son of the Holocaust Survivor (Act I: eighteen months) at first, but when he held me in his sea-sand eyes I felt myself divine. When he looked away I vanished and after that all I could see was the speed of his light. There was no lack of void. It was a crying shame.

We were smitten, The Son of the Holocaust Survivor and I. It was the first profound connection I had known since The Idol, so why didn't it work? We both came from 'broken homes', but plenty of long-term, successful unions are forged by people from fractured families. There was more to it than that. You guessed it.

His father was born a Hungarian Jew and, as a child, lost many family members to the camps, a fate he escaped by being sent to Transylvania to live with Protestant relatives. His grandfather in Budapest was conscripted into the German army and died at Stalingrad on the Russian front. As for his mother, well, she bailed at the tail end of the second wave in a fit of women's lib, leaving him and his younger sister in the care of their survivor dad, though in the spirit of challenging simplistic narratives about mothers who abandon their children we can perhaps assume there was more to it than this official family account allows. You wouldn't guess any of that to meet him. You'd likely be dazzled, as I was, by his smarts, his high-voltage smile, his quick wit and warmth. He was a pockmarked Lou Reed lookalike and a charmer. We laughed and frolicked through that summer, holing up in his room at night, fusing a deep, beatific bond that within a year became an airless trap, a boxing ring in which we threw verbal hooks till we collapsed back between the posts.

Drawing on the work of neuropsychologist Daniel J. Siegel and *Brain-Wise* author Bonnie Badenoch, Sharie Stines discusses the 'painful consequence of interrelational disconnection' that most of us, even those in the happiest of unions, have experienced.

These theories and clinical frameworks pay particular attention to the way trauma affects neurology and the nervous system, in turn manifesting in relationships as dysfunctional and conflict-based behaviours that over time cement into patterns that seem impossible to break. Badenoch conceptualises the systems theory commonly used in couples and family therapy into a multidisciplinary take on 'interpersonal neurobiology' that includes a focus on attachment styles, the 'neurobiology of shame' and a therapeutic engagement with the 'inner community' – a subjective multiplicity, formed in childhood, and adapted throughout adulthood. 'When a person is not properly attuned to as a child, secure attachment and healthy connection do not occur,' Stines explains. Traumas relating to insecure attachment surface when the honeymoon phase passes: cue corresponding painful consequences of interrelational disconnection.

Bradshaw calls the inevitable individuating phase of an intimate relationship 'the Hatfields vs. the McCoys'. No longer on a high, secure enough to risk not being on best behaviour, and cast out of the Garden of Eden of early bonding, couples find pesky differences emerging amid their familiarity and start bickering over how things should get done, how the kids should be raised, and how and in what measure they fall short of each other's expectations. The testy task of individuating while retaining a capacity for intimacy now begins, the Holy Grail of which is individual maturation and relational interdependency. But beneath surface tensions around daily rituals and damp towels left on bathroom floors, a more troubling Pandora's box of unmet childhood needs, abandonments and unconscious traumas jacks open.

A process of negotiating these trials ensues for each person and each couple somewhere on a sliding scale of consciousness and 'dysfunction'. If attempts at resolution prove unsuccessful or inadequate, either the intensity level ratchets up or one or both parties in the relationship retreat. Bradshaw coined the clever catchphrase 'Post-Romantic Stress Disorder' to describe the meeting of human-condition relational challenges and trauma-bound interference.

Trauma hinders emotional regulation, so it stands to reason that severely and chronically traumatised people often struggle to acclimatise in relationships. 'Unresolved trauma,' Stines says, 'contributes to persistent chaos and rigidity and inflexibility to adapt to the circumstance of present interactions.' In my adolescence and early adulthood, I was chaotic, perhaps mirroring and manifesting the tumultuous aspects of my childhood, but when I gave up drugs and alcohol I found out just how rigid, inflexible and fearful I could be. I became multi-phobic and unbecomingly uptight. These CPTSD symptoms fluctuate on a continuum, dependent on many factors, including general stress levels. Even now, I'm a high-functioning agoraphobe; even though I don't fit the stereotype of the housebound shut-in, peering out from behind a closed curtain, I hate being in crowds and I often feel unsafe in environments others view as routine. I have a fear of flying, and exhibit OCD-like symptoms around the house, craving cleanliness, order and impossible-to-attain-and-maintain perfection. It was decades before I understood the connection between my history of trauma and familial violence and this pathological need for order and control. The first signs set in soon after Al left: I began to ritualistically prepare for school each night, painstakingly ironing and laying out my uniform over a dining room chair and arranging all the other items I would need in a particular, precise formation on the dining table. These obsessive–compulsive behaviours came, and still come, with a payoff. I experience relief when I sense I have re-established order in some way. It feels as if I can finally – at least momentarily – relax (until the next threat of disorder attracts my attention). Intellectually I know this is illusory folly, that there can be no absolute order, no sustainable cleanliness, no guarantee of safety, but trauma is nothing if not illogical. Since I no longer live with violence, my deeply ingrained hyper-vigilance manifests around ridiculous trifles – a cup where it ought not to be, the affront of dust collecting on the surface of the piano, an insistence on the kitchen sink being wiped down to a gleaming finish. This means that, unchecked, I am domestically unreasonable.

Medicated – drunk, stoned or otherwise anaesthetised – none of this manifested. Back when I drank and did drugs I cared not for the minutiae of my abode. I walked around alone at all hours of the day, went out often and socialised madly, staying out for days at a time. I did not generally fear for my personal safety; in fact, I exhibited high-risk and sometimes downright hazardous behaviours, such as habitually walking out into heavy speeding traffic without looking left or right, cocktailing my drugs in life-threatening combinations, and occasionally partying with low-lifes and criminals. Sober, a different self emerged, one that I hardly recognised. A self preoccupied with safety (and perceived threats to it); a self who felt compelled to line shoes up against the wall with military-like precision, who found routine reassuring, who did Quixote-like battle with cat hair. I felt this version of myself was every bit as shameful as the out-of-control girl who blacked out and conned and game-played her way through life. In many respects this incarnation is still harder to live down than the deluded drug-ravaged one of my youth, which at least came with the balm of denial, and which has, in some circles, a little purchase on cool and romanticism.

Integration, according to Stines, requires synergy between the two types of memory – implicit and explicit. She explains: 'Implicit memory is perceptual, emotional, interactive, sensory, mental modelling, and priming. It is not aware of time. When a person experiences an implicit memory it feels as if it is happening in the now.' This is in contrast to explicit memory, which places the recollection in its historical, factual context: 'the person realizes that something is being recalled from the past'. In PTSD, implicit

:es hold, resulting in visceral sensations of the past that
) overwhelming, excruciating implosions of affect –
olence.

it parts of the brain are involved in the two types of
memory. The amygdala – an almond-shaped cluster of neurons
nestled deep in the brain – is crucial to implicit memory, and
also controls our reactions to external stimuli. As Stines puts it,
it is the 'alert system in the brain', and when it over-fires it can
lead to anxiety. Explicit memory, on the other hand, is controlled
by the hippocampus – elongated and ridge-like along the lateral
ventricles – which is the part of the brain that connects history
to memory. In order to make sense of the past, we need the
'intention, organization, and categorization' that explicit memory
enables, especially if the raw emotional aftershocks of trauma have
dominated via implicit memory.

Stines cites research suggesting that amygdala activity
decreases when a person can 'name an emotion accurately'.
In studies, this kind of internal labelling was associated with
the activation of the middle prefrontal cortex and ventrolateral
prefrontal cortex, which led to the release of inhibitory
transmitters that modulate the amygdala's response and,
perhaps, the subject's anxiety. Siegel, notes Stines, refers to this
process as 'name it to tame it'. This is, of course, nothing new
in a sense, harking back to the fundamentals of psychoanalytic
'talk therapy', which has long established the importance of
linguistic communication in addressing trauma-induced states
and neurosis.

For a couple who decide to seek help, there are now
myriad therapeutic models on offer, some departing from this
cognitive-focused approach and its narrative bent. Regardless
of the methodology, they all rely on neuroplasticity, or the
brain's potential for change. Stines says that 'attuned, empathic
relationships are what can aid in rewiring broken neural circuits',
which is why friendship, reading, therapy and support groups

(granted, not all therapeutic settings and support groups are places of healing) help many traumatised people. And it's also why tackling trauma in the context of a committed, intimate relationship, when both parties are willing to do so, can be especially soothing and rewarding. My longing to undertake that project with The Son of the Holocaust Survivor wasn't fulfilled. We were trapped in a power struggle we didn't understand.

When I was down for the count after several rounds with him, I came across a book by Pia Mellody, a vocal public advocate of twelve-step recovery programs. An addiction and relationships educator, Mellody is a senior clinical advisor at The Meadows in Arizona, a multi-disorder facility that has been a model for inpatient services the world over – it specialises in the treatment of trauma via tailor-made therapies. Mellody has written numerous self-help titles, including *Facing Love Addiction*, which I initially greeted with the usual combination of disdain and desperation that I reserved for books of this genre. When I started reading it, however, I readily identified my own reactions, and my partner's, in the destructive dynamic she outlined. A preface to introducing Mellody's thesis: the love addict–avoidant dichotomy is a broad conceptualisation of trauma-bound relational dynamics. As such, it's a framework that needs to be handled with care. Bleached of specificity and nuance, it can be applied too literally and heavy-handedly, as if we complex beings were a homogeneous mass easily split into two pre-fab typecasts, and as if there aren't shades of grey and surprises and slippages that unsettle such formulations.

Mellody describes relationship co-addiction as a debilitating and progressive process in which both partners compulsively play out the roles childhood experience has primed them for. One partner tends to crave love as a result of neglect or abandonment in formative years, having formed a survival fantasy that somebody (my father; the past in the present) will show up to fill the void, rescuing them from loneliness and the isolation of traumatic shame, and affirming that they matter. 'Love addicts', Mellody explains, unconsciously choose partners prone to 'avoidance': inclined to be unresponsive, to neglect the relationship, and to actively avoid the intimacy and enmeshment the love addict seeks. Though there are warning signs from the start, the love addict – in a state that combines the ingrained rescue fantasy with transference – initially denies the reality of their partner's unavailability.

When cracks inevitably appear in that denial, the love addict ramps up efforts to secure the attention and affection of the avoiding other. This happens even when there are opposing commitments: in the psyche of an ardent feminist, for example, or someone who intellectually values independence and self-sufficiency. Shit gets cray cray, escalating out of control, because the more the love addict pursues, the faster and further the avoidant runs, and the more the avoidant runs, blocks and walls off, the more the love addict pursues and hammers, flipping between manipulative and more overtly controlling strategies. Both roles play out across the gender spectrum but, with aeons of patriarchal conditioning, women are more prone to, and commonly identify with, love addiction, and men are more prone to, and commonly identify with, avoidance. Whichever way you cut it, the trajectory of each partner is rooted in formative traumata.

We crashed and burned. On the rebound, The Son of the Holocaust Survivor hooked up with a chic seventeen-year-old. I tried to weather the emotional fallout, but faltered and, demented with anguish, took up with Mr Wrong (five years). He stormed around the stage, part Pozzo, part Lucky. You find it tedious? He was younger than me and twisted by rage that simmered daily. Determined to be a better man than his brutish father and loathing of woman-beaters, he was loyal and could be caring (once driving from Brisbane to Sydney in one stretch to be with me when my mother was dying). But he was wrong for me and I got stuck. Scared of being alone I took the coward's respite and years passed, moving between restless sleep and discontented wakefulness.

The union of two people with corresponding traumas is, John Bradshaw insists, no accident. As he explained to Hay, it's the central paradox of an adult relationship informed by childhood trauma: 'A woman will find a man who basically treats her in the rejecting way that her father treated her ... A guy that had a controlling, dominating mother who hated it, marries a woman that's controlling and dominating.' It's not always quite so clear-cut or obvious. Sometimes people go the other way and choose a partner who seems to be the opposite of what they grew up with, but that can lead to a different set of problems or a mere reversal of roles in the dynamic.

During this draining dance, cycles of intensity and 'bombing' – acts or exchanges designed to engage the other, albeit in a dramatic manner – and withdrawal take the place of healthy intimacy and communication. According to Mellody, love addicts are often attracted to people with process (work, sex, gambling, gaming, etc.) or substance addictions. Through their process or substance addiction, the avoidant partner seeks to medicate their childhood history of engulfment by a needy, possessive or domineering caregiver, while the love addict seeks to medicate their childhood history of neglect or abandonment by obsessing about their partner. In other words, the love addict is addicted to the avoidant partner, who is addicted to [insert addiction of choice here].

When love addicts go cold turkey – either when their partner leaves, or when they end the relationship in an effort to maintain or reclaim their sanity and dignity – they experience harrowing pain and may seek relief in other people, other addictions, suicide or some form of revenge. Hard-core love addicts frequently end up dying prematurely, or being institutionalised in prisons and psych wards, and, according to Mellody, this dynamic underlies many cases of intimate-partner violence.

The tragedy is that both the love addict and love avoidant share the same fundamental fears of abandonment and engulfment, though they operate in different orders of priority. The primary fear for the love addict is abandonment and the flipside fear of engulfment lies dormant so long as the desired other is significantly unavailable. Conversely, the love avoidant predominantly fears engulfment until and unless the other pulls away, triggering a latent fear of abandonment. These secondary fears are not as baffling as they might at first seem because, as the theory goes, being engulfed by a caregiver as a child also involves abandonment since being forced to meet the needs of an adult means critical childhood needs go unmet, and for a person perversely bonded to abandonment and unaccustomed to deeper experiences of intimacy, it can, though craved, feel frightening and overwhelming. If two love addicts get together, they are likely to form a highly dependent and enmeshed relationship in which they lack individuation and differentiation. If two avoidants hook up, they usually form a very low-intensity relationship with minimal emotional engagement, each putting their addictions ahead of time and intimacy with one another. To make matters even more distressing and confusing, an individual can switch between love addiction and avoidance. When you get two people frequently doing that within the one relationship, it's loony tunes. If they're lucky, they'll break up or get to therapy.

Several of my significant relationships wound up in couples therapy. The ones that didn't weren't spared that fate because they were healthier, but because they were significantly less so. As seasoned at therapy as I became over the years, I still find partner therapy harder than any other to endure. If you're committed enough to each other, if you stay in the process long enough, if the relationship still has some juice in it, and if the therapist is any good, all the collusions and sickly micro-contracts, all the pettiness, the grudges, the housework gripes and ridiculous resentments come creeping out. You feel unbearably exposed, ambushed, ganged up on, misunderstood – and heard. The intimacy is, at times, intolerable, and in those moments when the dust settles you find yourself looking across the room at your partner and you see their suffering in its pulsing poignancy and you find out just how damn loveable they are. And of course, you discover your own story. You find out where it all began.

He comes to visit and takes me to my grandparents' place, where fairies live in the garden. My grandmother makes nice roasts and homemade ice-cream and I like the food. But I don't think she likes me. She grills me about my mother and she's always praising my aunt and cousins. They are prettier and cleverer and better in ways I can't see. My father leaves me alone with her in the sunroom for hours on end while he takes long naps and my grandfather tinkers away in the shed. I go home with tension migraines – until the day my mother announces he's not allowed to take me there anymore.

Sometimes I ask my mother why my father doesn't love me. He loves you, she tells me, he just doesn't like children – which is basically saying he doesn't like what and who I am. I try to understand. I do not exist. I do not have a father.

By the time my father returned from Brisbane after the collapse of his second marriage, I was a teenager, and it was my turn to disappear. In my compulsive travels, I all but forgot about him. He did not exist. I saw little of him in my comings and goings, and when I did it was the same as always, only I was older and I could escape and drink. I have a father. I am confused. I do not have a father.

In my late teens my father bought a property in an idyllic location in northern New South Wales. He transformed it into what he imagined to be a haven for the family come the Next

Big Depression. He badgered me to leave the city and move to the country. He built an extension that was never used and bought games for my brother's children that rotted unopened. It was his turn to wait. He spent almost two decades there alone and he did not understand. Eventually he moved closer to town and met a woman who did him a world of good, and with whom he now passes his days with great mutual respect and fondness.

I visit my father's house in my early twenties. He seems to want to bond, but I'm hard to reach and I remain uncomfortable in his presence. It's an unsettling mix of intimidation, unease and shame, and it renders me stilted at best and speechless at worst. He is disappointed I am like this. He drags me out on bushwalks, but I'm a city girl and I don't enjoy them. I feel a low, slow burn that I later identify as resentment. I do not feel I belong to him and yet he is of great importance to me. I no longer dance. I am depressed and I want to go home.

In my thirties, some years after I quit drinking, I went to live in a city nearer my father and for several years I saw more of him. There were times I found his presence surprisingly soothing. Age was mellowing him and loneliness was softening him, or maybe I was just growing up. I began to inhabit my skin. We became friends, even close. But the past in the present still continued when it came to my relationships with men. When it ended with Mr Wrong I went to live with my father while I finished my master's thesis and contemplated my next move. We hadn't lived together in decades, since I was four or five, but we made it work. Better: we forged a connection. It was as if we loved each other.

I married The New Yorker (six-and-a-half years) on a cold afternoon in February 2001 on the Upper East Side. I was thirty-seven and wore a champagne Audrey Hepburn dress from Barneys; the highlight of our small and hasty wedding was a gate-crashing by a posse of Long Island gossips, friends of his mother who showed up uninvited. We lived in Manhattan for two years before relocating to Sydney. He was a kind father figure, the kindest. We shared continents and lives for a time.

In many respects, that marriage was my most successful relationship to date. My American husband was smart, cultured, generous and gentle. He earned a decent income and was happy to financially support a writing wife struggling with chronic illness in the form of Hepatitis C, contracted years before during active addiction. It was a relatively peaceful union, but it failed to flourish. The honeymoon ended abruptly seven months after we wed, on a sunny Tuesday morning when terrorists flew two passenger planes into the Twin Towers of the World Trade Center, with a third hitting the Pentagon and a fourth crashing in a field in Pennsylvania. This event instantly triggered a major decline into severe CPTSD symptomology. For weeks I struggled to eat, battled diarrhoea and had trouble sleeping. Living through constant bomb scares and high alerts in Manhattan, the beating heart of the biggest city of the US, eroded the fragile sense of baseline safety I had managed to establish.

Large-scale traumatic events take place all the time, but never before had humanity experienced one quite like this. Wilfully causing horror and diabolical shock is inherent to terrorism – to conventional warfare too, but in terrorism the inflicting of trauma amid the general population is a prime objective, not regrettable collateral damage. The horror and diabolical shock of 9/11 was amplified by location: terror had struck New York and Washington, the centre of the so-called 'free world'. It was the first time a nation-state created in the image of white people had been directly and spectacularly attacked by a rogue entity. This was not the young man throwing rocks or the bus explosions by lone suicide bombers that had become routine in the protracted conflict of the Middle East, and nor was it traditional guerrilla warfare. This was a sophisticated and highly technologised organisation that had coordinated a suicidal visitation of multi-pronged mass destruction designed not only to kill and instil terror, but also to enact economic sabotage and unleash ideological mayhem. That this calamity unfolded in such a heavily mediatised period of civilisation resulted in real-time transmissions and a wildfire of affective distress – fear, anger, sadness – sweeping across the world, making the events of 9/11 an unprecedented global traumatic event that announced a new world order. Millions were traumatised in the world wars, in civil wars around the world, and in other long, brutal armed conflicts over aeons, but never before had so many far and wide been traumatised, to varying degrees, in one moment.

Katherine Harmon writes in *Scientific American*: 'Just watching television footage of the terrorist attacks of September 11, 2001, was enough to cause clinically diagnosable stress responses in some people who did not even live near the attacks – let alone the millions of people who did.' Quoting researchers Priscilla Dass-Brailsford and Yuval Neria, Harmon reports that traumatic reactions do not necessarily indicate PTSD, while the conventional wisdom on PTSD – that those closest to and most physically affected by an event will be the most traumatised by it – does not necessarily hold. Another article claims that while 90 per cent of people will experience traumatic stress in the wake of a major event like 9/11, symptoms gradually subside over a period of several weeks through a process of 'natural recovery'. In line with this, Harmon reports on a 2006 study in *The Journal of Nervous and Mental Disease* that showed PTSD rates in New York decreasing from about 5 per cent a year after 9/11 to 3.8 per cent two years later.

Socioeconomic factors are thought to play a part in the development and longevity of PTSD, along with the amount of graphic television footage people view (I still avoid watching footage of the planes hitting the towers). In 2011, *The New York Times* ran an article titled '10 Years and a Diagnosis Later, 9/11 Demons Haunt Thousands', in which Dr Margaret Dessau, who lives close to where the towers stood and witnessed the attacks first-hand, describes her experiences of trauma to journalist Anemona Hartocollis. Having heard the noise of the first hijacked plane hitting WTC 1, she had run naked from the shower, only to see the gaping hole in the tower. 'The flames get worse, and then I start seeing all these people hanging out there. The guy with this white towel, and he's waving it.' When he jumped, she heard children screaming from a nearby school. Therapy eventually helped ease Dessau's severe PTSD symptoms, but when her husband died in 2009 of lung cancer (possibly associated with the toxic fallout of the attack) Dessau found herself sliding backwards into the complicated grief and anxiety disorder often indicative of PTSD.

Hartocollis taps into the spooky resonance between stories of suffering when she writes that Dessau 'sees 9/11 and her husband's death as part of a continuum': Dessau's parents had escaped Nazi Germany, a relative had died by suicide, and she had been a student in Israel during the 1967 Arab–Israeli War. For Dessau, 9/11 was 'corroboration of the evil of human beings'. Hartocollis and Dessau gesture towards a principal reality: as random, as erratic, as crazed and surreal as events like 9/11 seem, they are, like the Arab–Israeli War, like Nazi Germany, like all of the mass traumatic events throughout history, grounded in the social system of patriarchy and its manifestations in institutionalised religion, politics, imperialism, and aggressive forms of liberalism and capitalism.

On the ground in New York in the aftermath, it seemed like everyone knew someone who had died in the attacks. In our case it was a family friend's son, who had been working in one of the towers. We heard many other accounts – from neighbours, conversations among passers-by, news reports. For many New Yorkers the eyewitness stories about the jumpers (those who jumped from the upper floors of the towers rather than burn) and the photos of 'the falling man' were the stuff of a wide-awake nightmare that, paradoxically, only dreamless sleep could relieve. There were scores of painful posters posted on buildings downtown, bearing once-smiling faces and pleading descriptions of the missing. For months afterwards I passed fire stations all over Manhattan with images of the fallen, wreaths of flowers, drawings from children and messages of gratitude. I thought of the helpers, galvanised and too busy to tend to their own trauma, of a city tenderised and unified by grief. At times it seemed like everyone I came upon was being braver than I was, but I knew that behind closed doors others were suffering unspeakable torments: I could only imagine the devastation of the families of those who were killed and the fresh PTSD of many who were closer than I was to Ground Zero on that infamous autumn day. I could only trouble over the injustices that American Muslims and other people of colour around the country faced, suddenly finding themselves cast as the enemy, abused or even murdered in hate crimes of deranged retaliation.

Born and raised in New York, my husband, along with millions of other Americans, must have felt the impact of 9/11 in ways I couldn't share. Even though I was living in Manhattan on the day of the attacks, they hit, in some psychic sense, on foreign soil: much as I loved New York, it did not yet feel like home. At the same time, I felt more directly threatened by the attacks than many of the Americans around me. It was a predicament both my husband and I struggled to make sense of. The months passed and his tolerance thinned. I felt ashamed and embarrassed that I was so disproportionately affected, and despite seeking counselling I remained in a state of hyper-vigilant anxiety until long after we left New York for Sydney. We relocated partly because my ageing grandparents were declining rapidly, but also because, in my unstitched state, I longed for whatever sense of security I could find, and that meant home.

I did what people so often do – I thought in terms of a hierarchy of suffering, concluding that I had no right to be as affected as I was, given the closest I came to danger was being on a bus travelling south towards the towers at the time of the attacks, before watching them fall in plumes of black smoke while standing in the shadow of the Empire State Building. I was waiting for my husband, who was making his way to me, along with the throngs of others fleeing downtown, so that we could get on a packed bus heading back uptown. Between the bus stop and our apartment building, we stopped to buy supplies at the near-empty store, which resembled a scene from one of those Armageddon films. We reached the sanctuary of our apartment, huddling in shock to watch the live coverage as the city shut down, bridges and tunnels closed, and fighter jets circled the sky overhead. I did what people so often do – I forgot to factor in the power of formative experience (the past in the present) and the difference between PTSD and CPTSD. As Judith Herman states:

> repeated trauma in childhood forms and deforms the personality. The child trapped in an abusive environment is faced with formidable tasks of adaptation. She must find a way to preserve a sense of trust in people who are untrustworthy, safety in a situation that is unsafe, control in a situation that is terrifyingly unpredictable, power in a situation of helplessness. Unable to care for or protect herself, she must compensate for the failures of adult care and protection with the only means at her disposal, an immature system of psychological defenses.

It felt as if I had been thrown back into this realm of immature psychological defences, as if at some level the healing or maturation or reasoned understanding I had achieved – patchy and incomplete at best – had been erased by the spectacular reminder on 9/11 of just how violent men can be, and just how unsafe our supposedly civilised society can be, despite the veneer of decency.

By the time my husband and I celebrated our first anniversary the damage was done; the fault lines had been exposed. There was a gulf between us that seemingly could not be traversed. Having grown up in a stable environment with no familial experience of violence, he found my reaction excessive, and hard as he tried he could not understand the tenacity of my distress and extra-heightened anxieties, which remained so for several years after that dark September. 'Most people,' continues Herman, 'have no knowledge or understanding of the psychological changes of captivity. Social judgment of chronically traumatized people therefore tends to be extremely harsh.' I don't blame my ex-husband for judging me, for being frustrated and falling short of meeting my endless neurosis with ample compassion. I judged myself just as harshly and felt equally frustrated by my seeming inability to snap out of the liminal tension between the traumatised past and the re-traumatising present, though I was also aware I was trapped inside it. I became increasingly lonely and isolated.

It's hard to know how the marriage might have panned out without that terrible day and its ongoing reverberations, but thinking back over my history with men I see an undeniable pattern of bonding followed by struggles around intimacy. Pia Mellody's figuring of love addiction offers some insights into understanding how the fundamental need for intimacy becomes deformed by early traumatic losses, re-emerging in adult life as an obsessive attempt to bridge a traumatic gap in relationship. In some ways, I successfully shut down that behaviour in my marriage to The New Yorker, but only by suppressing my need for intimacy. He was a rock in terms of commitment and stability, and attentive in his way, but despite being caring and sensitive he was, at some crucial level, also as emotionally impenetrable as a rock. I settled for the level of intimacy he was capable of and content with, but it meant sacrificing that desire for shared vulnerability, for emotional access, and it turned out that was a bigger sacrifice than I bargained for. I grew restless in a Madame Bovary kind of way, becoming persistently dissatisfied, depressive, and flirtatious with other men. It was a relatively tranquil relationship, but I felt a dogged irritation that increasingly erupted into angry outbursts, and most of the time I felt guilty for not being as happy as I thought I should be now that I enjoyed high-quality living, a partner everybody liked, and a share in a mortgage on a three-bedroom warehouse apartment in Surry Hills. We became more and more alienated from each other and I became more and more alienated from myself, and, as this twofold alienation gathered speed, the CPTSD symptoms that had flared up in the wake of 9/11 snowballed into frequent panic attacks. I became reliant on my husband for reassurance; in response, he behaved like an indulgent, resentfully repressed carer, measured impatience and impervious in the face of my inner turmoil. I was a mess of contradictions: child-like and leaning on him one minute, raging at him the next.

Among the many possible variables of a relationship, two dominant, negative models are often assigned to the committed het relationship: the domineering, controlling, possibly violent man to the submissive, oppressed little woman; and the angry, controlling woman to the sensitive, passive (and often passive–aggressive) man. If my relationships have tended towards one of these stereotypes it would be the second. I've lost count of the times I've witnessed a woman spoken of as a 'bitch' or a 'ballbuster', or how often I've heard a woman maligned for daring to be unsatisfied with the proffered passive alternative to traditional patriarchal machismo. Often politically left-leaning, this alternative man comes as a welcome relief from more toxic modes of masculinity, for he allows a woman independence and agency. She gets to express strength, and to define terms, but because the passive man is confused, ashamed of his kind, and suffering painful emotions from generations of patriarchal woundings, he represses his own strength and desire, lacks initiative, stays too safe, and lives on the surface. She wants more. He is baffled.

'A man works all his life to get it right, to be the strong, invulnerable warrior, and then someone says you've got it all wrong,' Bradshaw said in his interview with Sherry Von Ohlsen. He was speaking for the men of his generation, those who grew up trained to adopt patriarchal roles in the nuclear-het family only to have them upended by twentieth-century feminism. 'We men have been raised by women, and so our feelings about ourselves stem in large part from them. Women who have unresolved male issues affect how a male grows up to think about himself.' (But what woman can *not* have 'unresolved male issues' in a patriarchal society?) bell hooks reminds us that feminists began to use the word 'patriarchy' in place of 'sexism' and 'male chauvinism' as a conscious effort to highlight the ways in which patriarchy negatively affects everybody. She criticises 'antimale activists' for making men 'the enemy' instead of inviting them into a partnership in learning how to understand, and change, the deeply embedded and traumatically rooted attitudes and practices that perpetuate the cycle, generation in, generation out. When hooks says in *Feminist Theory*, 'Separatist ideology encourages women to ignore the negative impact of sexism on male personhood. It stresses polarization between the sexes', she's just warming up: 'Patriarchy promotes insanity,' she writes in *The Will To Change*. 'It is at the root of the psychological ills troubling men in our nation.' She also states: 'Until we can collectively acknowledge the damage patriarchy causes and the suffering it creates, we cannot address male pain. We cannot demand for men the right to be whole, to be givers and sustainers of life.'

Until the damage patriarchy causes and the suffering it creates is collectively acknowledged and formally stunted, toxic or neutered masculinities will continue to proliferate. There are exceptions and we need men who have forged, or are forging, new masculinities and capacities. Women, feminists, need to work with them, to acknowledge them. There's a difference between being expected to 'hand out cookies' every time a man isn't an arse and due recognition and regard.

When The New Yorker and I took our tattered marriage to counselling, it slowly dawned on us that we didn't seem to have a future. I wanted more (though I couldn't be sure if this wasn't a sign of my tendency to be discontented). There is no more, he said, this is it, this is all I am, all I got. Friends were shocked to hear me talk of leaving. It made no sense. And then one night in my early forties, as we made our way towards that conclusion, I was woken by a dream.

The Son of the Holocaust Survivor (Act II: twenty months) had grown paler and weary. The sand-sea eyes searched my face as if they'd found home. Why don't we hang ourselves? It was not a question of trust. Nor forgiveness. Apparitions – made flesh what were we? Alive? We dwelled in parallel dimensions, him married with child in the outer suburbs, me married, childless, urban.

I initiated a separation and my husband put up no fight. The Son of the Holocaust Survivor tried leaving his rotting marriage. He spoke of her, how she clung on, playing the child-pawn, one grim move after another. He flailed in limbo and then conceded defeat. He couldn't leave the boy like his mother had left him.

It was a question of faith. We lay in the darkened bedroom of my apartment, where I was living alone for the first time in years. I told him I would not see him again and I asked how I would go on without him. 'Think of me as dead,' he said, 'because I will be.' Then, and for the last time, he went home to the suburbs and his miserable wife. Astride a grave and a difficult birth.

It was then, in the following weeks, that I started to stop waiting for my father (the past in the present). There were nights when the upstairs neighbours would start. Nights when, no longer waiting, alone in the darkened room, I would hear them and plead telepathically: please, not tonight. Lying there, willing my neighbours to stop, I'd remember the way The Son of the Holocaust Survivor sometimes opened me up so much I'd cry when I came. *Think of me as dead*, he'd said. Then it would be over and quiet. You can tell a lot about a person by the way they come.

I cried for months after I turned him away, could barely manage routine daily tasks. I knew it was not just about the end of the affair and my marriage, but about the traumatic grief around the men of my childhood, and most especially my father, as it finally surfaced. It had made its way to light before, but I'd always managed to outrun it, to introduce yet another man into the space it demanded. This time it would not be stopped, and I had lost steam in trying to stop it. I had what my grandmother would have called a nervous breakdown. I think of it more as an exposé, a rite of passage, a trial by fire. The floodgates broke and there was no stemming the gushing flow.

I am standing in the centre of my apartment so assailed by pain I want to die (I should not exist). I don't know what to do, where to go, and can't think straight to gather my things and get out the door. I don't know what to do so I stand there, staring ahead. Without thought, without intention, I cross the room and watch as my hand reaches for the phone. By the time my father answers I am sobbing uncontrollably. He says hello and I hear myself speak, the words coming out all on their own, breaking soft through the snot and the tears and the hard-to-breathe breath: why didn't you love me when I was a child? Oh my darling girl, he says.

I have a father.

We talked. I told him about the waiting and the men. He told me what went on behind the scenes, the marital theatrics and the back-story I'd never known, his errors of judgement, his regrets.

I didn't think I'd be missed, he said. We counted the cost. For the first time I understood his life as a younger man, the other side of his failure to father in the way I needed, and I felt relief and I felt forgiving, but I couldn't stop weeping. I spent a week in a psychiatric hospital. After I returned home, for the next two years, in the eternal time of passing nights in the darkened room while listening to my neighbours fuck, I was alone.

There have been many men. I have a father and I have never loved him more than I do now. It is not for nothing I lived through this long day. Sometimes I am the happiest girl in the world. *Think of me as living.*

But when I reflect on the men I shared my life with, between my sexual awakening with The Idol at twenty and the gruelling grieving of my mid-forties, I'm still not sure how much of what passed between us was desire, love or addiction.

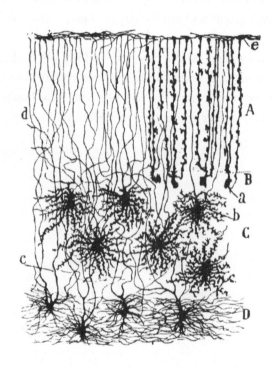

Looking back, it's easy to see that the demise of my relationship with The Idol, my first ardour, my first true fuck, was what finally brought me undone.

I'd already weathered a speed bender during the course of our relationship, between the ages of twenty-one and twenty-three, mainlining till I saw glimpses of speed psychosis and reached a paranoid, whimpering end, by which point heroin had become my go-to crutch. I didn't think myself a proper junkie, supposing I wasn't as bad as some of the people I ran with. I was a lowly poly-addict, not tough or street or armoured like the hardcore junkies, but more unruly than the lightweights and more blatantly self-destructive than your average dedicated 'alchy', for I thought nothing of consuming lethal chemical cocktails, the kind that left a friend's twentysomething sister with brain damage so severe she's spent the past few decades being cared for in a nursing home. I didn't think myself a proper junkie, insisting I had class, that there were things I wouldn't do for a fix (in rehab they called these 'yets'). Is there any way to avoid cliché? This is not about *my* numbing. It's about the big numbing: patriarchy, with its endemic traumata.

How Childhood Trauma Creates Life-long Adult Addicts (The Fix)

The US-based organisation Addiction Campuses, a Christian network of comprehensive addiction treatment services, set out to determine which kind of traumatic experience would most likely lead to a substance addiction. An Addiction Campuses blog post by Brittany Meadows rhetorically poses an extended question: do particular traumatic experiences have links with particular substances? I say rhetorical, because they go on to conclude, without citing actual studies, that the obvious answer is that 'any type of trauma can be just as damaging as the next'. Trauma affects individuals differently: you and I might experience the same event with one of us emerging traumatised and the other relatively unscathed; according to the piece, 'the crucial factor isn't what the event was, but how the person perceived and was able [or not able] to cope with it'. We don't usually get to choose our formative traumas, but most addicts have a 'drug of choice'. Even those not socially tagged as addicts tend to lean on something: those extra glasses of wine at the end of a hard day, that shopping binge when you're feeling blue, the work jag that leaves you depleted and alienated from the family. What's your poison?

We don't usually get to choose our formative traumas, but they're what sticks most. In *The Argonauts*, Maggie Nelson quotes psychoanalyst Donald Winnicott: 'Babies do not remember being held well – what they remember is the traumatic experience of not being held well enough.' That is to say that the met need does not wound, and even if you don't 'remember' a traumatic experience, even if you suffer from traumatic amnesia, it has wounded and has been registered in implicit memory. For Nelson, Winnicott's observation is an incitement, an invitation to the maternal goal to leave her child no memory, by which she means no traumatic memory (whether that memory be conscious or remain buried even in the midst of its raising hell).

Having qualified their position, the Addiction Campuses' 'addiction professionals' go on to list some of the traumatic experiences most commonly associated with addiction: sexual assault, emotional and/or physical child abuse, 'complicated' grief (which is when the normal grieving process following the loss of a loved one has pathological characteristics), violent crime or accidents, and natural disasters, almost all of which are symptoms, either directly or indirectly, of the traumata of patriarchy (from the inside out). Even natural disasters, once described as 'acts of God', are, in the epoch of the 'Anthropocene', potentially and increasingly associated with the works of industrialised, globalised and capitalist 'mankind'.

Thoughout my extended binge of chemical excess, I spent my days indulging pop culture obsessions and playacting the role of a coquette across several coteries.

The Idol has left me, but I can't let go and I get to him the only way I still can: sex. We're hanging by this thread. Thankfully, he has bad boundaries and things drag on for months. Eventually, he meets someone else and that last filament is severed. I go mad (I mean madder), wracked by a blood-deep grief I'd rather die than feel. My flat is a glorified bedsit on Liverpool Street. I've toyed with the Czech down the hall and an army of others in an effort to get over The Idol as I spin out of control. Now I take a new lover.

My new partner in crime and inamorata is a leggy beauty with a killer smile. Ona is of Chinese-English-Irish descent, and she has, by happy coincidence, moved into the hovel-room next door, as we'd already met – back when she was the girlfriend of my friend Ben, who was deliriously in love with her. We pass time hanging in my flat, or drinking Lambrusco on the roof, looking down on the city streets. We sit around like a couple of witches, cooking up in our makeshift cauldron: dessert spoon resting on the laminex table, the delicate pouring of a small pool of water from a nearby glass, the tapping of a tiny mound of powder from the creases of an alfoil square, the dab of cotton-like matter torn from the filter of a cigarette, the lighting of a match held under the raised silver spoon, the belt tourniquet, the needle sucking up the cloudy water, the rising vein, the droplet of blood on the pale inside of my arm, the steel sliding out, the melting down and closing eyes, the unyielding back of the vinyl chair against my spine, the surrender to the welcome tranquillity of a warm nod, the stopping of time, the dissolving of fear and memory, the unreserved relaxation, the finally feeling safe. Our days are devoted to getting on and rampaging around the city with a chain of jokers who have one foot in the grave.

Addiction tribute #1: Uncle Hugh. I remember your cravats and pipe and biting wit, and the way you never ate. Just the whiskey and milk and waking with the shakes. I didn't make your funeral (it's a long story and not one I think you'd understand). I hope you know I cared. I'm still writing after all these years, as you can see.

Ona and I scrape, scam and seduce our way through the world of H, and lately we've been bartering a double act for a Harley-riding dealer in exchange for junk, and passing the wee hours some nights with a lonely humanities professor who likes to talk and who pays us for our time.

If you've suffered childhood trauma, you're 4600% more likely to become an injecting drug user than if you haven't. (Open Democracy)

Some days scoring is hard, exhausting work, in an ever-shifting network of acquaintances, friends and frenemies, but when we're holding and it's just the two of us, and the rush spreads through me like a summer storm surge, we soften down on my bed, her creamy thighs against mine.

I get sick (I mean sicker).

Addiction tribute #2: Skateboard Danny. I hardly knew you but saw you often, on Victoria Street, at the coffee shop, where we gathered in those early days, when our de-medicated bodies shook with wakefulness and we'd shield our eyes from the brightness of life with perpetual sunglasses. I heard you went back for more and then I read you had been murdered, a small-time dealer fatally stabbed in a botched robbery. Your killer was an addict, no doubt known to you, ravaged by ice and H. So was his girlfriend, the messed-up daughter of a retired politician, who will always be known as the messed-up daughter of a retired politician, and their accomplice who went at your flatmate with a hammer. A petty plan hatched by addicts that escalated to horror. In a letter to the court your killer wrote of the drugs: *they just have a hold on me.* I know you know exactly what he meant. You're a tragic figure now, perished on the cross of toxic patriarchy, but know this: there are those who remember another you, the you when life was winning.

Ona and I touch toes on rock bottom and take turns trying to get clean. One of us is always avoiding the other, drying out, determined to quit. We disappear, reappear, drift, reunite, sink lower, change tactics. No H. No drinking before six p.m. Only one hit a week. Only wine. Only every three days. Only if bestowed by a friend in a generous mood.

I get clean for days, weeks, even months at a time, but then I 'bust', as they say in addict parlance, sometimes nudging the line between life and death. I OD on the floor of a friend's place, surrounded by records. I OD in the flat of the muse of a famous musician and her new dealer boyfriend. I've befriended their flatmate, a slight, silent country boy, the better to be near the white. They carry me around the apartment to wake me, splashing cold water on my face, and I come back. I OD on the bed of the hovel and my five-minute friend phones an ambulance before taking off in case I cark it. One minute Charlie Parker's 'Salt Peanuts' is playing in the background; the next, the smack and benzos get the better of me and I'm lights out on the bed with my outlaw companion leaving the door ajar for the paramedics. I come to, groggy, on a trolley in a hospital hallway. As I try to sit up a nurse appears. I ask what happened, my words slurring. You've had your stomach pumped, she says; because there are indications of attempted suicide, I am to see a hospital social worker. As soon as she leaves I get up and stagger the three blocks home in nothing more than a T-shirt and undies as first light tips the city skyline.

Meanwhile, the Hep C was busy eating away at my liver. I'd been infected at twenty, the second time I injected. There was no treatment for what was then called 'Non-A, Non-B Hepatitis', though a concerned addiction specialist I'd been referred to did offer a course of methadone, which I declined. It would be close to two more decades before successful treatment would declare me cured. In the meantime, there would be stigma, around both the drugs and the Hep C. There would be judgemental doctors and nurses (always wanting to know how I got it), and hypocrisy – stones thrown by those who lived in alcohol-fuelled, prescription-drug-run glass houses. Stigma/stigmata.

Addiction tribute #3: Christine. You came from Melbourne to get off H. We counted clean days together. Sharing our shit lists. Gossiping. We never did drugs together, but we did get drunk one time, making a pact to keep our 'bust' secret. I buckled and confessed. I don't know if you ever did. You took up with a rock star and now you run a cafe and you seem to be doing well. The eldest of your four daughters, whom I remember as a quiet child of five or six, is now older than we were back then.

I recall the children of friends I used H with, kids who saw stuff they shouldn't have seen, the daily desperations, amateur dramatics and sordid deals of addiction, and I know I'm part of their traumatic memories.

My body breaks down. The constipation from the H gives me haemorrhoids. The liver groans in pain. Ona and I hardly see each other. Our paths cross less and less. I resolve to try a new strategy: a respectable boyfriend. I get together with a close friend of The Idol's. The Businessman runs an indie record company from a huge terraced house in Paddington. This means I'm okay, right?

I'm thinking with the deluded mind of an addict in decline. I am incapable of original thought; worse, I'm incapable of any thought, only circular self-hating mantras, justifications, rationalisations, self-deceptions and self-obsessions, careening into and around each other like cars in peak-hour traffic, sparking along the dying cells of a shrinking brain.

... treatment for women's addictions is apt to be ineffective unless it acknowledges the realities of women's lives, which include the high prevalence of violence and other types of abuse. A history of being abused increases the likelihood that a woman will abuse alcohol and other drugs.
(Dr Stephanie S. Covington)

The Businessman doesn't approve, so I try going straight, but I'm sneaky. I think I can have it both ways, think I can fool him, fool myself. He picks me up for dinner. I have a hit stashed away. Shoot up on the sly before we leave. Nice courtyard garden. Try not to look stoned. Gulp down the wine. Force myself to eat. He talks about work: this errant band, that dodgy venue. We leave and as he opens the car door in the breaking spring breeze I hurl my undigested dinner up in the gutter before him. By now he's put two and two together, and I look up, eyes pinned. I'm *trying*. He deposits me at the hovel, says not to call till I clean up my act. I sit and snivel and drink, but as I get more and more maudlin, a subterranean struggle of almighty magnitude ensues.

The breakthrough comes as I'm walking down Darlinghurst Road at dawn, morning unfolding between the buildings, light changing around me, glowing rose-gold and settling on trees and surfaces, sharpening everything, as if it were the atmosphere of another planet. I stop inexplicably at the church I walk by daily without so much as a glance (I know what you're thinking; rest assured, I won't be claiming to have been saved by the Lord). I shake the gates, but they're locked. I don't know what I might want in there. More than anything, it's a sign of desperation, the longing for a moment's repose among the candles and dark wood and silence. I cross the road and a heel snaps off one of my stilettos. I fish out my key and hobble inside like a walking metaphor. Inside, my all-consuming despair is interrupted. I am visited by a lucid moment, a crossroad. Something shifts, as if the track my life runs on has switched and I'm compelled to go in another direction. I phone a detox for the last time.

I debouched into a future met by many: a multitude of convalescing addicts and helpers; nurses on nightshifts in detox; understanding doctors; therapists whose cornball sayings bemuse me, who out shame when my eyes dart from theirs or when I laugh or smile while disclosing something unfunny. And the counsellor who uttered the words that reached me at the right time.

I had been clean some weeks in the safety of a rehab for women. It was all the platitudes rolled into one: it was touch and go, a daily grind, a close call, one step forward and five steps back, hard-going but worth it, etc., etc. I wanted the new life they spoke of, but I held back till the day I let my guard down and reached my yes.

The counsellors, two women who were themselves 'recovering addicts', had taken us away for the weekend, a little holiday. I don't recall enjoying it and I've forgotten where we went. I can't picture all of the women. I can't visualise the beach. But I do remember the moment I confessed my reservation to the counsellor I was closest to. We were standing in the kitchen. We were alone. It was very quiet. Leaning against the bench I told her I was scared I couldn't write sober, that I worried I'd never write again, that life would be boring and predictable without drink and drugs. She locked her eyes onto mine and spoke: *everything is possible.* You're not being offered the old life polished up, she said. This will be a completely different life, and its future and potential are unimaginable from where you stand.

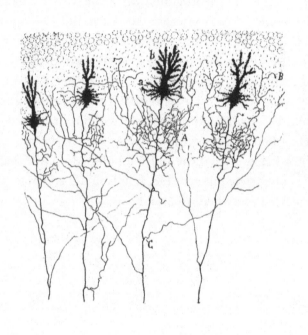

It's spring now. Bees buzz round the crabapple tree. A fierce, warm wind blows, and butterflies and wasps bat at the windowpanes in frenzied flight. *Eucalyptus oreades*, Blue Mountains ash, are clustered in a far corner of the yard, stripped to their skirts of ribboned bark. Their misty pale trunks stand tall with green-grey leaves and buds awaiting the white flowers of summer. In turn, they will become the woody fruit of the gumnut. A pair of rosellas feast on the wisteria, and the garden's fecundity commands reverence: the inexplicable genius of everything knowing how to do what it does, how to be what it is.

I don't know why I'm still here when other lives were cut short. I don't believe in the word 'God', though I sometimes catch myself using it as empty shorthand. I can't abide an anthropomorphic God of fear or wrath or bargains, a God who kindly arranges parking spaces and other miracles of convenience for adherents of the New Age while signing off on genocide in West Papua and turning a blind old-man-in-the-sky eye to clergy raping children, but if I did I would say it was a deity of terrible games and unconscionable riddles.

My father has a theory about time. He thinks the reason it seems to pass so slowly in childhood and so quickly as we age – speeding up with every year – is metabolism. For a fast metabolism, time moves in slow motion; the slower the metabolism, the swifter the passage of time.

I remember the way a day stretched on, and the endless wait between one birthday and the next. Galaxies formed as the summer surf tossed me in its liquid folds, but now I grow older as a spider weaves its web.

You want to know where this book has taken you and if there's a happy ending to this story. I'm thinking about how to respond.

The question is: are we powerless over the toxic effects of a history of patriarchy, powerless over the addictions we distract and medicate ourselves with, powerless over traumata and its symptomology? The answer is yes and no.

When Nietzsche, the German philosopher, became ill, he was taken into the care of his sister Elisabeth, who also took control of his unpublished work. *The Will to Power* is a collection of his thoughts and writing that was collated, contaminated and published by Elisabeth after his death. Elisabeth was a Nazi and she actively established an historical association between Nietzsche's philosophy and the Nazi regime that most contemporary scholars agree would have mortified Nietzsche. (I proceed with caution.)

The ideas about power in Nietzsche's allegorical novel, *Thus Spoke Zarathustra*, pre-date the less-than-reliable material in *The Will to Power* (though educated guesses can be made, it is impossible to know which words are Nietzsche's and which were added or rearranged by Elisabeth). In the novel, *Macht* (power) is related to Nietzsche's notion of 'self-overcoming' and his vision of the *Übermensch* ('the Overman', embodied in the character of Zarathustra) as the highly evolved person who dares to become an individual. The Overman is radical in defining their own values and rejecting inherited authority and conditioning, and as such exemplifies a higher order of humanity. Such a person represents an alternative to entrenched ideologies and they naturally serve as a beacon to those enslaved by what Nietzsche controversially called 'the herd instinct' (especially prevalent in institutionalised religions). The Overman is, above all, an artist, but not necessarily or merely in the sense that they produce art, though they are quite likely to. The Overman is an artist in that they live creatively, actively, rather than reactively: they are life-affirming rather than life-negating. In Nietzsche's view, religions that cast this life as sinful and the afterlife as heavenly are life-negating – rather, if there is a divinity, if there is salvation, it must be found and exercised in this life, here in the imperfect realm of sentient being in which he declared he could only believe in a God who dances.

This is not power sought for personal gain – money, social status or scheming political influence – but, for want of a less loaded term, a kind of spiritual awakening. It comes from breaking free of 'herd' morality and its repressive institutionalised gods, coupled with the energetic release of having also challenged the doctrine of rationality, that God of the Enlightenment, by engaging with emotions and other orders of experience consciously. Nietzsche envisioned the Overman as a historic figure, in that such a person is destined to shape history, to be, in a sense, immortal, in that they are likely to reappear again and again through the thoughts and values and works of others. Nietzsche saw the Overman as a future potential, and not one that all people could fulfil. This attracted accusations of elitism (and also seemed to give weight to those associations with Nazism). Some view the figure of the Overman as the fantastical ramblings of an unbalanced albeit supremely intelligent man, but if ever there was a time in which such an emergence is needed it is now, at the brink of catastrophic human-induced global warming and the widespread meltdown of the political and economic systems – the consequences of aeons of patriarchy.

Nietzsche's thinking on the will to power builds upon Arthur Schopenhauer's concept of the 'will to live', essentially a vision of universal vitality, and it perhaps in turn informed what Freud later called the 'life force,' an expression of which is 'libido'. Nietzsche's 'will to power' does not necessarily equate to obvious manifestations of power and it is not defined by dominance. 'I have found strength where one does not look for it,' wrote Nietzsche in one of his notebooks (translated by Walter Kaufmann), 'in simple, mild, and pleasant people, without the least desire to rule.' Nietzsche adds, in a statement that seems to predict Trump: 'conversely, the desire to rule has often appeared to me a sign of inward weakness: they fear their own slave soul and shroud it in a royal cloak (in the end, they still become the slaves of their followers, their fame, etc.).' Following on from Schopenhauer's 'will to live', viewed as driving both the desire to live and procreate, and the avoidance of death, Nietzsche's 'will to power' recognises that threats to one's ability to live to the utmost and avoid death don't always come in the form of rampaging bears; the tendency to avoid challenge, pain, conflict, to conform at the cost of integrity, to give in to all manner of human weaknesses are life-denying formulae for shrinkage and decline.

The Overman has achieved a state of 'self-overcoming', and if most of us fall short of the zenith of self-realisation, Nietzsche declares that many of us can lay claim to having achieved a degree of self-overcoming, which he conceived as an impassioned, proactive will to live. For Nietzsche, self-overcoming is redemption, and if there is redemption in my story, it is in my summoning, somehow, and with a great deal of support, enough of that will to live, those flashes of self-overcoming, which over time have fused into a radically re-inscribed sense of self. But it is far from absolute and I'm still plagued by unanswered questions. Are we doomed to be divided and fighting? Can we transform the traumata of patriarchy (from the outside in and the inside out) in time? Can we transform it at all? Can enough of us make not just art, but artists of ourselves and art of our communities? Nietzsche wrote:

> My idea is that every specific body strives to become master over all space and to extend its force (its will to power) and to thrust back all that resists its extension. But it continually encounters similar efforts on the part of other bodies and ends by coming to an arrangement ('union') with those of them that are sufficiently related to it: thus they then conspire together for power. And the process goes on …

Thus the noble, natural life force of the will to power has two potentials: it can become corrupt, divisive, political, during the process of 'coming to an arrangement'; or it can form unities that remind us what we are and, at best, who we can be. Trauma and the will to power jostle side by side, agitating for attention, racing each other to the surface, riding on waves of energy emanating all the way from the Big Bang. 'This world is the will to power,' Nietzsche pronounced, 'and nothing besides!' The question is, what wave will you ride? Which potential?

Do you think it odd this recourse to dead men of the western canon? Unseemly? Does it make me a 'bad feminist'?

Two centuries before Nietzsche's rise to prominence, Baruch Spinoza first borrowed from and then challenged other Enlightenment philosophers, including the influential René Descartes. A Dutch Jew, Spinoza was declared a heretic and excommunicated from Jewish society at the age of twenty-three because he dared to suggest that God didn't make us in 'His' image but that we made 'Him' in ours. His radical notion of a non-institutional God was equated with blasphemous atheism in a society not long emerged from the Dark Ages. Spinoza rejected the tenets of Judeo-Christian theology, controversially questioning the received authority of the scriptures in favour of a philosophical and impersonal God. He described God as one substance, encompassing the universe and everything in it, manifesting as infinite attributes (or evolving over time into different entities, as Darwin would later scientifically clarify), but let's not imagine Spinoza a monotheist or pantheist – he was less religious than that.

In a move crucially shifting away from Descartes' dualism, Spinoza 'denies that the human being is a union of two *substances*. The human mind and the human body are two different expressions – under Thought and under Extension – of one and the same thing: the person', as the *Stanford Encyclopedia of Philosophy* puts it. For Spinoza, it made no sense to speak of a 'mind–body split'. Patriarchal societies tend to put a great deal of stock in the conviction that the lofty mind is superior to the lowly body, but to Spinoza that was a reductionist fiction, a falsehood. He was concerned with exploring the complex ways in which these expressions and operations could correspond and behave either productively or destructively, intelligently or reactively. Enter Spinoza's theory of the affects in *Ethics*, his posthumously published magnum opus (he died aged only forty-four). Postulating power as beingness, he argued that power/beingness is either increased or decreased by a given action. His move vis-à-vis ethics is stunning in its simplicity:

that which increases the well-being or power of a being is ethical; that which diminishes it is unethical. It's here that Nietzsche's will to power, expansive rather than domineering, comes to mind.

It's a fearsome business, this tryst with the works of bygone philosophers (someone is bound to point out my mistakes – in my mind it's a man, white and tenured). There's a reason I'm taking that risk.

In *Ethics*, Spinoza claims that the more the body is rendered capable of affecting others and of being affected, the more the mind can perceive. The formulation continues. The capacity to consciously experience affect (emotion and the senses) leads to perception, which leads to reason or understanding (he uses both words alternately). For Spinoza, the most valuable form of self-esteem, perhaps the only true form, comes about through a reflective 'power of understanding'. I can claim to have achieved something of this power of understanding, but as for a tidy dénouement, there is none; neither my story nor my trauma has yet concluded.

The trials of traumata survived and surmounted is the tried and true formula for many Hollywood movies, but in the real world the film keeps rolling past the happy ending and I continue to show up in all my flawed, neurotic glory. I no longer seek to purge the most stubborn seeds of my trauma, but to live as peacefully and as compassionately with them as possible. Discussing how he came to be an expert in traumatic stress in an interview, Bessel van der Kolk recounts the moment in which a Vietnam vet led him to the realisation that working with trauma was not as straightforward as issuing a 'cure'. 'People become living testimonials for things that no longer exist,' he says. Trauma is not a blight to be lasered over; it involves a 'loyalty to the dead, to what was'. If I changed (and I have), if I became more of who I always was (and I have), if I have surpassed survival to live (and I have to some degree), this is how it happened. In the rooms of therapists, in the community halls of support groups, feeling it, on the phone to friends, in the arms of lovers, practising yoga, writing, doing shit jobs, feeling it; in the heat of the moment, in the sensation of a smell, during a long walk, at the cinema, reading, singing, patting a cat, feeling it, looking at a painting, feeling it, listening to music, making music, feeling it, bearing body-splitting, mind-twisting pain, casting doubt, writing, love, feeling it. This is how I weather patriarchy and heal from its traumatic effects (as best as I can, given that I continue to live inside the wound that is our culture) – one day at a time, one person at a time, one action at a time, one point of connection at a time.

I toss through the night, hot with dream-memories. Wake up with a start, a cry carrying forth.

Spinoza envisions ethical and what Joan Wynn Reeves calls 'insightful action' as the aptitude to override affects resulting from external causes (which may be experienced as positive or negative – in the case of trauma, they are usually heartbreaking or violating) through a process of scrutinising the misunderstandings they generate and discernment from within the grips of the resulting misery. Though not always sufficient to change damaging circumstances over which one has no or little control, this process has the potential to bring relief from suffering and an increase of power (beingness). In his view, this capacity to insightful action is innate to human beings, as an expression of vitality, of life force. It therefore necessarily has positive or joyful resonances. It is ethical because such a development not only benefits the individual, it also benefits others and contributes to the common good. This in turn informs action and self-overcoming. When affect resulting from external stimuli is traumatic and overwhelming, like that generated from toxic patriarchy, an individual or community manifests what Spinoza called 'the passions' or 'bondage'. This is affect run riot, detached from perception, discernment and understanding. This is toxic masculinity and absent fathers and raging stepfathers and neglectful, abusive mothers. This is war and suicide statistics. This is terrorism and jails. This is trolling and cyber-bullying. This is sexism and depression and the glue of our social structures that keeps inherited bigotries in place. This is where we find ourselves. This is where I found myself at the age of twenty-four, thirty years ago, as I walked up the path of a halfway house for women with histories of addiction.

I look out the window to see the arms of gum trees shaking fists of leaves in the wind. I'm unsettled by the association between Nietzsche and the Third Reich and the appearance of anti-Semitism and sexism in those passages of his writings where, in biting and fervent cultural critique, he rails against the constructions and constrictions of Judaism and gender-conditioned femininity in such a way as to seemingly disparage Jews and women. I worry that perhaps I've been too eager to buy into blaming his sister, too keen to castigate her for polluting and misrepresenting his ideas, too quick to absolve him. I think about Nietzsche breaking down, as it is said, on a Turin street at the sight of a brutally whipped horse, about his decline, the once monumental mind desolately isolated, decaying slowly, beyond words, beyond philosophy, depleted of its will to power.

For those of us not yet beyond reach, there's good, if tempered, news: thanks to our brain's capacity for change, recovery is possible (though not guaranteed as an absolute). Miki Perkins' profile of Dr Bruce Perry in *The Sydney Morning Herald* reveals his life-changing work as a psychiatrist and leading expert on the long-term effects of trauma in children. His research on the way trauma in childhood changes the biology of the brain confirms that 'prolonged stress can literally shrink the brain and alter its functioning'. The neurological baseline of the stress response becomes elevated and stays that way. Some parts of the brain stop functioning. The more threatened such a person feels, the more primitive their reactions and behaviours become, the more 'scared and scary'. Conversely, though, that also suggests that the less threatened a traumatised person perceives themselves to be, the safer they feel, the less scared and scary they'll become. It's something worth remembering as ideological warfare rages and a host of socio-political tensions tear communities around the world apart.

Brain plasticity means that even the most severely traumatised people can, under the right conditions, re-wire at least some neural pathways malformed by chronic stress, and thus find some reprieve. Neuroscientist Bessel van der Kolk postulates three key differences between the functioning of individuals with post-traumatised brains and those with relatively healthy brains. First, people with PTSD have enhanced threat perception, which means they tend to see danger (the past in the present) where less traumatised people see a manageable challenge. This is not controllable at the level of conscious cognition because it stems from the fear-driven primitive part of the brain, wired to protect physical safety (Bradshaw referred to this as the 'lizard brain'). Second, the brain's filtering system, which helps to distinguish between relevant and irrelevant data, gets messed up. Consequently, a PTSD-affected person is prone to focusing on details that less traumatised people ignore, and may find it difficult to fully engage in everyday situations (the past in the present). Finally, the self-sensing system is numbed, most likely due to a defensive response activated by terror during the traumatic experience. This numbing can be further heightened by drugs or alcohol, and van der Kolk links this effect most directly with the post-traumatic impulse to self-medicate and the addictive tendencies so common to people with C/PTSD. But this solution, this salve, exacts a toll, compounding trauma's deathliness by repressing positive feelings along with the negative ones, and diminishing the capacity to love and empathise (and the ability to undertake the insightful understanding/action Spinoza espouses).

This is what I can tell you. I no longer self-destruct. I know myself well. I often like myself, but not always. My experience of chronic trauma is commonplace to people born and socialised as female and to people born to addiction-affected families. It's not growing up in a ghetto surrounded by gang warfare. It's not a child crying under siege in Aleppo. It's not wasting away in the indefinite detention of a refugee camp, or being held hostage in a basement for years, forced into sexual slavery by a sadist. I live and write from a foundation of relative lifelong comfort. There were many needs and wants my family did meet, care unremembered, unmentioned in this book. I've made peace with family members alive and dead and I love them unreservedly today. I enjoy gains hard-won by feminist foremothers and those forefathers who also fought for my rights. I am the beneficiary of relentless goodness: caring teachers, patient nurses, helpful cabbies, and the kindnesses big and small of innumerable people whose names I may not recall or perhaps never knew. I contribute. I know love.

There are still bone-deep cracks and bruised vulnerabilities and injurious trauma-bound habits. Of van der Kolk's three areas of damage to the post-traumatised brain, I've made the most progress on the second and third. I remain most affected by the first, my lizard brain at the ready, forked tongue flicking. My preoccupation with physical safety has proved resilient in the face of various kinds of therapy. I have an array of daily micro-madnesses, obsessive-compulsions, anxious overreactions and hypersensitivities, and a self-protective need to limit my time out and about in the world.

If you go walking among the ghost gums in the wildfire winds of spring, beware. Fire, as they say, starts with a spark.

This is what I ask myself: can you dedicate your life to changing what is in your power to change, what needs to be changed? Can you love life despite the ugliness, the unfairness, the injustice? Can you meet traumata in tenderness? There are moments of grace, good days, in which I can answer yes, emphatically, whole-heartedly, but most of the time I still struggle towards those elegant hours. Could I bring myself to ask these questions of the family in the refugee camp, the family under siege in Aleppo, or the parent whose child has been killed in the crossfire of warring drug lords? These are questions I ask, philosophies I entertain, as one who has endured a privileged kind of traumata, a childhood of well-resourced neglect in the context of white, western womanhood.

In his concept of 'the eternal return', which relates to the will to power, Nietzsche puts to us a puzzle.

> What, if some day or night a demon were to steal after you into your loneliest loneliness and say to you: 'This

life as you now live it and have lived it, you will have to live once more and innumerable times more; and there will be nothing new in it, but every pain and every joy and every thought and sigh and everything unutterably small or great in your life will have to return to you, all in the same succession and sequence – even this spider and this moonlight between the trees, and even this moment and I myself. The eternal hourglass of existence is turned upside down again and again, and you with it, speck of dust!' Would you not throw yourself down and gnash your teeth and curse the demon who spoke thus?

He poses an impossible, trickster question: 'how well disposed would you have to become to yourself and to life to crave nothing more fervently than this ultimate eternal confirmation and seal?'

You're thinking about how to respond.

Nietzsche was mad, of course, by the time he died, and perhaps much earlier than that, for he served as a medical orderly in the Prussian forces during the Franco-Prussian War and returned profoundly traumatised. His thoughts and ideas are, like many productive and provocative thoughts and ideas, open to dispute (and compromised in the hands of the dreadful Elisabeth), but I will always love him for throwing himself on the beaten horse against the whip of the patriarchy.

The winds have died down and evening falls again, with its dome of popping stars. A halo of cloud circles the moon as it drifts across the night sky. I stand looking up, exhaling mist into the still air.

I think of that girl, the one who wandered round the playground in a daze, the one who got into the car of strangers on the trail of Sherbet, who flew to London on her own, who fled the seedy Bondi hotel room naked, who rode the highways in a puce-pink EK station wagon, who fell in love and spiralled down into drug-culture crisis, and I marvel that she survived.

In the early 1990s, when I had not long turned thirty, there was a time when this girl often knocked at my door, keeping me up at night, unruly, unreasonable. When her demands for attention wore me down and I could no longer ignore her, I wrote her a love letter in the form of a poem.

To the girl

You turned one summer
into a car too fast,
an empty house, a gang of
lost children looking for home.

You turned,
golden-skinned, and
sent your smile out like a servant
to gather wood for fires that
did not warm you.
From blaze to blaze
they did not know you,
covered in ash, and
melting them
your flame was hidden.

You turned then
into one who speaks
too much and too loud of
all but what needs to be said.
You,
small-bellied, lately fleshed, suddenly seen,
ran away from the castle of dead kings and queens

and leaving behind their costumes and jewels
you became a beggar, as orphans often do.

You turned one winter
into rain that never stopped.
Cold-limbed and tired you sat still.
It was lonely time full of days
and ticking clocks.
Music slipped down stairs
or laughter in the hall
but your room was quiet
as a funeral.
You waited and guessed for what.
Girl, you are my girl
I will not bury you.

All that you guessed was not it
and you waited too long for me,
like a burning bridge between
there and here
       in a tired
          old war.

In a photo taken by my father, I'm standing on a grassy knoll, aged four, maybe five. I don't recognise the place and my father can't remember. I'm standing on a grassy knoll on First Nation country, on country stolen from people who once roamed those rocks and that sand.

I'm standing on a grassy knoll. It's a windy, cloudy day. I'm looking out across the living sea. Most of my story is not yet written, and I have no knowledge of what is to come. There's some part of me that will be untouched by it, or rather that will remain untainted. There's some part of us that continues being, continues becoming, like the wind and the sea and the cloud, no matter what madness, what brutality, what traumata surrounds us. It has no name. It can't be caged, there where breath meets love. Can you feel it?

Acknowledgements

This book would likely not exist were it not for Julianne Schultz and *Griffith Review*. Julianne first encouraged me to write memoir and has championed my writing since I first published in *Griffith Review 4: Making Perfect Bodies*. And it was Julianne's prompting to write a book-length memoir that led to my undertaking *Traumata*. I am profoundly grateful for her support over the years. Varuna, the National Writers' House, is a treasure and was a vital resource during the writing of the book. Winning a Varuna residency in the *Griffith Review* Contributors Circle competition in 2016 enabled me to start this book. Soon after, I submitted the first three chapters in application for a Varuna Residential Fellowship and was awarded the Dr Eric Dark Flagship Fellowship for non-fiction 2017, which granted me another three weeks' retreat. This allowed me to complete the first draft. I thank the Dark family, Varuna staff, and the peer panel who honoured and assisted this work by selecting it for the Flagship Fellowship.

As a first reader, Sylvia Johnson has been a great friend to me and to this book. I thank her warmly for her generosity in giving of her time and talent, for lending her sharp eye and ear to these pages, and for her astute suggestions. I am also indebted to other readers and supporters: Deb Shaw, Kate Cole-Adams, Tanya Vavilova, Lex Hirst and Carol Major. I have been heartened by the way my agent, Jane Novak, and my publisher, Alexandra Payne, embraced this book, and I am grateful for their guidance.

I warmly thank Ian See for his deft and attentive edit, and salute all at UQP who helped get *Traumata* to print and beyond.

I heart my family for accompanying me through the wild ride of life, and for what I hope will be their understanding. There can be few things as confronting for a family as to find they have a memoirist in their midst. I hope too for the understanding of others who might have recognised themselves in these pages. I appreciate they will have their own version of shared experiences and I'm aware my telling mine may cause some discomfort. I have changed some names to protect identities in an effort to minimise that. Gregory Atkinson supplied many breakfasts, lunches, dinners and cups of tea as I worked on this book in time I barely had to spare. I will not forget his crucial practical support, or his steadfast faith in me and in this work.

Finally, I want to acknowledge the many women who, in different capacities, have buoyed me and educated me over the past three decades of mindful wrangling with both trauma and patriarchy. I dedicate this book to them, to all those wranglers who came before us, and to those who will follow.

The drawings of human brain neurons throughout are from *Texture of the Nervous System of Man and the Vertebrates* Vols I and II (edited by Pedro Pasik and Tauba Pasik and originally published around the turn of the twentieth century) by the Spanish scientist, medical artist and Nobel Laureate Santiago Ramón y Cajal. Cajal reportedly referred to neurons as 'mysterious butterflies of the soul'. I thank Antonella Franchini and the Fisher Library at the University of Sydney for practical assistance in obtaining digital versions of them.

The cover photos were taken by Christopher Wright and are used with kind permission from Christina Lena Wright. The photo on page 181 was taken by my grandfather, John Clayton (neé Denzil Bertram Wilmot Carvalho). Permission to use the photo on page 247 compliments of Lisa Walker. The photographers of images on pages 45, 148, 211 and 221 are unknown. My father, Russell Frank Atkinson, took the remaining photographs and I thank him for permission to use them. He's a bloody good sport.

Parts of this book were previously published in various forms: 'Child's Play: The Biggest Sherbet Fans Ever', *Griffith Review 33: Such Is Life,* 2011; 'Waiting for Dad-o', *Meanjin Quarterly,* vol. 69, no. 2, 2010; 'The Exiled Child', *Griffith Review 15: Divided Nation,* 2007; 'Girls Talk', *Griffith Review 11: Getting Smart,* 2006; 'From a Moving Car', *Griffith Review 9: Up North,* 2005; 'Beauty and the Bête Noire', *Griffith Review 4: Making Perfect Bodies,* 2004.

The poem 'Circle' was previously published in *Map of Skin: Selected Poems,* a chapbook published by Pink Flamingo Press in 1995. 'To the girl' was published in *Heat,* no. 5, Giramondo, in 1997, and 'Writing a Dear John letter while reading Abraham and Török' was published in *The Best Australian Poems 2010* (edited by Robert Adamson), Black Inc., 2010.

Bibliography

Abraham, Nicolas, and Török, Mária (ed. N.T. Rand), *The Shell and the Kernel: Renewals of Psychoanalysis*, University of Chicago Press, Chicago, 1994.

Adamson, Joseph, and Clark, Hilary (eds), 'Introduction: Shame, Affect, Writing', *Scenes of Shame: Psychoanalysis, Shame, and Writing*, State University of New York Press, New York, 1999, pp. 1–34.

Adorno, Theodor W., *Negative Dialectics*, Bloomsbury Academic, New York, 1981.

—— (tr. Shierry Weber Nicholsen and Samuel Weber), *Prisms*, The MIT Press, Cambridge, 1983.

—— (ed. Rolf Tiedemann, tr. Edmund Jephcott), *Metaphysics: Concepts and Problems*, Stanford University Press, Stanford, 2000.

Ahmed, Sara, 'Speaking Out', *feministkilljoys*, 2 June 2016. https://feministkilljoys.com/2016/06/02/speaking-out/

American Society of Plastic Surgeons, 'Briefing Paper: Plastic Surgery for Teenagers', 2015. https://www.plasticsurgery.org/news/briefing-papers/briefing-paper-plastic-surgery-for-teenagers

Andrews, Kylie, 'Epigenetics: How Your Life Could Change the Cells of Your Grandkids', *ABC Science*, 21 April 2017. http://www.abc.net.au/news/science/2017-04-21/what-does-epigenetics-mean-for-you-and-your-kids/8439548

Astbury, Jill, Atkinson, Judy, et al., 'The Impact of Domestic Violence on Individuals', *The Medical Journal of Australia*, vol. 173, no. 8, 2000, pp. 427–431.

Atkinson, Alan, *Camden: Farm and Village Life in Early New South Wales*, Oxford University Press, Melbourne, 1988.

Australian Human Rights Commission, *Change the Course: National Report on Sexual Assault and Sexual Harassment at Australian Universities*, AHRC, Sydney, 2017.

The Australian Women's Weekly, 'The Macarthurs of Camden', 21 August 1957, p. 8. http://trove.nla.gov.au/newspaper/article/48530028

Badenoch, Bonnie, *Being a Brain-Wise Therapist: A Practical Guide to Interpersonal Neurobiology*, W.W. Norton & Company, New York, 2008.

Bagshaw, Dale, Campbell, Alan, and Jelinek, Lena, *Children and Domestic Violence: An Evaluation of Jannawi Resources*, Department of Human Services South Australia, Adelaide, 2002.

Barthes, Roland (tr. Richard Howard), *A Lover's Discourse: Fragments*, The Noonday Press, New York, 1978.

Bataille, Georges (tr. Mary Dalwood), *Eroticism*, Marion Boyars Publishers, London, 1987.

Beauchamp, Paula, 'Girls Bigger Bullies: Teen Queens More Hurtful, Conference Told', *Herald Sun*, 31 October 2005.

Birney, Ewan, 'Why I'm Sceptical About the Idea of Genetically Inherited Trauma', *The Guardian*, 12 September 2015. https://www.theguardian.com/science/blog/2015/sep/11/why-im-sceptical-about-the-idea-of-genetically-inherited-trauma-epigenetics

Blanch, Anna, 'Make a Whistle from My Throat: Giving Voice to the Voiceless', *Transpositions: Theology, Imagination and the Arts*, undated. http://www.transpositions.co.uk/make-a-whistle-from-my-throat-giving-voice-to-the-voiceless/

Bradshaw, John, *Homecoming: Reclaiming and Championing Your Inner Child*, Bantam, New York, 1990.

——, *Creating Love: The Next Great Stage of Growth*, Bantam, New York, 1994.

——, *Where Are You Father?*, audiobook, John Bradshaw Media Group, Houston, 2008.

Brennan, Teresa, *The Transmission of Affect*, Cornell University Press, New York, 2004.

Brett, Lily, *The Auschwitz Poems*, Scribe, Melbourne, 1986.

——, *After the War: Poems*, Melbourne University Press, Melbourne, 1990.

Buczynski, Ruth, 'How Does Childhood Trauma Impact Adult Relationships?', National Institute for the Clinical Application of Behavioral Medicine, undated. https://www.nicabm.com/could-childhood-trauma-affect-adult-relationships/

Burnett III, James H., 'Racism Learned', *The Boston Globe*, 10 June 2012. https://www.bostonglobe.com/business/2012/06/09/harvard-researcher-says-children-learn-racism-quickly/gWuN1ZG3M40WihER2kAfdK/story.html

Butler, Judith, 'Performative Acts and Gender Constitution: An Essay in Phenomenology and Feminist Theory', *Theatre Journal*, vol. 40, no. 4, 1988, pp. 519–531.

——, *Gender Trouble: Feminism and the Subversion of Identity*, Routledge, New York, 1990.

Carter, Angela, *The Sadeian Woman: And the Ideology of Pornography*, Virago Press, London, 1979.

Caruth, Cathy, *Unclaimed Experience: Trauma, Narrative, and History*, Johns Hopkins University Press, Baltimore, 1996.

Catsoulis, Jeannette, 'Review: "Tony Robbins: I Am Not Your Guru" Depicts a Self-Help Prophet', *The New York Times*, 12 July 2016. https://www.nytimes.com/2016/07/13/movies/tony-robbins-i-am-not-your-guru-review.html

Collins, Patricia Hill, *Black Feminist Thought: Knowledge, Consciousness, and the Politics of Empowerment*, Unwin Hyman, Boston, 1990.

Corbett, Alan, 'The Last Hold-Out Caves: The Slow Death of Corporal Punishment In Our Schools', *New Matilda*, 28 June 2016. https://newmatilda.com/2016/06/28/the-last-hold-out-caves-the-death-of-corporal-punishment-in-our-schools/

Crandall, Diana, 'Feminist Columnist Jessica Valenti Quits Social Media After Trolls Threaten to Rape Her 5-year-old Daughter', *New York Daily News*, 27 July 2016. http://www.nydailynews.com/news/national/columnist-quits-social-media-threats-rape-5-year-old-article-1.2728374

Crenshaw, Kimberlé W., 'Demarginalizing the Intersection of Race and Sex: A Black Feminist Critique of Antidiscrimination Doctrine, Feminist Theory and Antiracist Politics', *University of Chicago Legal Forum*, vol. 1989, no. 1, 1989, pp. 139–167.

——, 'Mapping the Margins: Intersectionality, Identity Politics, and Violence Against Women of Color', *Stanford Law Review*, vol. 43, no. 6, 1991, pp. 1241–1299.

D'Angelo, Mike, '*I Am Not Your Guru* Is Compelling Enough for a Glorified Tony Robbins Commercial', *AV Film*, 13 July 2016. https://film.avclub.com/i-am-not-your-guru-is-compelling-enough-for-a-glorified-1798188315

Davey, Melissa, 'Study to Determine Sexual Assault Prevalence in Australian Universities', *The Guardian*, 23 August 2016. https://www.theguardian.com/australia-news/2016/aug/23/study-to-determine-sexual-assault-prevalence-in-australian-universities

Davidson, Helen, 'Northern Territory Youth Detention: No Excuse for Not Knowing of Abuse, *The Guardian*, 26 July 2016. https://www.theguardian.com/australia-news/2016/jul/26/northern-territory-youth-detention-no-excuse-for-not-knowing-of-abuse

Deerchild, Rosanna, 'Lasting Effects of Trauma Reaches Across Generations Through DNA', *Unreserved*, CBC Radio, 27 September 2015. http://www.cbc.ca/radio/unreserved/buffy-sainte-marie-wab-kinew-and-how-dna-remembers-trauma-1.3242375/lasting-effects-of-trauma-reaches-across-generations-through-dna-1.3243897

Didion, Joan, *Slouching Towards Bethlehem*, Farrar, Straus and Giroux, New York, 1968.

——, 'Why I Write', *The New York Times Book Review*, 5 December 1976, p. 270.

Diu, Nisha Lilia, 'Suicide Is Now the Biggest Killer of Teenage Girls Worldwide. Here's Why', *The Telegraph*, 25 May 2015. http://www.telegraph.co.uk/women/womens-health/11549954/Teen-girls-Suicide-kills-more-young-women-than-anything.-Heres-why.html

Doherty, Ben, and Marr, David, 'The Worst I've Seen – Trauma Expert Lifts Lid on "Atrocity" of Australia's Detention Regime', *The Guardian*, 20 June 2016. https://www.theguardian.com/australia-news/2016/jun/20/the-worst-ive-seen-trauma-expert-lifts-lid-on-atrocity-of-australias-detention-regime

Evershed, Nick, 'What We're Dying From: The Leading Causes of Death in Australia', *The Guardian*, 20 October 2015. https://www.theguardian.com/news/datablog/2015/oct/20/what-were-dying-from-the-leading-causes-of-death-in-australia

Felitti, Vincent J., Anda, Robert F., et al., 'Relationship of Childhood Abuse and Household Dysfunction to Many of the Leading Causes of Death in Adults', *American Journal of Preventive Medicine*, vol. 14, no. 4, 1998, pp. 245–258.

Felman, Shoshana, and Laub, Dori, *Testimony: Crises of Witnessing in Literature, Psychoanalsyis, and History*, Routledge, New York, 1992.

Fogarty, Siobhan, 'Suicide Rate for Young Indigenous Men Highest in the World, Australian Report Finds', *ABC News*, 12 August 2016. http://www.abc.net.au/news/2016-08-12/indigenous-youth-suicide-rate-highest-in-world-report-shows/7722112

Ford, Clementine, 'The Epidemic of Rape Culture in Schools Can No Longer Be Ignored', *The Sydney Morning Herald*, 18 August 2016. http://www.smh.com.au/lifestyle/news-and-views/opinion/the-epidemic-of-rape-culture-in-schools-can-no-longer-be-ignored-20160817-gquv53.html

Freud, Sigmund, 'On Transience', *On the History of the Psycho-Analytic Movement: Papers on Metapsychology, and Other Works*, The Hogarth Press, London, 1950, pp. 305–307.

Funnell, Nina, 'Students from 71 Australian Schools Targeted by Sick Pornography Ring', *News.com.au*, 17 August 2016. http://www.news.com.au/lifestyle/real-life/news-life/students-from-70-australian-schools-targeted-by-sick-pornography-ring/news-story/53288536e0ce3bba7955e92c7f7fa8da

Gibbs, Anna, 'Contagious Feelings: Pauline Hanson and the Epidemiology of Affect', *Australian Humanities Review*, December

2001. http://australianhumanitiesreview.org/archive/Issue-Decem ber-2001/gibbs.html

Gross, Thomas J., 'Hippocampus Involvement in Explicit Memory Processes Related to Trauma', *School Psychology: From Science to Practice*, vol. 6, no. 3, 2013, pp. 21–27.

Haig, Matt, 'There Is No More Shame In Mental Illness Than Having Tonsilitis', *The Guardian*, 21 July 2017. https://www.theguardian. com/books/2017/jul/21/reformation-2017-matt-haig-mental-health-physical-integrated-healthcare

Harmon, Katherine, 'The Changing Mental Health Aftermath of 9/11 – Psychological "First Aid" Gains Favor over Debriefings', *Scientific American*, 10 September 2011. https://www.scientificamerican. com/article/the-changing-mental-health/

Hartocollis, Anemona, '10 Years and a Diagnosis Later, 9/11 Demons Haunt Thousands', *The New York Times*, 9 August 2011. http:// www.nytimes.com/2011/08/10/nyregion/post-traumatic-stress-disorder-from-911still-haunts.html

Hay, Veronica M., 'An Interview with John Bradshaw', *People and Possibilities*, undated. http://www.peopleandpossibilities.com/ John-Bradshaw.html

Hegarty, Kelsey, Hindmarsh, Elizabeth D., and Gilles, Marisa T., 'Domestic Violence in Australia: Definition, Prevalence and Nature of Presentation in Clinical Practice', *The Medical Journal of Australia*, vol. 173, no. 7, 2000, pp. 363–367.

Herman, Judith, *Trauma and Recovery: The Aftermath of Violence – From Domestic Abuse to Political Terror*, Pandora, London, 1998.

Hirsch, Marianne, *Family Frames: Photography, Narrative, and Postmemory*, Harvard University Press, Cambridge, 1997.

——, 'The Generation of Postmemory', *Poetics Today*, vol. 29, no. 1, 2008, pp. 103–128.

Holt, Melissa, 'Bullying and Its Relation to Child Abuse, Sexual Victimization, Domestic Violence, and Witnessing Community Violence', *Education.com*, 3 March 2016. http://www.education.com/ reference/article/bullying-child-abuse-sexual-domestic-violence/

hooks, bell, *The Will to Change: Men, Masculinity, and Love*, Simon and Schuster, New York, 2004.

Hush, Anna, 'Sexual Assault on Campus Is Systemic. But Sydney Uni Has Failed to Act for Decades', *The Guardian*, 23 August 2016. https://www.theguardian.com/commentisfree/2016/aug/23/sexual-assault-on-campus-is-systemic-but-sydney-uni-has-failed-to-act-for-decades

Irvin, Jim, and McLear, Colin (eds), *The Mojo Collection: The Ultimate Music Companion*, fourth edition, Canongate, Edinburgh, 2007.

Kianpoor, Mohsen, and Bakhshani, Nour Mohammad, 'Trauma, Dissociation, and High-Risk Behaviors', *International Journal of High-Risk Behaviors and Addiction*, vol. 1, no. 1, 2012, pp. 9–13.

Kristeva, Julia (tr. Leon S. Roudiez), *Black Sun: Depression and Melancholia*, Columbia University Press, New York, 1989.

—— (tr. Jeanine Herman), *Intimate Revolt: The Powers and Limits of Psychoanalysis*, Columbia University Press, New York, 2002.

LeDoux, Joseph, 'The Amygdala and Unconscious Memories', *Big Think*, 16 September 2010. http://bigthink.com/videos/the-amygdala-and-unconscious-memories

MacNell, Lillian, 'Online Students Give Instructors Higher Marks If They Think Instructors Are Men', *NC State News*, 9 December 2014. https://news.ncsu.edu/2014/12/macnell-gender-2014/

Massumi, Brian, 'The Autonomy of Affect', in Patton, Paul (ed.), *Deleuze: A Critical Reader*, Blackwell, London, 1996, pp. 217–239.

Meadows, Brittany, 'The Top Trauma That Causes Addiction', *Addiction Campuses*, 4 May 2015. http://www.addictioncampuses.com/resources/addiction-campuses-blog/the-top-trauma-that-causes-addiction/

Meares, Russell, *Intimacy and Alienation: Memory, Trauma and Personal Being*, Routledge, London, 2000.

Mitchell, Natasha, 'The Secrets Inside Your Cells: Epigenetics, Trauma, and Ancestry', *Science Friction*, radio program, ABC RN, 22 April 2017. http://www.abc.net.au/radionational/programs/sciencefriction/the-secrets-inside-your-cells/8430922

Morgan, George, 'Dangers Lurk in the March Towards a Post-Modern Career', *The Sydney Morning Herald*, 18 October 2016. http://www.smh.com.au/comment/dangers-lurk-in-the-postmodern-career-that-is-missing-job-security-20161017-gs3u5o.html

Myles, Eileen, *I Must Be Living Twice: New and Selected Poems 1975–2014*, Ecco, New York, 2015.

Negri, Antonio (tr. Martin Joughin), 'Control and Becoming: Gilles Deleuze in Conversation with Antonio Negri', *Futur Antérieur 1*, 1990. http://www.generation-online.org/p/fpdeleuze3.htm

Nietzsche, Friedrich (ed. Walter Kaufmann, tr. Walter Kaufmann and R.J. Hollingdale), *The Will to Power*, Vintage, New York, 1968.

Paglia, Camille, 'It's a Man's World, and It Always Will Be', *Time*, 16 December 2013. http://ideas.time.com/2013/12/16/its-a-mans-world-and-it-always-will-be/

Pearl, Anne, and Weston, Jane, 'Attitudes of Adolescents About Cosmetic Surgery', *Annals of Plastic Surgery*, vol. 50, no. 6, 2003, pp. 628–630.

Perera, Suvendrini, and Pugliese, Joseph, 'Offshore Detention "Black Sites" Open Door to Torture', *The Conversation*, 26 August 2015. http://theconversation.com/offshore-detention-black-sites-open-door-to-torture-46400

Perkins, Miki, '"Scared and Scary": How Trauma Changes a Child's Brain', *The Sydney Morning Herald*, 28 October 2015. http://www.smh.com.au/national/scared-and-scary-how-trauma-changes-the-child-brain-20151027-gkjulx.html

Powers, Abigail, Ressler, Kerry J., and Bradley, Rebekah G., 'The Protective Role of Friendship on the Effects of Childhood Abuse and Depression', *Depression and Anxiety*, vol. 26, no. 1, 2009, pp. 46–53.

Reeves, Joan Wynn, *Thinking About Thinking: Studies in the Background of Some Psychological Approaches*, Routledge, Abingdon, 2015.

Robson, Kathryn, *Writing Wounds: The Inscription of Trauma in Post-1968 French Women's Life-Writing*, Rodopi, New York, 2004.

Sayrafiezadeh, Saïd, 'How to Write About Trauma', *The New York Times*, 13 August 2016. http://www.nytimes.com/2016/08/14/opinion/sunday/how-to-write-about-trauma.html

Schwab, Gabriele, 'Writing Against Memory and Forgetting', *Literature and Medicine*, vol. 25, no. 1, 2006, pp. 95–121.

Shen, Aviva, 'Students See Male Professors as Brilliant Geniuses, Female Professors as Bossy and Annoying', *ThinkProgress*, 7 February 2015. https://thinkprogress.org/students-see-male-professors-as-brilliant-geniuses-female-professors-as-bossy-and-annoying-5dd018d5a785

Smith, Karen Ingala, 'Counting Dead Women', blog post, undated. https://kareningalasmith.com/counting-dead-women/

Smith, Michelle, 'Friday Essay: Double Standards and Derision – Tracing Our Attitudes to Older Women and Beauty', *The Conversation*, 7 July 2017. http://theconversation.com/friday-essay-double-standards-and-derision-tracing-our-attitudes-to-older-women-and-beauty-79575

Spinoza, Baruch de (tr. Edwin Curley), *Ethics*, Penguin, London, 1996.

Stein, Joel, 'How Trolls Are Ruining the Internet', *Time*, 18 August 2016. http://time.com/4457110/internet-trolls/

Stines, Sharie, 'Trauma, Differentiation and Integration, and Neuropsychology', *PsychCentral*, 6 January 2016. http://pro.psychcentral.com/recovery-expert/2016/01/trauma-differentiation-and-integration-and-neuropsychology/

Stockton, Nick, 'Your Brain Doesn't Contain Memories. It Is Memories', *Wired*, 19 July 2017. https://www.wired.com/story/your-brain-is-memories/

Strohecker, Dave Paul, 'Body Modification, Gender, and Self-Empowerment', *Cyborgology*, 22 September 2011. https://thesocietypages.org/cyborgology/2011/09/22/body-modification-gender-and-self-empowerment/

The Sydney Morning Herald, 'She's a Girl Named Phoebe', editorial, 24 February 1957, p. 63.

Thomson, Helen, 'Study of Holocaust Survivors Finds Trauma Passed

on to Children's Genes', *The Guardian*, 22 August 2015. https://
www.theguardian.com/science/2015/aug/21/study-of-holocaust-
survivors-finds-trauma-passed-on-to-childrens-genes

Tippett, Krista, 'Bessel van der Kolk: How Trauma Lodges in the Body',
On Being, radio program, 9 March 2017. https://onbeing.org/
programs/bessel-van-der-kolk-how-trauma-lodges-in-the-
body-mar2017/

Tomkins, Silvan S., *Affect, Imagery, Consciousness, Volume II: The
Negative Affects*, Springer Publishing, New York, 1993.

Triple J Hack, 'Victim of Schoolgirl Pornography Ring Says Police
"Laughed" at Her', 17 August 2016. http://www.abc.net.au/
triplej/programs/hack/victim-of-pornography-ring-says-police-
laughed-at-her/7760578

Valenti, Jessica, 'Worldwide Sexism Increases Suicide in Young
Women', *The Guardian*, 28 May 2015. http://www.theguardian.
com/commentisfree/2015/may/28/worldwide-sexism-increases-
suicide-risk-in-young-women

van Alphen, Ernst, 'Second-Generation Testimony, the Transmission
of Trauma, and Postmemory', *Poetics Today*, vol. 27, no. 2, 2006,
pp. 473–488.

van der Kolk, Bessel, *The Body Keep the Score: Brain, Mind, and Body in
the Healing of Trauma*, Viking, New York, 2014.

van der Kolk, Bessel, and Buczynski, Ruth, 'The Neuroscience of
Traumatic Memory', *National Institute for the Clinical Application of
Behavioral Medicine*, 2016. http://www.nicabm.com/neurobiology-
trauma/free-confirmed/

Von Ohlsen, Sherry, 'On Fathers: An Interview With John Bradshaw',
The World and I, 1991. https://www.worldandischool.com/public/
1991/june/school-resource19328.asp

Waites, Elizabeth A., *Trauma and Survival: Post-Traumatic and Dissociative
Disorders in Women*, W.W. Norton & Company, New York, 1993.

Weale, Sally, and Batty, David, 'Sexual Harassment of Students
by University Staff Hidden by Non-Disclosure Agreements',
The Guardian, 26 August 2016. https://www.theguardian.com/

education/2016/aug/26/sexual-harassment-of-students-by-university-staff-hidden-by-non-disclosure-agreements

Webb, Jonice, *Running on Empty: Overcome Your Childhood Emotional Neglect*, Morgan James Publishing, New York, 2012.

Wiesel, Elie, *Night*, Bantam, New York, 1982.

Wolf, Naomi, *The Beauty Myth: How Images of Beauty Are Used Against Women*, HarperCollins, New York, 2002.

Yehuda, Rachel, Daskalakis, Nikolaos P., et al., 'Holocaust Exposure Induced Intergenerational Effects on FKBP5 Methylation', *Biological Psychiatry*, vol. 80, no. 5, 2016, pp. 372–380.

Züst, Marc Alain, Colella, Patrizio, et al., 'Hippocampus Is Place of Interaction Between Unconscious and Conscious Memories', *PLoS One*, vol. 10, no. 3, 2015. https://www.ncbi.nlm.nih.gov/pmc/articles/PMC4380440/